THE SENATE OF THE UNITED STATES
A Bicentennial History

By
Richard Allan Baker
Director
U.S. Senate Historical Office

AN ANVIL ORIGINAL

Under the general editorship of
Louis L. Snyder

ROBERT E. KRIEGER   PUBLISHING COMPANY
Malabar, Florida

1988

Original Edition 1988

Printed and Published by
ROBERT E. KRIEGER PUBLISHING COMPANY, INC.
KRIEGER DRIVE
MALABAR, FLORIDA   32950

Library of Congress Cataloging-in-Publication Data

Baker, Richard A.
    The United States Senate.

    "An Anvil original."—
    Bibliography: p.
    Includes index.
    1. United States. Congress. Senate—History.
I. Title.
JK1158.B35   1988   328.73'071'09   87-3740
ISBN   0-89874-865-X

10   9   8   7   6   5   4   3   2

*This book is for
H. Allan and Eleanor Baker
with love and appreciation.*

CONTENTS

PREFACE

On the eve of the Senate's 150th anniversary in 1939, George H. Haynes published his classic two-volume *The Senate of the United States* (Boston, 1938). Over the past nearly half-century that study has served as an invaluable starting point for those seeking to understand the historical development of this complex and colorful institution. Regrettably, Haynes' study is now out of date and out of print.

Although the present volume differs from that of Haynes in scope and focus, it shares a common purpose. It is designed to make the Senate's rich history more accessible to a broad audience. That audience includes modern-day senators, congressional staffs, domestic and foreign visitors to the Capitol, students, and the American electorate. This work also differs from Senator Robert C. Byrd's vastly more detailed series of historical lectures delivered in nearly one hundred installments before the Senate since 1980.

The Senate's 1989 bicentennial has stimulated broad popular interest in that body's history and its institutional capacity to cope with modern challenges within a framework fashioned late in the eighteenth century. The ability of the Senate to adapt and grow during its first two centuries stands as a monumental tribute to the framers of the Constitution and to the 1,800 men and women who have served as senators since 1789.

I gratefully acknowledge the contributions of colleagues who have assisted me in the preparation of this manuscript. They include David Corbin, James T. Currie, James R. Ketchum, Maeva Marcus, Donald A. Ritchie, and Raymond W. Smock. I am particularly indebted to Senate Majority Leader Robert C. Byrd, whose perceptive conversations about the Senate's history have greatly aided my understanding of this unique legislative body. Finally, I extend my deepest appreciation to Patricia K. S. Baker, Christopher A. Baker, and David R. Baker.

PART I

THE SENATE OF THE UNITED STATES

CHAPTER 1

CREATION OF THE SENATE: 1787–1789

For two hundred years the United States Senate, "the world's greatest deliberative body," has been a source of national pride and national frustration. It has risen to meet enormous challenges and, on occasion, it has fallen to a state of functional paralysis. The 1,800 members who have served during the first one hundred Congresses count among their number statesmen and politicos, brilliant legislative tacticians, and fiery demagogues. Most commonly, however, United States senators have been individuals of a more modest nature doing their best to meet the demands of their times with available resources. The Senate of the late 1980s, in many of its fundamentals, bears a close resemblance to that of the late 1780s. In other respects, it is a profoundly different body, having developed in ways that its first members could never have anticipated. The story of this complex body's growth over two centuries richly illustrates the resilience of the government under the Constitution of 1787. Throughout the nation's history, in its relationship with the other branches of the federal establishment, the Senate has played both dominant and subordinant roles. It began in a decidedly secondary position.

COLONIAL AND STATE ANTECEDENTS. When the framers of the Constitution assembled at Philadelphia in May 1787, most assumed that the new charter of government would include a two-house legislature. Although the prevailing government under the Articles of Confederation lacked a second house, such chambers were found in most of the thirteen state governments. These bodies had taken their form from the earlier colonial-era governors' councils.

The English monarch customarily made appointments to colonial councils on the basis of governors' recommendations. Generally men of wealth and status, the councilors usually served without pay and could be expected to support the established regime. Yet, they also exercised a decided measure of independence. Although convened by the governor, colo-

3

nial councils possessed the power of free and unlimited debate and the obligation to provide advice and consent to gubernatorial appointments and other actions. They also functioned as the highest court of appeal within each colony, with the governor acting only as presiding judge. Finally, and most importantly, councils operated as upper houses[1] within the colonial legislatures. Their powers nearly equalled those of the popularly elected assemblies with the exception, following English parliamentary practices, that they lacked authority to initiate or to amend revenue legislation.

The American Revolution overthrew both the royal governors and their councils. Within the newly established states, however, the practice survived of an upper house representing property rights and acting as a check on both the governor and the lower house. All but three state constitutions provided for two legislative chambers, with the three unicameral states— Vermont, Georgia, and Pennsylvania—continuing the councils as executive rather than legislative bodies.

The country's first central government evolved under circumstances that did not require a council or second legislative body. The First Continental Congress, which assembled in Philadelphia on September 5, 1774, was an emergency assembly that existed only to formulate recommendations for collective action by individual colonies. After meeting for seven weeks the Congress adjourned, providing for a Second Continental Congress to convene the following year. Assembling in May 1775, less than a month after the hostilities at Lexington and Concord that brought the infant republic to a state of open war with Great Britain, the legislature quickly expanded its role to meet the wartime emergency.

ARTICLES OF CONFEDERATION. On June 11, 1776, while debating a draft of the Declaration of Independence, the Second Continental Congress agreed to establish a committee ''to prepare and digest the form of a confederation to be

---

[1]The term ''upper house'' applied to bicameral legislatures suggests the body of more restricted membership. These assemblies were frequently located on the less spacious upper floors of legislative buildings.

entered into between these Colonies." Nearly five years passed before all states finally agreed to the resulting Articles of Confederation. The articles recognized the structural status quo of the emerging Congress. The legislature would continue to be composed of a single chamber, with an elected president, in which each state had but one vote. It would perpetuate the notion of state sovereignty, exercising only those powers that the states, by unanimous vote, had expressly delegated. State legislatures would determine the qualifications and method of electing their representatives to Congress and would pay their salaries and expenses. A state could replace any of its delegates at any time. Each state could send from two to seven members, but no person could serve for more than three years in any six-year period. Thus, under the Articles, state legislatures tightly controlled the national legislature's exercise of power.

As the Revolutionary War drew to an end, and the resulting need for unity between the states diminished, weaknesses within the Confederation Congress became dramatically apparent. States refused to comply with congressional requests for funds, leaving the fragile central government to contend with rising indebtedness and inflation. By 1786 many congressmen acknowledged that significant revisions in the Articles would be necessary to deal with the nation's mounting crises in the areas of finance, commerce, and foreign affairs. Observing that Congress lacked the independent authority to raise armies, regulate commerce, and levy taxes, Virginia's James Madison called the Articles "nothing more than a treaty of amity and of alliance between independent and sovereign states."

CONSTITUTIONAL CONVENTION. This crisis led the states to send delegates to Philadelphia in the spring of 1787 to consider a revision of the Articles that would "render the constitution of the Federal Government adequate to the exigencies of the Union." Plans simply to revise the Articles perished quickly in the early sessions at Independence Hall. Once the delegates accepted the necessity of a stronger national government with a separate chief executive and a legislative chamber elected directly by the people rather than by state assemblies, the need became apparent for a "council of revision'' to examine and refine the handiwork of the popularly elected body and of the president. Accordingly, the issue before the framers was not whether to have a senate, but how the senate could best be devised to protect the interests of men of property from the dictates of the larger citizenry and from the arbitrary designs of the central executive. The ''first branch,'' or House of Representatives, would be constituted along the lines of the Confederation Congress, with popularly elected members serving relatively short terms to ensure their responsiveness to public sentiment. In shaping the ''second branch,'' which by resolution was to be called the ''Senate,'' the framers debated such issues as the method of election, length of term, basis of representation, and specific legislative powers.

METHOD OF ELECTION. Framers of the ''Virginia Plan,'' the first working draft of the Constitution, proposed that the House of Representatives select senators from candidates nominated by the respective state legislatures. A few delegates suggested selection by the president, or by direct popular vote. Most believed, however, that involvement by the House or the president would deprive the Senate of its necessary independence. Beyond that they felt popular election would leave the relatively small commercial classes vulnerable to the dictates of the country's predominant agricultural interests. Connecticut's Roger Sherman noted, ''The people should have as little to do as may be about the government. They lack information and are constantly liable to be misled.'' Consequently, the framers concluded that selection by state legislatures, with their greater ''sense of character,'' would provide the necessary ''filtration'' to produce better senators. They expected that this would tie those potentially troublesome bodies closer to the national government. In agreeing on this method, with the actual manner of choosing senators left to the individual legislatures, the framers had simply copied the system under which they had been chosen, as had most of the members of the Continental and Confederation Congresses.

QUALIFICATIONS. Early in the convention James Madison observed: ''The use of the Senate is to consist in its proceeding with more coolness, with more system, and with more wisdom, than the popular branch.'' To ensure that senators would be less subject to the presumed transitory passions of youth, the framers set the minimum membership age at thirty, five years greater than for House members. Senators were also required to have been citizens for nine years, two years longer than popularly elected members of the House. Madison explained that these distinctions were based on ''the nature of the senatorial trust, which requir/es/ greater extent of information and stability of character.'' (*See Reading No. 1.*)

TERM OF SERVICE. The framers agreed that senators should serve longer than House members to ensure independence from short-term pressures. None believed that the Senate should follow the practice of the British House of Lords with hereditary service, and only Alexander Hamilton suggested lifetime appointments. The delegates sharply divided over the specific number of years, advancing proposals ranging from three to nine. Edmund Randolph argued that a seven-year term would ensure that the Senate could control the consequences of House action. ''If it not be a firm body,'' he reasoned, ''the other branch being more numerous, and coming immediately from the people, will overwhelm it.'' James Madison added that the Senate, with its special role in foreign affairs, would appear more respectable to other nations if its members served longer terms. The framers then settled on a six-year term with one-third of the terms to expire every two years, thus combining the principles of continuity and rotation in office.

BASIS OF REPRESENTATION. The framers paid close attention to the Senate's role in balancing interests of both large and small states. Disagreement over the issue of whether states would be represented equally or in proportion to their population threatened to destroy the convention at its midpoint. Small-state delegates went to Philadelphia determined not to yield the advantage they enjoyed under the Articles in which each state had an equal vote regardless of size. Delaware's John Dickinson asserted that these delegates ''would sooner submit to a foreign power, than to submit to be deprived of an equality of suffrage in both branches of the legislature, and thereby be thrown under the domination of the large states.'' (*See Reading No. 2.*)

The case for equal state representation gained strength from the convention's decision to allow the states, through their legislatures, to elect senators. This confirmed the view that senators were to be ''ambassadors'' of their state governments, rather than of the people at large. Small states were particularly fearful that large states would combine and conspire to obtain commercial advantage. They saw the Senate as their sole check on such competition, for only the Senate could consent to ratify the treaties necessary to establish trade agreements, and only with the consent of two-thirds of its members. This would allow one-third of the states to block treaties objectionable to a significant minority. Similarly, small states feared that the Senate's unique power to confirm presidential appointments would work to the advantage of large states if members were apportioned according to population. They therefore advocated equal representation among states in the Senate to ensure that larger states, with their greater numbers in the House, would not unduly influence appointments to key government administrative posts.

On the weekend of July 14–15, 1787, cool breezes relieved a month-long siege of uncommonly hot weather in Philadelphia. Delegates slept well and the ever-present mosquitoes seemed to disappear. On Monday, July 16, after nearly three weeks of deliberation, during which Gouverneur Morris declared ''the fate of America was suspended by a hair,'' the refreshed framers reached general agreement, by a one-vote margin. Under the ''Great Compromise,'' states were to be represented equally in the Senate and in proportion to their populations in the House. Each state would be allotted two senators, as three would be too costly and would work against the desired efficiency of a smaller body. They were to vote as individuals rather than as a state bloc. The framers intended that the Senate would not be simply another council of states, as was the Confederation Congress, but rather an independent body beholden to no single source of influence or pressure. To ensure that senators would be more than merely the instructed pawns of state legislatures, they as well as House members would be paid by the central government and could not be recalled. With a six-year term, members were thus offered a degree of independence greater than that of any other elected national office holder.

LEGISLATIVE POWERS. As the convention neared its end, the delegates took up the Senate's role in treaty making. Earlier the Committee on Detail had recommended that the Senate "shall have power to make treaties and to appoint ambassadors, and Judges of the Supreme Court." On September 4, the convention transferred treaty-making power to the president "with the advice and consent of the Senate." James Wilson urged the delegates to extend that power to the House as well, but Roger Sherman successfully argued that "the necessity of secrecy in the case of treaties forbade a reference of them to the whole legislature." On the question of whether approval should be by two-thirds vote of all members, or a simple majority, the convention compromised on two-thirds of those present and voting.

Early in the convention, delegates agreed that the Senate should appoint all federal judges, for only senators as statewide officials would have enough knowledge of suitable candidates. Plans to have the Senate try all impeachment cases eventually undercut this proposal, as that would place the Senate in the position of being able to fill vacancies that it had created through the impeachment process. Finally, following the successful model of Massachusetts, the convention agreed to divide responsibility between the president and the Senate. In so doing the delegates accepted Gouverneur Morris's reasoning that "As the president was to nominate, there would be responsibility, and as the Senate was to concur, there would be security."

The small states in the "Great Compromise" had conceded that all revenue bills would originate in the House and that the Senate would be explicitly denied the power to alter or amend such legislation. James Madison, in opposition, observed that this arrangement had proven troublesome in Great Britain and in those states that had followed it. Others agreed that this provision violated the maxim that "the least numerous body was the fittest for deliberation; the most numerous for decision." They argued that it would remove significant legislative responsibility from the Senate, "the great security for good behavior," and that it would lead to endless disputes between the two bodies. After much discussion, the framers adopted the language of the Massachusetts constitution: "All bills for raising revenue shall originate in the House of Representatives; but the Senate may propose or concur with amendments as on other bills."

The convention accorded the Senate one major judicial function—the trial of impeachments. Originally, the framers had vested the Supreme Court with jurisdiction over impeachments of national officers. When they turned to the question of who would try impeachments of Supreme Court justices, the framers decided to give that power to the Senate upon receipt of articles of impeachment from the House. Near the convention's end, delegates shifted all impeachment trials, including those of a president, from the Supreme Court to the Senate. Some argued in opposition that this placed the president at the mercy of Congress. They predicted that "If he opposes a favorite law, the two houses will combine against him, and under the influence of heat and faction, throw him out of office." In preference to moving presidential impeachments to a trial by the Supreme Court, whose members were presidential appointees, the framers resolved that "When the President of the United States is tried, the Chief Justice shall preside: And no person shall be convicted without the concurrence of two-thirds of the members present." This kept the vice president, who as president of the Senate would normally preside in impeachments, from the impropriety of presiding over a trial that might result in his own elevation to the presidency.

RATIFICATION. The convention conducted its deliberations in secret. Consequently, when the framers completed their work on September 17 (*see Reading No. 3*), neither the members of Congress sitting in New York, nor the legislatures of the thirteen states were aware of the delicate mixture of compromise and sheer luck that had propelled this remarkable document to their attention. The framers feared, with good reason, that as soon as members of the state legislatures read the proposed Constitution they would regard it as a fundamental assault on their sovereignty. Accordingly, the Philadelphia delegates provided, and the Confederation Congress agreed, that the Constitution would be sent to special ratifying conventions within each state rather than to the various legislatures. As with the Philadelphia convention, these conclaves would most likely include advocates of change rather than defenders of the status quo. The framers followed the requirements of the Articles of Confederation for passing a major measure by stipulating that nine of the thirteen states must ratify the document to bring the new government into being for those states.

The thirteen state conventions met during the final months of 1787 and during 1788. Provisions for the Senate received sharp scrutiny. Supporters characterized the Senate as a bulwark against tyranny, a source of stability and legislative wisdom, and the states' ultimate guarantee of sovereignty. Contrary to the views, asserting senatorial independence, expressed behind the convention's closed doors, the Federalists—as the Constitution's defenders came to be called—assured the conventions that senators would serve as state ambassadors. State legislatures would be able to "instruct" their senators in matters of consequence.

Despite these assurances, critics feared that the Senate might evolve into an unreachable aristocracy with its longer terms, greater powers, and smaller numbers. Of the twenty-six initial members, only fourteen would have to be present to establish the quorum necessary to conduct business. Of that number a majority could be formed with only eight members. These opponents, within the ratifying conventions, sought to limit the Senate's independence. (*See Reading No. 4.*) One frequently proposed amendment would have enabled state legislatures to recall senators, with or without cause. James Madison sought to ease these fears, explaining in his anonymously written *Federalist* 62 that the Senate represented the portion of sovereignty residing with the states. He assured the legislatures that "No law or resolution can now be passed without the concurrence, first, of a majority of the people, and then, of a majority of the states." In *Federalist* 63, he stressed the stronger "sense of national character" that senators would display in comparison with House members, owing to their longer terms and more distant ties to their constituencies.

Critics also focused on the six-year term and the Senate's treaty powers. In an effort to prevent the creation of a senatorial aristocracy, opponents sought to restrict senators to one six-year term in any twelve-year period. (*See Reading No. 5.*) Defenders of the Constitution's provisions countered that such limits would drive away the best men and that biennial elections for one-third of the body's members would be sufficient to check abuses of power. Those opposing the treaty provisions argued that two-thirds of a quorum—ten senators— would be in a position to sacrifice the nation's commercial and military interests to a foreign power through bribery and other corrupt enticements. Southern states in particular feared that northern and mid-Atlantic states would betray them. William Grayson warned the Virginia convention that if southern members were absent from the Senate for ''just one hour'' a treaty might be concluded giving Spain control over Missis- sippi River navigation, preventing development of the south- west, thus ensuring continued northern domination.

The Constitution's defenders dismissed these arguments, explaining that the Senate's actions were subject to restraint by the state legislatures, which selected senators, the House of Representatives that shared the Senate's approval power, and the president who alone had the power to nominate key officials and to negotiate treaties. Even the impeachment power was limited, as the Senate could try only those cases that the House presented.

When the state conventions completed their work, they submitted proposed constitutional amendments. Of the ten that were subsequently adopted in 1791, none affected the Senate's structure. As preparations went forward to convene the First Congress in March 1789, there was general agreement that the Senate represented a reasonable distribution of power and that it should be given a chance to prove itself.

CHAPTER 2

THE FIRST SENATE: 1789–1791

The Senate of the First Congress established the traditions, precedents, and institutional structures that would define its unique role in the federal system over the next two centuries. Ever sensitive to its relations with the presidency, as well as to the House of Representatives and the individual state legislatures, the Senate engaged these rival bodies with an awareness that each decision would have long-range consequences for the success of the new experiment in constitutional government. During the First Congress, from 1789 to 1791, the Senate confronted virtually every problem that would arise to test the United States government in the two centuries ahead. These included threat of war, taxation, sectionalism, the administration of public lands, congressional salaries, tariff reform, Indian affairs, and slavery.

On June 21, 1788, New Hampshire became the ninth state to ratify the Constitution, thus ensuring the new government would come into existence. The Confederation Congress began an extended debate on the location of the capital city. This debate dragged on for months due in part to sectional jealousies, and in part to the need for individual states to hold legislative elections in the expectation that the new assemblies would be more favorably inclined to the freshly minted Constitution than the old. Ultimately unable to decide on a new seat of government, the Confederation Congress designated its own location—New York City—as the temporary capital. On September 13, 1788, the Confederation Congress signed its death warrant, setting the first Wednesday in January 1789 as the date for states to select presidential electors. Those electors were then to cast their ballots for a president on the first Wednesday in February. The new Congress was to convene on the first Wednesday of the following month—March 4, 1789. (*See Reading No. 6.*)

SENATE ELECTIONS. The ensuing contests for presidental electors and for members of the House stimulated great public interest. By contrast, the selection of senators, in which the people had no direct role, occurred in the various state legislatures with little fanfare. Senate elections generally were held earlier than those for the House, allowing defeated Senate candidates to seek House seats. The Constitution's framers had left details of the selection process to the individual assemblies. Most legislatures decided that senators should be elected in a joint session of both houses—a common means of selecting certain state officials. New Hampshire, Massachusetts, and New York believed, to the contrary, that the selection of senators should be handled, as any other legislative act, by proceeding concurrently. This latter method gave equal weight to the smaller upper houses, unlike the joint voting in which they would be overwhelmed by the numerically larger lower houses.

In New York both houses fought bitterly over procedure for electing senators. After weeks of futile debate between the Federalist upper house and the Anti-Federalist lower chamber, the legislature adjourned on March 3, 1789, unable to select its senators. As a result, New York went without Senate representation for most of that year until the legislature, with both houses safely in Federalist hands following statewide elections, finally agreed to the concurrent method.

In choosing their senators, many states openly recognized existing economic and geographical divisions. Some elected one senator from candidates favorable to their more aristocratically inclined upper houses and the other suitable to their popularly elected lower chambers. The Maryland assembly divided its Senate representation according to geography, stipulating that one senator was to be chosen from the state's Eastern Shore and the other from the larger region west of the Chesapeake Bay. New York, Pennsylvania, and Georgia followed similar regional divisions.

Supporters of the new Constitution took heart in the results of the first Senate elections. With the exception of Virginia, which selected two vigorous opponents of that charter, state legislatures chose men commited to give the new governmental structure a fair chance. Of the twenty senators who had been elected by March 4, 1789, ten had served as delegates to the constitutional convention. Many others had worked to secure ratification in their states. The First Senate's oldest member, William Samuel Johnson (CT), 61, was president of Columbia College. Its youngest, Rufus King (NY), 34, had served in the Revolutionary War, the Massachusetts and New York legislatures, the Confederation Congress, the Constitutional Convention, and the Massachusetts ratifying convention. Among the other senators, whose average age was 48, seven had been officers in the Continental Army, four signed the Declaration of Independence, and nineteen had served in the Continental and Confederation Congresses. Three-quarters had state legislative experience. Eleven were college graduates, with four from Harvard and three from Princeton.

INITIAL ACTIVITIES. State delays in selecting senators and difficult late winter travel conditions along the east coast combined to frustrate the old Confederation Congress' plan to launch the new government on March 4, 1789. Only eight senators-elect responded to the first quorum call. Days stretched into weeks as impatient members appealed to absent colleagues to hasten their arrival. The House of Representatives experienced a similar difficulty until April 1 when it finally mustered a quorum. The arrival of Virginia's Richard Henry Lee permitted the Senate to began its work on April 6.

The men of the First Senate had reason to be pleased with their new meeting place. In an effort to convince Congress to select New York City as the permanent seat of government, local merchants and others underwrote a handsome restoration of the old city hall. The Senate chamber, located on the second floor, occupied a richly carpeted space forty feet long and thirty feet wide. The chamber's most striking features were its high arched ceiling, tall windows curtained in crimson damask, fireplace mantels in handsomely polished marble, and a presiding officer's chair elevated three feet from the floor and placed under a crimson canopy. The ceiling was adorned in the center with a sun and—expressing optimism that Rhode Island and North Carolina would soon join the Union—thirteen stars. Noticably absent from the lavishly ornate chamber was a spectators' gallery—a sign that the Senate's deliberations were to be closed to the public.

The Senate's first order of business was the election of a

presiding officer—a president *pro tempore*—who could act
until the electoral votes for vice president had been counted
and the winner could be certified and sworn into office. The
Senate chose handsome, 48-year-old John Langdon of New
Hampshire and proceeded to its first constitutional duty—
tallying, with the House, the electoral ballots for president and
vice president. Langdon announced that Virginia's George
Washington received sixty-nine votes and thus secured the
presidency. John Adams from Massachusetts, with thirty-four
votes, became vice president. As Senate messengers were
dispatched to notify the winners, senators turned to matters of
internal organization. The Senate chose as its first secretary,
Samual A. Otis, brother of Massachusetts patriot James Otis
and an associate of the new vice president. For doorkeeper, an
essential position in a body that would meet in secret, the
Senate selected James Mathers. Following the procedure of
the Confederation Congress, the Senate selected a chaplain—
the Rev. Samuel Provoost, the first Episcopal bishop of the
New York diocese and a former chaplain of that earlier
Congress. The House chose a chaplain of a different denomi-
nation and agreed with the Senate to interchange the ministers
on a weekly basis.

SENATE-HOUSE RELATIONS. On April 7, 1789, the
Senate established a five-man committee to draft rules of
procedure. Committee members, all lawyers, had served in
state legislatures, the Confederation Congress, and the Constitutional Convention. The influence of these bodies, and British
parliamentary practice, was readily apparent in the resulting
code of twenty rules adopted within the next two weeks. (*See
Reading No. 7.*) Many of the rules were taken directly from the
1778 rules of the Confederation Congress. These rules reflected the emerging distinctions between the twenty-
two-member Senate and the fifty-nine-member House. In the
Senate each member was permitted to participate in the
assignment of members to the temporary committees established to consider legislation. In the House the Speaker alone
exercised that prerogative. Any senator could seek and generally obtain permission to introduce legislation. In the House,
only the *ad hoc* committees could do this. Unlike the Senate,

the House quickly centralized its decision-making processes, and placed emphasis on action at the expense of deliberation.

In these formative weeks, the Senate tried to underscore its presumed exalted status over the House in matters of protocol. The Senate proposed, for example, that two members of the House deliver all communications from that body, while the Senate secretary would suffice to carry the upper chamber's messages down to the House. When the House ignored such pretensions, the Senate added an enticement providing that when one House member presented a message, he would be admitted into the chamber itself. When the desired two members arrived, the entire Senate would rise in acknowledgement. *(See Reading No. 8.)* The Senate also sought, in vain, to establish for its members a higher rate of pay. Ultimately both bodies, reluctant to deal at all with such a touchy issue, agreed on the rate paid to members of the Confederation Congress and the Constitutional Convention—$6 for each day they were in session and $6 for every twenty-five miles of travel to and from the capital.

PROTOCOL AND PROCEDURE. Precedent and etiquette concerning Senate relations with the House and the president consumed a great deal of time in the first months of the Senate's existence. The inauguration of Vice President John Adams on April 21, 1789, *(see Reading No.9.)* raised additional quandaries. Influenced by his recent experience as minister to Great Britain, Adams suggested that senators be addressed as the "Right Honorable." On April 30, the date Congress had set for Washington's inauguration, Adams pleaded with the Senate for guidance as to proper form. As he was speaking, members of the House arrived and took seats in the Senate chamber. After an hour's delay, the presidential entourage appeared. Washington took his oath, delivered his inaugural address, and retired with members for a church service. *(See Reading No. 10.)* Senators then returned to debate the proper form for responding to the presidential address. More than two weeks passed as the Senate considered successive drafts, arguing such matters as whether John Adams should sign the document as vice president or as president of the Senate. On May 18, the Senate traveled to the president's residence where Adams awkwardly read the message (*see Reading No. 11.*) and Washington responded with equal stiffness.

Early in May the Senate addressed two key procedural matters. The Constitution provided that the terms of one-third of the Senate's members would expire at the end of each two-year Congress. Consequently, the Senate moved to divide its members into three "classes." The terms of those in "Class I" would expire at the end of the First Congress in March 1791. "Class II" members would serve until 1793 and "Class III" would expire at the end of the Third Congress in 1795. On May 15 the twenty senators whose credentials had been received drew lots in a specially designed arrangement that ensured each class would contain no more than one member per state and that its members would be drawn from all sections of the country. As additional senators arrived, they would choose lots to retain the sectional and numerical balance between the states. On May 5 the Senate passed its first bill, which set forth the time and manner of administering an oath in support of the Constitution for all national and state legislators, executives, and judicial officers. The president signed this first act on June 1, 1789, and on June 4, Senate President Pro Tempore John Langdon administered the oath to Vice President Adams, who in turn gave it to the entire Senate.

KEY LEGISLATION. In this late spring period the Senate also busied itself with important substantive legislation. The Confederation Congress had set the early March date for the new Congress to begin its work in anticipation that it would be able to establish import duties in time for the spring trading season. This would provide necessary operating revenue for the embryonic government. When the House presented such a measure to the Senate, members of the upper chamber drastically amended the bill, changing the duties on most items. The House, in turn, refused to accept most Senate provisions. Within three weeks a conference committee of both houses forged a compromise that gave the legislation the dual focus of providing needed revenues and serving as a protective device to shield American products from foreign competition. The debate over tariff legislation disclosed ominous sectional strains pitting northern manufacturing and shipping interests against southern agricultural producers.

While this important revenue legislation was drafted in the House, as the Constitution provided, the Senate was at work on the Judiciary Act of 1789. On the day following the first quorum, the Senate appointed Oliver Ellsworth (CT) as chairman of a committee to draft legislation creating the entire federal judicial structure. This measure created a delicately balanced mechanism including a Supreme Court with a chief justice and five associate justices, a federal district court for each of the thirteen states, and three travelling circuit courts of appeals composed of two Supreme Court justices and the judge of the district court in which the appeals court was sitting. This act also established the principle of federal judicial review over state legislation, although such power had not been specified in the Constitution. The Senate passed the measure on July 17 and the House concurred two months later. In late September, the Senate confirmed New York's John Jay as the nation's first chief justice.

NOMINATIONS. The nature and extent of the Senate's constitutional power to provide "advice and consent" to the president's nominations and to his ratification of treaties received several key tests during the initial months of the First Congress. On June 17, 1789, John Jay, serving temporarily as secretary of foreign affairs prior to the creation of the State Department, visited the Senate. He announced that President Washington wished to appoint William Short to replace Thomas Jefferson who was returning on leave from his post as minister to France. The Senate set a key precedent in deciding on the manner in which such a vote would be conducted. Pennsylvania's acerbic William Maclay, whose journal provides the only direct record of the First Senate's closed proceedings, argued that the vote, as with any other election, should be conducted by secret ballot. A senator who openly voted against the president's wishes, he believed, would certainly lose his place in the presidential "sunshine." He feared that some members would be tempted to vote with the chief executive, against their better judgment, to win the president's "warmth." In spite of spirited opposition to the secret ballot,

Maclay's forces carried the day and William Short became the first executive nominee to win Senate confirmation.

A few weeks later the Senate exercised its confirmation power in a manner less satisfactory to the president. On August 3 the Senate began consideration of a list of nearly one hundred presidential nominations for positions as naval officers, customs collectors, and surveyors. After two days of discussion, the Senate approved all but one nominee. That individual, Benjamin Fishbourn, had been appointed naval officer for the Port of Savannah, Georgia. The specific grounds for Fishbourn's rejection were never made clear, although it was presumed that one or both of Georgia's senators found him unsatisfactory. In an era before nominees were summoned by Senate committees to explain their "fitness," the Senate relied heavily on the views of senators from the appointee's home state. Although Fishbourn was the only nominee rejected during the First Congress, the Senate established the principle of "senatorial courtesy" in which senators from the nominee's state exercised a decisive influence. On the following day, the president submitted a new nomination for the Georgia post without attempting to force a Senate reconsideration. In his message to the Senate, however, Washington asked that senators who had a problem with one of his nominees consider whether "it would not be expedient to communicate that circumstance to me, and thereby avail yourselves of the information which led me to make them, and which I would with pleasure lay before you."

TREATIES. Several months later President Washington provided the Senate an opportunity to test its role in reviewing treaties. On August 22, 1789, the president, undoubtedly mindful of the Fishbourn rejection, visited the Senate with General Henry Knox to gain that body's advice and consent for pending treaties with southern Indian tribes. That session sorely tested presidential and senatorial assumptions about the nature of such proceedings. Intimidated by Washington's presence, the Senate reversed its earlier decision for secret ballots and agreed to vote openly on each of the seven treaty articles.

Knox began the session by handing Vice President Adams a treaty document, which the presiding officer attempted to read to the assembled senators. Maclay reported in his journal that "Carriages were driving past and /made/ such a noise /that/ I could /only/ tell it was something about 'Indians'." Senators asked Adams to repeat the first article. When he had done this, he asked for their advice and consent. The result, according to Maclay, was "a dead pause." Senators, in awe of Washington, had been unable to absorb the substance of the treaty. After some whispered coaxing from colleagues, Maclay asked for a reading of various documents referred to in the treaty. At this point, wrote Maclay, "I cast an eye on the President of the United States. I saw he wore an aspect of stern displeasure." Following the reading of the requested documents, senators, growing bolder, voted to postpone a decision several days until a committee could review the issues at hand. Speaking to the senators for the first time during the proceedings, Washington angrily proclaimed, "This defeats every purpose of my being here." Accustomed to the practice of governors' councils deciding such executive matters without recourse to committee deliberation, the president observed that Knox was an expert on the subject, and that he possessed all the information that was necessary for a decision to be made.

The presidential temper eventually cooled and he returned as requested on the following Monday. As he looked on, senators debated various amendments and approved the treaties. This exchange established that the Senate would not act, in the manner of governors' councils, as a rubber stamp for executive proposals. It also convinced Washington never again to visit the Senate. In the future, with the exception of his annual message, he would send his requests in writing. The chief exeuctive also decided not to seek Senate aid in the process of treaty making, but only to give that body the opportunity to accept or reject the finished document.

WORKLOAD AND ACCOMPLISHMENTS. The Senate's workload increased greatly in the final weeks of the first session. This accorded with the framers' notion that the House would serve as the principal workshop for crafting legislation, while the Senate would pass on the lower chamber's handiwork, polishing and reworking in consideration of what were presumably the nation's broader and longer term interests.

With the essential machinery of government in place, the Senate and House adjourned on September 29, 1789. Following a three-month break, both houses reconvened on January 4, 1790. On January 8, President Washington delivered his first annual message to a joint session of Congress assembled in the Senate chamber. The Senate replied within three days, demonstrating greater efficiency than in its earlier response to the president's inaugural message.

During the second session, which continued until August 12, Treasury Secretary Alexander Hamilton played a central role with his plan to place the nation on a firm financial footing. Congress, through a complex set of compromises, agreed to establish the seat of government at Philadelphia for a period of ten years. Subsequently the capital would be located to the south in a federal district at a site along the Potomac River. The second session also authorized the first census of population, defined crimes against the federal government, established a government for the western territories south of the Ohio River, and devised offices for the registration of patents and copyrights. During this session, North Carolina and Rhode Island ratified the Constitution and sent members to the Senate and House. This gave each chamber its full complement of twenty-six and sixty-five members, respectively. At last the Union seemed secure.

On December 6, 1790, the First Congress began its brief final session in new quarters in Philadelphia's recently constructed county court house. Newly named "Congress Hall," this bulding offered the Senate accommodations considerably more elegant than those a floor below in the larger House chamber. In addition to the double row of members' desks and chairs upholstered in red leather, the room's furnishings included a large carpet brightly designed with an eagle clutching an olive branch and thirteen arrows. There were also full-length portraits of Louis XVI and Marie Antoinette, gifts in 1784 of the pre-revolutionary French government. These portraits had adorned the Senate's New York City chamber in recognition of vital French aid during the American Revolution. In Philadelphia, perhaps in deference to the French Revolution, they were outfitted with curtains that could be drawn as protective covering.

CHAPTER 3

THE FORMATIVE YEARS: 1789–1819

In its first thirty years of existence, the Senate expanded the limits of its authority under the Constitution, growing from a small advisory body to the position of equal standing with its two governmental rivals—the House of Representatives and the presidency. Between 1789 and 1819 its membership doubled, rising from twenty-two at the time of the first quorum to forty-four with the admission of Alabama in 1819. This era brought the development of political parties, the absolute guarantee of unlimited debate, creation of permanent standing committees, and expanded public access to chamber proceedings. In this period, the Senate, with the rest of the national government, sat in three capital cities, moving from New York to Philadelphia in 1790 and then, in 1800, to the new federal city of Washington. In 1814 invading British burned the Capitol and the Senate's chamber, forcing a relocation until 1819 when restoration was completed.

POLITICAL PARTIES. In this formative period political parties quickly emerged to shape issues in a way that often cut across the north-south or large state–small state basis of cohesion that the framers thought would prevail. Treasury secretary Alexander Hamilton in 1791 stated the philosophy of the emerging Federalist party on the issue of national development in his "Report on Manufactures." The report's outline for transforming the nation's economic base from agriculture to industry evoked heated opposition from Anti-Federalists led by Secretary of State Thomas Jefferson. These opposition forces, who began to call themselves "Republicans" in contrast to the aristocratic Federalists, sought to retaliate in 1792 by denying Vice President Adams a second term. Adams easily turned aside that challenge and the Federalists retained control of the Senate by a 17-13 margin.

Simmering partisan antagonisms erupted in the Senate when the Third Congress convened in December 1793. The clash came over the seating of Pennsylvania's Albert Gallatin.

Shortly after the Swiss-born Republican took his oath, Vice President Adams presented a petition challenging his eligibility on grounds that he had not been a citizen the required nine years. A committee of five Federalists considered the challenge, under the Constitution's provision for the Senate to be the ultimate judge of its members' fitness to serve. Early in 1794, the Federalist majority, by a strict party division, voted 14-12 to deny Gallatin his seat.

PUBLIC ACCESS. The Gallatin case raised the issue of whether the Senate should continue its policy of conducting its sessions behind closed doors. The Constitution's framers simply assumed that the Senate would follow their own practice, as well as that of the Continental and Confederation Congresses, of meeting in secret. They believed that publication of an official annual journal, with information on how members voted on legislative matters, would be sufficient to keep the public informed. In the Senate, defenders of secrecy looked with disdain to the House where members were tempted to play to the gallery, whose occupants routinely cheered and hissed as issues were debated. In an era before shorthand reporting achieved reliability, press accounts of House activity were notoriously incomplete and distorted along partisan lines.

Opposition to the closed-door policy emerged during the final session of the First Senate and grew in intensity over the following five years. It took particular strength from the Republican minority and from state legislatures whose members felt they could not effectively assess the behavior of those senators whom they had elected. Eventually, the Senate's Federalists recognized that their views could more easily win popular support if publicly aired rather than privately concealed. The notion of the Senate as a "lurking hole" in which conspiracies were hatched against the public interest had to be put to rest. Additionally, press coverage of the House helped popularize that body's role and the public began to use the words "House" and "Congress" interchangeably. The Senate was in danger of becoming the forgotten chamber. Consequently, when the Republicans gained control of the House in 1793, Senate Federalists were ready for a change.

The opportunity for change arrived with the dispute over

Gallatin's seating. Senators, meeting in Philadelphia, realized the delicacy of the situation in which they were questioning the action of the Pennsylvania legislature in selecting Gallatin. Wishing to avoid the charges of "Star Chamber" that would surely follow a secret vote to reject Gallatin, the Federalist majority agreed to open Senate doors just for that occasion. Several weeks later, the Senate decided to open its proceedings permanently as soon as a suitable gallery could be constructed. The Senate never intended, however, to open its discussions of treaties and executive nominations and it reserved the right to close regular legislative sessions at any time. When the gallery opened in December 1795, the public paid little attention.

In the years that followed, the press showed little sustained interest in covering Senate debates, which lacked the fire of those in the lower chamber. (*See Reading No. 12.*) On the few occasions when a dramatic debate attracted reporters, they were consigned to the crowded and noisy gallery. This situation only worsened when the Senate moved to Washington in 1800. The gallery was farther from the floor. Republican editor Samuel Harrison Smith petitioned the Senate in 1802 to permit reporters access to the floor. The Senate, then under Republican control, agreed and Smith began providing readers of his *National Intelligencer* modestly reliable stenographic accounts of congressional debates. His poor health and lack of qualified assistants resulted in uneven coverage, for the reporter's illness or more interesting debate in the House left the Senate unreported.

JAY'S TREATY. Debate over John Jay's 1794 peace treaty with Great Britain placed the spotlight of national attention on the Senate's treaty powers and its evolving party divisions. No other issue in the closing years of the eighteenth century so inflamed partisan animosities. Rumors of the treaty's provisions, which were perceived as favorable to the hated British, circulated widely before President Washington called the Senate into special session on June 8, 1795. Following two weeks of bitter debate, the Senate barely approved the treaty by the necessary two-thirds majority. Several days later Virginia Republican Stevens Mason provided a copy of the still-secret document to a Philadelphia newspaper. An intense public outcry resulted. The senators who had voted in favor became targets of angry mobs while the "virtuous and patriotic ten" who had opposed it became national heroes for their refusal to sign this "death warrant of America's liberties." While House members debated Washington's possible impeachment for signing the treaty, the Senate declined to its lowest point in public esteem.

Weary from those partisan battles, Washington retired to Mount Vernon following the March 1797 inauguration of Federalist President John Adams and Republican Vice President Thomas Jefferson. Adams convened a special session in May 1797 to address worsening relations with France. The Senate agreed to a special negotiating commission and strengthened national defense measures in the event these discussions failed. Early in 1798, the public learned of the insulting treatment of American negotiators by French agents. Immediately, as popular sentiment turned against France, the pro-British Federalists in the Senate regained their popularity. As the Senate pushed through measures enlarging the nation's armed forces, it also initiated four bills known collectively as the "Alien and Sedition Acts." These bitterly nationalistic and intolerant laws threatened severe punishment to those judged disloyal. They temporarily quieted Republican dissent. By 1800, President Adams had successfully negotiated a peace treaty with France, but at the cost of a severe and ultimately fatal split within his Federalist party.

JEFFERSON'S MANUAL. Throughout the turbulent years of the Adams administration, Vice President Jefferson had little to do but preside over the Senate. During that period he devised a manual of parliamentary practice to deal with the chaos that often characterized the Senate's proceedings. His predecessor, John Adams, generally followed British parliamentary experience in making his rulings to settle disputes. Jefferson believed the Senate needed a more specific system of practice. Although he had helped establish the 1776 rules for the Continental Congress, Jefferson was dissatisfied with their application. Accordingly he collected those British precedents that seemed in harmony with the Constitution and the existing code of Senate rules. When the latter two authorities offered no guidance on a particular matter, Jefferson applied the appropriate British precedent. As Jefferson's four-year term as the Senate's president drew to a close in 1801, a local printer collected and published the manual to guide future Senates. Ironically, in 1837 the House incorporated the *Manual* as part of its rules, while the Senate determined that it would not be considered a direct authority on parliamentary procedure or a part of its own rules. (*See Reading No. 13.*)

THE MOVE TO WASHINGTON. On November 21, 1800, the Senate took up residence in basement quarters of the unfinished Capitol in the new federal city on the Potomac. This chamber, smaller than that of Philadelphia, seemed appropriate in dignity and refinement to the Senate's requirements. In 1800 only the Senate wing of the Capitol had been completed, so the House, the Supreme Court, the Library of Congress, and a host of other offices were crammed into the building's north wing.

With a majority of members in both houses, Jeffersonian Republicans set out to undercut Federalist control of the judiciary. Their chief target was the Judiciary Act of 1801, enacted in the closing days of the Adams administration. This law reduced the size of the Supreme Court from six to five members, thus delaying the opportunity for the Republican president to make his own appointments. Adams had also filled newly created judicial posts with Federalists. Early in 1802 the Senate, following a bitter battle in which Vice President Aaron Burr voted with the opposition Federalists, agreed to repeal the act. This ended Burr's career with the Republicans.

IMPEACHMENT. The Senate then turned its attention to another partisan-based fight—the impeachment of Federalist Supreme Court Justice Samuel Chase. On March 12, 1804, the Senate, by a strict party vote, had found Federalist U.S. District Court Judge John Pickering guilty of decisions contrary to law and of drunkenness and profanity on the bench. By all accounts, Pickering was insane. On that same day, the House voted to impeach the eloquent and intemperate Justice Chase for biased conduct and an ''anti-Republican'' attitude. The trial began on February 4, 1805, in the Senate chamber, specially fitted out for the event with a ladies' gallery. Adding to the occasion's drama was the appearance of presiding officer Aaron Burr who only months earlier had killed Alexander Hamilton in a duel and had subsequently fled to avoid an arrest warrant. On March 1 the Senate failed to convict Chase by a single vote, effectively insulating the judiciary from further congressional attacks based on disapproval of judges' opinions. (*See Reading No. 14.*) If the Republicans had removed Chase, there was little doubt that their next target would have been Federalist Chief Justice John Marshall. Two days after the conclusion of the Chase trial, Burr moved members to tears with his stirring farewell address. (*See Reading No. 15.*) Mindful of the just-concluded impeachment proceedings, he described the Senate as "a sanctuary, a citadel of law, of order, and of liberty." (*See Reading No. 16.*)

EXPULSION OF MEMBERS. Within its first two decades, the Senate had several occasions to pass on the fitness of its own members for continued service. In 1794 the Senate had refused to seat Albert Gallatin. In 1797 the body, for the first time, expelled a member. Tennessee's William Blount, a signer of the Constitution, was charged with conspiracy in his efforts to aid Great Britain in a plot to take the vital port of New Orleans from Spanish control. In concluding that this was entirely unsuitable behavior for a member, and thus grounds for expulsion, the Senate nonetheless rebuffed a House move to impeach Blount, ruling that its members were not impeachable officers under the Constitution. Nearly a decade later, Aaron Burr cast his long shadow over the career of another senator. In January 1807, President Jefferson sent the Senate a message describing Burr's alleged conspiracy with Great Britain and Spain to separate western territories into a new nation. Burr surrendered to federal authorities, but was acquitted in a trial presided over by Chief Justice John Marshall. Ohio Senator John Smith had been indicted along with Burr. Despite the acquittal, the Senate decided to discipline Smith following an unfavorable report by a special committee led by Senator John Quincy Adams. After three months of testimony and deliberation, with Baltimore lawyer Francis Scott Key leading Smith's defense, the Senate voted 18-10 for expulsion—one vote short of the required two-thirds. At the request of the Ohio legislature, however, Smith resigned his seat shortly thereafter.

MEMBERSHIP AND LEGISLATIVE LIFE. During its formative years, the Senate consisted of relatively young men with extensive experience in their state legislatures and in previous national Congresses. In 1801, 71 percent had prior congressional service. The average age of a senator, by 1810, had dropped to 40 from the 1789 average of 48. Members normally conducted committee work in the mornings and on Saturdays. They held regular legislative sessions daily from 11 a.m. until 2 p.m. (*See Reading No. 17.*) Senators worked either at their desks in the chamber or in their Capitol Hill boardinghouses. Each member was given writing materials and the privilege to "frank" or send at government expense letters weighing not more than two ounces. (*See Reading No. 18.*) The Senate provided up to three newspaper subscriptions per member. The legislative year generally began in December of the odd-numbered years and lasted until April or May. The final session of a two-year Congress convened the following December and expired three months later on March 3. Unless the president called a special Senate session to confirm cabinet appointees, as was customary at the start of his four-year term, the new Congress would begin the cycle again the following December.

Most legislative activity in this period took place in the House as representatives originated more bills and conducted a greater number of roll call votes. During the Tenth Congress (1807–09), the House originated 173 bills, while the Senate introduced only 54. While the House focused on revenue-related measures, the Senate tended to be most active in matters related to courts and judicial procedure, organization of state and territorial governments, foreign affairs, and banking. Much as the Constitution's framers had intended, senators tended to see themselves as a "Supreme Executive Council of the Nation." (*See Reading No. 19.*) While substantial power resided in the House, true prestige remained with the Senate.

FOREIGN RELATIONS. Relations with Great Britain

and France dominated the Senate's foreign policy agenda during the first three decades. This period coincided with the French Revolution and the Napoleonic Wars. In 1803, following demands within the Senate that the government take action necessary to expel the Spanish from the port of New Orleans, President Jefferson concluded a treaty to purchase the entire Louisiana Territory from France. Although the Senate quickly approved that treaty, it split over providing the $12 million promised to France. Federalists, in the minority and fearing further erosion of their political base through westward expansion, argued that the president had no authority under the Constitution to buy territory from foreign governments. Eventually, the Republican-controlled Senate agreed to the funding measure.

Foreign policy issues during the remainder of Jefferson's administration focused on British interference with American shipping. The Senate passed a series of trade embargoes. These ultimately proved futile as New England-based smugglers, firm in their Federalist opposition to administration policies, delivered essential goods to European buyers. Shortly after James Madison assumed the presidency in 1809, the Senate addressed the legality of taking West Florida from Spain. The administration argued that it had been included in the Louisiana Purchase. Federalist opposition leader Timothy Pickering quoted an 1804 letter from the French foreign minister to support his view that it had not been included. The majority immediately turned on the irascible Pickering, charging that he had violated Senate rules by reading from a confidential document without prior Senate permission. Then, by a vote of 20 to 7, the Senate censured the Massachusetts Federalist, making him the first member to be so scorned.

On June 17, 1812, by a 19-13 margin, the Senate approved Madison's declaration of war against Great Britain. This action, in response to continued British depredations against American traders, went badly for the United States from the outset. With the abdication of Napoleon in 1814, the British intensified their campaign against the Americans. British troops moved into Washington and, on August 24, set fire to the White House and the Capitol. A quick-thinking Senate clerk commandeered a wagon and removed priceless Senate records to the safety of the Virginia countryside. When members returned to the building in September, they found their chamber a charred ruin. Meeting in temporary quarters, the Senate in 1815 unanimously approved the Treaty of Ghent ending this most frustrating conflict.

COMMITTEES. The war of 1812 demonstrated the need for consistent availability of expertise based in permanent standing committees. For the first twenty-seven years of its existence, the Senate operated without such committees. Senate rules required members to obtain majority permission for introduction of bills. In debating the merits of the issue under consideration, the Senate shaped a general consensus and then formed a temporary committee to draft specific legislative language. This accounted for the high percentage of committee-approved bills subsequently enacted by the full Senate.

Committee members were elected in secret balloting by vote of the entire Senate. The member receiving the highest number of votes, generally the senator who initiated the proposal, usually became the chairman. Most committees were composed of three members, although more significant or complex matters were assigned to panels of five or seven members. Over these early years a small number of senators tended to dominate committee work. In the session of 1805–1806, eight senators filled 325 of the 442 committee assignments and held 87 of the 120 chairmanships. Thus, one-quarter of the senators held three-quarters of the committee assignments. Members tended to be reappointed to committees covering subject areas in which they had prior experience. A few senators served on no committees and a larger minority never chaired a committee.

Committees met before and after full Senate sessions, seldom heard witnesses, and never kept transcripts of their proceedings. Originally the Senate sent only the most controversial of the presidential nominations to committees. By 1809, however, it routinely referred all nominations for committee review. This increased workload plus the burdens of national defense that accompanied the War of 1812 placed a premium on specialization. The House of Representatives, with its larger numbers, had established permanent committees early in its existence. As its members moved to service in the Senate, they attested to the greater efficiency of standing committees. In 1815, the Senate created select committees to examine various sections of the president's annual message. Rather than disbanding those panels when they completed their assignments, the Senate continued them to consider legislation on related topics for the remainder of the session. In December 1816 the Senate agreed, for the first time, to establish "standing" committees. These bodies would review the president's annual message as before, but they would remain in business. These panels included the committees on Foreign Relations, Finance, Commerce and Manufactures, Military Affairs, the Militia, Naval Affairs, Public Lands, Claims, Judiciary, Post Offices and Post Roads, and Pensions. As permanent committees, they were able to conduct long-term studies as well as to consider specific legislation. In 1823, the time-consuming process of electing chairmen and members by secret ballot gave way to a system in which the presiding officer appointed members. This remained in effect until 1845.

TERRITORIAL EXPANSION. In 1817 James Monroe became the first senator to be elected president. His arrival at the White House ushered in the so-called "Era of Good Feelings" with the temporary suspension of two-party politics as a result of the demise of the Federalists. In that year, his secretary of state, John Quincy Adams, successfully concluded a treaty with Spain transferring Florida to the United States. The Senate quickly approved that treaty and turned its attention to the problems of settling its new empire west of the Mississippi River. As of 1819, all of the land east of the Mississippi, with the exception of the Michigan Territory, had been divided into two groups of states: slave and free. This situation would dominate the Senate's proceedings over the next four decades.

CHAPTER 4

THE "GOLDEN AGE": 1819–1859

Three senators and a theater-like chamber symbolize the Senate's so-called "Golden Age" during the four decades prior to the Civil War. Nearly a century after this period ended, in 1957, a Senate committee, chaired by Sen. John F. Kennedy, selected the all-time five most "outstanding" senators. Of the five chosen, three served in the first half of the nineteenth century. They were Henry Clay (KY), Daniel Webster (MA), and John C. Calhoun (SC).[1] The chamber in which these and other men confronted the problems of a rapidly expanding nation was located on the second floor of the Capitol's northern wing. The Senate first moved to that location in 1810 after a decade in smaller quarters on the floor below. When the British burned the building in August 1814, the Senate took up temporary residence a block away, until 1819 when restoration was completed. This large semicircular room, with its plain walls and low-vaulted domed ceiling, provided an ideal setting, both acoustically and dramatically, for the Senate during the troubled years ahead. (*See Reading No. 20.*)

In the years from 1819 to 1859 the Senate moved from a position of relative equality with the House of Representatives and the presidency to a preeminent position as balance wheel in the delicate mechanism of American constitutional government. In the face of growing national tensions associated with the issues of slavery, economic development, and sectional parity, the Senate devised the major compromise agreements. These measures bought time for a maturing nation so that when the scourge of civil war could no longer be held back, the national government had amassed the experience, balance, and strength to help it endure and rebuild on the Constitution's original foundations.

---

[1]The other two were Robert La Follette, Sr. (R-WI) and Robert A. Taft, Sr. (R-OH).

HENRY CLAY. Henry Clay's congressional career illustrates the relative growth of the Senate's importance in the early nineteenth century. The Kentucky state legislature sent him to the Senate in 1806 to fill the remaining months of an unexpired term, although he was three months short of the constitutionally mandated age of thirty for Senate service.[2] He then returned to his state legislature, where he was elected speaker. In 1809, at a time when U.S. senators commonly resigned to pursue more attractive options at the state level, the Kentucky legislature again sent Clay to Washington to complete an unexpired term. Although Clay loyally represented the legislature's views in Washington, he decided that he would rather serve the people of his state directly. In 1810 he announced his candidacy for the U.S. House of Representatives, explaining that "In presenting myself to your notice, I conform to sentiments I have invariably felt, in favor of the station of an immediate representative of the people." At the beginning of Clay's House service, that body, in an unprecedented step, elected this first-term member as its speaker. There he became a leader of the "War Hawks," determined to uphold national honor in the face of continuing British hostilities. He also greatly expanded the speaker's powers.

During the 1820s Clay remained in the House while seeking to achieve his principal ambition—the presidency. His three attempts to win that position—in 1824, 1832, and 1844—ended in failure. In 1825 he accepted from President John Quincy Adams the position of secretary of state. This triggered charges from his rival, Andrew Jackson, of a "corrupt bargain" when Clay's House of Representatives decided the close election in favor of Adams. In 1831 Clay returned to the Senate where he remained until 1842. Following his last try for the presidency in 1844, Clay served in the Senate from 1849 until his death in 1852.

From 1831 until the end of his life, Clay viewed the Senate

---

[2]Several years later, in 1816, Virginia sent Armistead Mason at the age of twenty-eight years and five months. In 1818, John Henry Eaton (TN) became the youngest person ever sworn in to the Senate at age twenty-eight years, four months and twenty-nine days.

as the best spring board to higher office and the forum in which to realize his "American System" plan of national development. This plan combined a protective tariff, encouragement of home manufactures, and a national program of internal transportation and communications improvements. A bitter foe of Democrat Andrew Jackson, Clay became a leader from the 1830s of the new opposition Whig party. In an era before the formal designation of party floor leaders, Clay effectively served that role. Members looked to him for signals of how to vote on key issues. A man of great personal magnetism, the tall Kentuckian was the Senate's preeminent tactician. Although not a profound thinker, he excelled in basing his arguments on common sense and expressing them with fearless conviction. (*See Reading No. 21.*)

DANIEL WEBSTER. Daniel Webster (MA) entered the Senate in 1827 after serving in the House, first from New Hampshire and then from Massachusetts. The Senate's outstanding orator, with his great organ-like voice, Webster in common with Clay, longed for the presidency, served as secretary of state, became a leader of the Whig party, and spent the majority of his productive years in the upper body. He rose to national prominence as a result of his 1830 debates with Sen. Robert Y. Hayne (D-SC). On December 20, 1829, Sen. Samuel Foot (CT), a member of the anti-Jackson opposition, introduced a resolution to limit public lands available for sale to those previously surveyed. Sen. Thomas Hart Benton (D-MO), a champion of western expansion and a firm supporter of President Jackson, immediately denounced the Foot resolution as an effort to keep cheap labor available to the industrialists of the northeast by limiting opportunities for the poor to escape to the frontier. Vice President John C. Calhoun (D-SC), who had sought to build an alliance between the South and West against northern manufacturing interests, strongly supported Benton's position.

As the Senate's presiding officer, Calhoun lacked the right to address the body without its permission. His fellow South Carolinian, Sen. Hayne, labored under no such limitations. Considered a master of sustained argument, the thirty-eight-year-old Hayne on January 19, 1830, addressed the

Senate in support of the Foot resolution. In an effort to reinforce ties between the South and West on the issue of public land, he bitterly attacked the northeast, high protective tariffs, and especially Daniel Webster, who had abandoned his earlier support for low tariffs. On the following day, Webster responded briefly, defending the resolution and tariff while challenging the South's apparent willingness to subvert the Union for regional economic gain. In doing so, he broadened the debate beyond land, tariffs, and slavery to a consideration of the very nature of the federal republic. Webster argued that the North had always been the West's ally. He successfully shifted the debate to one of states' rights versus national power. Following Hayne's affirmation of a state's right to openly defy an act of Congress, Webster returned on January 27, 1830, with his classic "Second Reply to Hayne." (*See Reading No. 22.*)

Speaking from twelve pages of notes, during two afternoons, Webster delivered an eloquent and powerful defense of constitutional nationalism. The nation, in his view, was no mere association of sovereign states, but a "popular government, erected by the people; those who administer it responsible to the people; and itself capable of being amended and modified, just as the people may choose it should be." To hold that states could selectively obey federal laws was, in Webster's view, to take a giant step toward civil war. Overnight, Webster became a national figure, respected by friends and enemies alike. In the wake of his dramatic address, the Senate shelved the Foot resolution and chances of an alliance between the South and West evaporated.

JOHN C. CALHOUN. John C. Calhoun emerged as the South's chief theorist and leading statesman during this dramatic period in the Senate's history. As with Clay and Webster, he developed an early interest in public affairs. All three had served together in the House during the War of 1812. Before entering the Senate in 1833, Calhoun had been secretary of war and then Jackson's vice president. He remained in the Senate for the rest of his life, except for a brief period as secretary of state in 1844–1845. His strength as a debater emerged from his powerful philosophical talents. Not a naturally gifted public speaker, Calhoun worked to cultivate his voice, "as to make his utterance clear, full and distinct . . . and while not at all musical, it fell pleasantly on the ear."

In 1832, Congress enacted a major tariff measure. Although milder than the 1828 "Tariff of Abominations," it contained few concessions for southern cotton farmers, while continuing to protect New England wool growers. This prompted Calhoun, as vice president, to reiterate the theory, propounded in 1828, that a state could "nullify" those acts it considered to be unconstitutional. South Carolina then convened a state convention that promptly adopted an ordinance nullifying the new tariff and banning collection of duties within the state. President Jackson condemned this action and alerted federal troops in South Carolina. Realizing that the issue would be played out in the Senate, Calhoun carried out a plan in which Sen. Robert Hayne resigned. The state legislature then elected Calhoun to the vacancy and Hayne won election as governor. With his Senate seat secured, Calhoun resigned the vice presidency.

Weeks earlier, Jackson had been reelected, defeating Henry Clay by a large margin, and Martin Van Buren (D-NY) had won the vice presidential term to begin on March 4, 1833. On January 4, Calhoun arrived at the Senate amidst rumors that the president had vowed to have him hanged. Several weeks later, in response to Jackson's "Force Bill," providing for use of the nation's armed forces to ensure obedience to acts of Congress, Calhoun delivered a vigorous speech supporting states' rights. (*See Reading No. 23.*) This set the stage for a replay of the Webster-Hayne debate, this time without Hayne as Calhoun's surrogate.

Calhoun spoke for two days in defense of his belief that the Union existed as a compact between sovereign states. In his opinion, each state retained the ultimate power to decide whether the laws of the United States were to apply to it. He flatly denied that the United States had ever been intended as a union of people. Webster responded calmly with familiar arguments from his earlier debate with Hayne. (*See Reading No. 24.*) To Webster, the Constitution was no mere "compact" among states, but rather an "executed contract" to set up a permanent government, supreme within its own sphere, acting directly on the people as a whole. On February 24,

1833, as Calhoun and his allies withdrew from the chamber in protest, the president's "Force Bill" passed by a 32-1 margin. Crisis was averted on this occasion with a compromise tariff measure that, over a decade, would lower rates across the board so that they would decline to the 1816 level. Calhoun agreed to this face-saving measure, realizing that his own state was divided on the issue and that it lacked support from other southern states.

RETURN TO PARTISANSHIP. The "Missouri Compromise" of 1820–1821 preserved the Senate's role as the debating forum for control of slavery in the territories and new states. With the addition of Maine and Missouri, the Senate's membership rose to forty-eight. Half of the states permitted slavery and half did not. Compared with the House's 213 members (it would rise to 242 after the 1830 census), the Senate offered a forum better suited to lively and discursive debate. Until the late 1820s, in the so-called "Era of Good Feelings," there was little distinct political party identification in the Senate, or elsewhere on the national political stage. The 1828 election of Andrew Jackson, however, led to the reemergence of two distinct national political parties. Those Jackson supporters who formed the new Democratic Party sought to identify themselves with the Jeffersonian ideals of states' rights, strict interpretation of the Constitution, and economic independence.

Shortly after taking office, Jackson, espousing the virtue of "rotation in office," replaced a large number of federal officials with men loyal to his regime. More than three hundred of those posts required Senate confirmation. When the Senate convened in December 1829, anti-Jackson forces succeeded in rejecting many of the president's nominees. The chief executive subsequently renominated a large number of the better qualified men, who had been holding office under "recess appointments," during the nine months prior to the Senate's convening. On the second try, in the face of growing Senate concern about public reaction to its treatment of a popular president, Jackson won confirmation for his appointees.

Within a few months of the Webster-Hayne debate, Jackson vetoed a bill providing federal funds for construction of a turnpike in Kentucky. He acted on the grounds that the federal government should not support projects of purely local importance. The Senate, with its nearly even balance between Democrats and National Republicans, failed to muster the necessary two-thirds vote to overturn Jackson's veto. This brought Kentucky's Henry Clay out of retirement to challenge Jackson in the 1832 election.

That campaign began with Senate debate over confirmation of a former secretary of state, Martin Van Buren, to be minister to England. Van Buren had won out over Vice President Calhoun in the battle for Jackson's affections. Calhoun knew that he stood no chance of being Jackson's running mate for a second term. In a bitterly partisan debate over the Van Buren appointment, the combined anti-administration forces of Clay, Webster, and Calhoun set out to embarrass Jackson and to wound his favored lieutenant by defeating the nomination. Administration supporters, led by Thomas Hart Benton, believed that opposition attacks on Van Buren would backfire and might actually increase his stature. Accordingly, they arranged for the confirmation vote to end in a tie, forcing Calhoun, as presiding officer, to cast the deciding vote. Calhoun gladly voted against Van Buren and boasted, within Benton's hearing, "It will kill him, sir, kill him dead; he will never kick, sir, never kick." Benton happily and prophetically contradicted him. "You have broken a minister and elected a vice president."

It was at this period in the Senate's history that the French visitor Alexis de Tocqueville described the body, in contrast to the "vulgar demeanor" of the House, as "composed of eloquent advocates, distinguished generals, wise magistrates, and statesmen of note whose arguments would do honor to the most remarkable parliamentary debates of Europe." (*See Reading No. 25.*) Benton took issue with this view. He argued that the Frenchman's opinion was based on an elitist belief that state legislatures selected better men than did the masses through popular election. The Missouri senator observed that most senators had originally been House members and thus had passed the test of popular scrutiny. (*See Reading No. 26.*)

THE BANK WAR. Henry Clay had believed he had a

ready-made issue for his 1832 campaign against Jackson in the president's opposition to the Bank of the United States. This federally chartered private financial institution exercised exclusive control over the government's deposits. Jackson and his Senate supporters, led by Benton, argued that the bank was an unconstitutional elitist institution benefitting commercial classes in the northeast at the expense of southern and western interests. Although the bank's charter was not up for renewal until 1836, Clay convinced its aristocratic president, Nicholas Biddle, to apply in 1832. Congress passed the necessary legislation, which Jackson promptly vetoed. Clay's National Republican forces failed, in July 1832, to override the veto. They also failed in November in their bid to capture the presidency. Believing that his massive reelection victory gave him a mandate to destroy the bank, Jackson in 1833 announced a plan to transfer government funds from the institution to selected state banks. Biddle responded by restricting loans and tightening credit in an effort to create a financial crisis that would force the president to end his war with the bank.

CENSURE OF PRESIDENT JACKSON. As the Senate convened in December 1833, the pro-bank forces of Clay, Webster, and Calhoun counted a majority of twenty-eight members, against twenty for Jackson's Democratic Party. On December 11, the Senate adopted Clay's resolution directing the president to provide a copy of a bank document that he had read to his cabinet. Jackson responded that the Senate lacked the constitutional authority ''to require of me an account of any communication, either verbally or in writing, made to the heads of departments acting as a cabinet council.'' (*See Reading No. 27.*) Clay then took the unprecedented action of introducing a resolution of censure condemning the president's behavior. In a classic assertion of legislative prerogative, Clay charged the president with usurping congressional power to override vetoes, to confirm appointments, and to control the government's financial management. (*See Reading No. 28.*) On March 28, 1834, by a vote of 26-20, the Senate—for the first time and only time in its history—censured a president.

Jackson responded to his censure with a message to the Senate denying its power to pass such a resolution. (*See*

Reading No. 29.) The Senate immediately voted to reject the president's message—an indication of the intense bitterness between the two branches. (*See Reading No. 30.*) The upper house then took another precedent-setting step, decisively defeating a cabinet nomination—for the first time in its history. Anticipating this outcome, Jackson had been reluctant to send to the Senate his nomination of Roger B. Taney to be treasury secretary. Finally, on June 23, 1834, the president forwarded the nomination. The next day, the Senate, by a 18-28 vote, rejected Taney. That this slap was directed at Taney for his role in aiding Jackson in the bank war became evident days later when the Senate unaminously confirmed the president's second nominee to that post.

DOCTRINE OF INSTRUCTION. The censure of Jackson revived debate on the right of state legislatures to "instruct" senators. Many at the constitutional convention in 1787 believed senators would serve as their states' ambassadors, as had members of the Confederation Congress. In February 1834 the Whig majority in the Virginia legislature instructed its senators to fight Jackson's removal of deposits from the Second Bank. Sen. John Tyler, who favored restoration, gladly followed the instructions, but Sen. William C. Rives, a strong supporter of the president, refused and resigned rather than vote against his convictions. The legislature immediately replaced him with a Jackson opponent who was willing to comply with its wishes. Later, when the legislature returned to Democratic control, Tyler resigned rather than follow its instructions to support Jackson.

Many state legislatures ordered their senators to try to overturn the censure resolution. In reaction to these instructions, Whig senators developed a body of theory supporting senators' rights to follow their consciences in defending both the Constitution and the independence of the Senate. Sen. Willie Mangum (W-NC) agonized over the issue and concluded that the Senate served as the only barrier to the executive's virtually absolute power. In rejecting his legislature's directions, he argued that the doctrine of instruction would undermine the Senate's immunity to frequent changes in popular opinion that the Constitution had conferred. Other senators distinguished between matters of "policy," in which they would follow instructions, and those involving "constitutional questions," in which they would not. By 1860 the doctrine of instruction, subject to repeated abuses, had been thoroughly discredited.

CENSURE EXPUNGED. For nearly three years Senate Democrats, under Benton's leadership, sought to expunge the blot of censure from Jackson's presidency. Finally, on January 16, 1837, as the ailing Jackson was preparing to turn the White House over to Martin Van Buren, the Democrats, now with a majority in the Senate, got their way. By a vote of 24-19, the Senate directed its secretary to produce its 1834 journal of proceedings and therein to draw heavy black lines around the original resolution, with the notation, "Expunged by order of the Senate." The Democrats thrilled to their great symbolic victory, while Henry Clay, dressed in black to mourn the death of the Constitution, noted "The Senate is no longer a place for any decent man." Despite Clay's momentary frustration, his leadership, along with that of Webster and Calhoun, brought into existence the new opposition Whig Party. The Whigs, predominately representative of aristocratic and commercial interests, drew their strength from the battles over the tariff, bank recharter, and the resulting presidential censure. For the next two decades, until the mid-1850s, these two parties helped define the nature of debate within the United States Senate.

THE WHIG PARTY. The Whig Party, in the wake of financial hard times in the late 1830s, sought to capture supporters from the Democratic Party by running without a clearly stated platform. Only in the Senate did Whig leader Henry Clay set forth a consistent program. From his position as chairman of the Senate Finance Committee, Clay sought to implement his "American System" through legislation to reestablish the Bank of the United States, raise tariffs, and provide federal funding for river, harbor, and other projects that would improve transportation between the sections to make them interdependent. In 1840 the Whigs, for the first time, elected a president. With a seven-vote Whig majority in the Senate and a similar margin in the House, Clay succeeded in 1841 in getting a bank bill passed. John Tyler, who had become president on the death of William Henry Harrison after only a month in the White House, quickly broke with Clay. He vetoed the bill, insisting that any bank legislation include a provision allowing states to reject the establishment of bank branches within their borders. Failing to override the veto, Clay got a modified version of the measure passed, but Tyler, seeing Clay as a likely rival for the Whig nomination in 1844, again vetoed it. The war between the two men continued as Clay sought, unsuccessfully, the passage of constitutional amendments allowing Congress to override a presidential veto by a simple majority rather than two-thirds and giving the Senate and House sole authority to appoint the secretary of the treasury. Clay believed that the president should have no authority to formulate laws, but only to administer them.

UNLIMITED DEBATE. In 1841 the right of unlimited debate in the Senate became entwined in Henry Clay's legislation to recharter the Bank of the United States. Sen John C. Calhoun and other opponents of the bill, between June 21 and July 12, launched the Senate's first extended filibuster. On July 12 Clay, following earlier House procedure, called for the "previous question" to end what he considered abuse by the minority of the right of unlimited debate. Calhoun responded with a promise of a lengthy fight against efforts to impose a "gag rule" on the minority's "undoubted right to question, examine and discuss those measures which they believe in their hearts are inimical to the best interests of the country." Clay, acknowledging his own previous efforts to draw out debate, yielded to the opposition's desire to continue talking. Eventually his bill passed. For the first time, the principle of minority rights was applied in defense of extended debate. In 1856 the Senate considered a rule requiring that floor discussion be relevant "to the question under debate." Reflecting its entrenched belief that the only limit on debate should be members' sense of decorum, the Senate quickly defeated that resolution. Over the following decades, the Senate consistently killed similar efforts to adopt a rule of germaneness, similar to that followed by the House.

CONFRONTATION WITH THE TYLER ADMINIS-TRATION. The low state of relations between the Senate and the Tyler administration became dramatically apparent in March 1843, during the final hours of the congressional session. Tyler nominated Rep. Caleb Cushing (W-MA) to be secretary of the treasury. Cushing had emerged as a determined supporter of the unpopular president and an opponent of the party's Clay faction. Although Clay had resigned from the Senate in 1842 to prepare for another presidential bid, his influence among the chamber's Whigs was still great. Consequently, for only the second time in its history, the Senate rejected a cabinet nomination. Tyler quickly renominated Cushing, and the Senate again, by a greater margin, rejected him. Within an hour of this defeat, the president submitted Cushing's nomination for a third time. Voting 2-29, the Senate finally put an end to the president's hopeless gesture. The Senate also rejected Tyler's nominations for secretaries of the navy and war, a Supreme Court justice, and ministers to France and Brazil.

Tyler sought to bolster his own reelection prospects by supporting annexation of the independent Republic of Texas. Daniel Webster, who had left the Senate in 1841 to serve the Whig administration as secretary of state and to promote Massachusetts's commercial interests, decided his usefulness had come to an end and resigned. Tyler eventually reached into the Senate and selected Calhoun. The South Carolinian desired to use Texas as an area for the expansion of slavery. When the treaty of annexation was sent to the Senate in April 1844, Calhoun associated protection of the institution of slavery with the "peace, safety, and prosperity of those states of the Union in which it exists." Abolitionist Sen. Benjamin Tappan (D-OH) leaked confidential treaty correspondence to the press setting off an uproar in the North and linking the issues of Texas annexation and the preservation of slavery. Annexation then became a volatile political issue. Opposition to it cost Van Buren the 1844 Democratic nomination and Clay the election, placing dark-horse pro-annexationist James K. Polk in the White House. The 1844 election had provided a mandate for annexation and Tyler signed an authorizing joint resolution as his term drew to a close.

COMMITTEES AND PARTY STRUCTURE. Prior to 1823 the Senate had elected members of its committees by secret ballot. In that year, this time-consuming practice gave way to an arrangement in which the presiding officer appointed members. This gave particular influence to the executive branch, as the vice president generally exercised his constitutional responsibility as the Senate's presiding officer. On December 4, 1845, the Senate defeated, by a single vote, a motion to allow the vice president to continue making committee appointments. Following several weeks of futile balloting for individual assignments, the Senate decided to adopt lists of names prepared by majority and minority party caucuses. This new method of selection greatly enhanced the influence of parties in the Senate. It also placed greater emphasis on seniority. As long as committee members had been selected by ballot or appointed by the presiding officer, a member's experience offered no absolute guarantee that he would be selected. From 1846 onward, seniority became the key determinant in selection of committee chairmen, thus reducing fierce intraparty struggles for committee control. At the same time a clear sense of party consciousness emerged as party members began to sit together in the chamber, with Democrats to the presiding officer's right and Whigs to his left.

TERRITORIAL ANNEXATION. Texas dominated the Senate's agenda in the mid-1840s. A boundary dispute with Mexico led in 1846 to hostilities that Whigs, suspicious of administration plans for expansion of slavery in the southwest, were quick to dub "Mr. Polk's War." This action greatly troubled Calhoun, who returned to the Senate in 1845. Although he had argued in favor of annexation while secretary of state, he did not wish to see the United States seize additional lands. His goal was to consolidate rather than to expand the South's territorial gains.

On August 8, 1846, David Wilmot, a House member from Pennsylvania, introduced a resolution providing that "neither slavery nor involuntary servitude shall ever exist in any part" of the territory won from Mexico as a result of the war. The Senate repeatedly blocked passage of the Wilmot Proviso. That measure took on great significance for it brought the slavery issue back into Senate deliberations after a quarter-century hiatus. Prior to the mid-1840s the Whig and Democratic parties included senators from all sections. The Whigs, with greater strength in the North, were held together by a general aversion to unchecked territorial expansion. The Democrats, with particular strength in the South, also operated as a genuinely national party.

Throughout 1847 the Senate, under Calhoun's leadership, blocked adoption of the Wilmot Proviso. On March 10, 1848, the Senate agreed to ratification of the annexation treaty. The Treaty of Guadalupe Hidalgo, ending the war with Mexico, brought the United States vast new territories from Texas to California. The Senate immediately confronted the issue of how these territories would be organized with particular regard to the existence of slavery within their borders. The Polk administration proposed simply to extend the Missouri Compromise line to the Pacific. This question engaged presidential candidates in the 1848 election. Free Soil Senator Lewis Cass (MI) devised the doctrine of "popular sovereignty" which left the decision to the territories' residents. The Democratic Party adopted this solution and nominated Cass as its presidential candidate. Van Buren organized an independent antislavery coalition thereby splitting the Democrats and handing the election victory to Whig General Zachary Taylor who had drawn support from the North as a war hero and from the South as a slaveholder.

Despite Taylor's southern roots, he took a national view and soon began to seek advice from antislavery Whigs such as Sen. William H. Seward (NY). The president hoped to avoid reawakening the slavery crisis by an arrangement that would allow California and New Mexico (including the present state of Arizona) to enter the Union immediately, bypassing the territorial stage. The absence of slaveholders in these regions ensured that they would join as free states. This plan ignited explosive opposition among southern senators who realized that it would destroy the Senate's equal sectional division between slave and free states.

COMPROMISE OF 1850. In January 1850 the Senate was confronted with an array of conflicting proposals for

settling this menacing situation. Henry Clay, recently returned
to the Senate following his abortive quest for the presidency,
set to work on a compromise similar to the one he had helped
devise as a House member in 1820. With the support of Daniel
Webster and numerous southern senators, Clay proposed a
series of eight resolutions. They provided that California
would enter the Union as a free state. Residents of New
Mexico territory would determine the status of slavery in that
region. Slavery would be continued within the District of
Columbia, but the slave trade there would be abolished.
Congress would enact a strengthened fugitive slave law and the
federal government would pledge not to interfere with slavery
where it existed. In his address to a packed Senate at the end
of January and early February, Clay, waved a fragment of
George Washington's coffin and concluded, "I have said what
I solemnly believe—that the dissolution of the Union and war
are identical and inseparable. . . . Such a war, too, as that
would be, following the dissolution of the Union! Sir, we may
search the pages of history, and none so furious, so bloody, so
implacable, so exterminating . . . was ever conducted." (*See
Reading No. 31.*)

On March 4, John C. Calhoun, gravely ill and emaciated,
arrived in the Senate chamber to respond to Clay's proposals.
Too weak to read his own remarks, he entrusted the task to
Virginia's James Mason. Calhoun challenged the Senate to
respect the South's institutions and to protect her economic
vitality against northern efforts to limit slavery and to favor
industrial over agricultural products. (*See Reading No. 32.*)

Three days later, on March 7, 1850, Daniel Webster
delivered his reply, one of the most notable addresses ever
presented before the Senate. (*See Reading No. 33.*) Webster
argued that the issue of slavery in the territories had been
settled long ago when Congress exercised its right to prohibit
it in the Northwest Ordinance of 1787 and to divide regions
into slave and free in the 1820 Missouri Compromise. He
called on northerners to respect slavery in the South and to
assist in the return of fugitive slaves to their owners. He joined
Clay in warning that the Union could never be dismembered
peacefully. Webster immediately earned the praise of moderates in both sections, along with the hatred of northern

abolitionists who believed he had sold his soul to the devil of the South's "peculiar institution."

BENTON-FOOTE CLASH. On March 31, 1850, the death of John C. Calhoun removed one of the strongest opponents of Clay's compromise. In mid-April Thomas Hart Benton rose in opposition to Henry S. Foote's (D-MS) proposal to create a special Senate committee to look into the compromise. Benton argued that Congress lacked the power to interfere with slavery and that the country was "alarmed without reason and against reason" over the slavery issue. Foote took this as a slap at the memory of the late Calhoun. Benton, a large bearlike man, responded by advancing on the diminutive Mississippi senator. As Foote retreated backwards down the aisle toward the presiding officer's desk, he instinctively drew a pistol. The chamber erupted in cries of astonished disbelief. While senators called for order, Benton shouted, "I have no pistols. Let him fire! Stand out of the way and let the assassin fire!" Other senators intervened and the crisis passed. Foote later threatened to write a very small book in which Benton would play a major role. Benton responded that he would write a very large book in which Foote would have no part whatsoever. With the publication of his classic *Thirty Years' View,* Benton fulfilled this pledge.

On April 18, following the Benton-Foote confrontation, the Senate passed Foote's resolution 30-22 and established a Select Committee of Thirteen, chaired by Henry Clay. Within three weeks Clay reported back to the Senate with a proposal virtually identical to his original compromise measure. The debate dragged on into the sweltering summer months. President Taylor's opposition to the Clay plan ended abruptly with his sudden death on July 9, 1850. Clay eventually abandoned his efforts to pass a single omnibus bill in the face of sectional fears. In his place, Sen. Stephen A. Douglas (D-IL), chairman of the Senate Committee on Territories, adopted a new strategy. He separated the major components of Clay's bill and, by tieing together temporary majorities for each measure, succeeded in getting them passed, one by one. By September 1850, both houses of Congress had completed the compromise, admitting California as a free state, adopting a tough fugitive slave law, and agreeing on territorial status for the remaining western regions. President Millard Fillmore readily approved all these Senate-engineered measures.

KANSAS-NEBRASKA ACT. The Compromise of 1850, the handiwork of Douglas rather than Clay, merely postponed for another few years settlement of the slavery issue in the remaining western territories. Douglas was particularly interested in resolving the territorial issue to clear the way for construction of a transcontinental railroad that would link his own city of Chicago with California. Southern senators blocked legislation providing for a route through the Nebraska Territory, which had been closed to slavery under terms of the Missouri Compromise. To counter southern proposals for an alternate route through Texas, Douglas moved, in January 1854, to exempt the Nebraska Territory from restrictions against slavery.

Reponding to southern pressure for repeal of the 1820 Missouri Compromise, Douglas modified his legislation to include an end to outright prohibition of slavery in the territories. He introduced Lewis Cass's concept of "popular sovereignty" under which a territory's residents would decide whether to allow slavery when those territories became states. He provided for the creation of two territories, Kansas and Nebraska, believing that Kansas to the south would likely become a slave state. Antislavery senators, led by Charles Sumner (W-MA) and Salmon P. Chase (Free-Soil/D-OH) lashed back with their "Appeal to Independent Democrats," charging Douglas with capitulating to southern demands. This document, widely circulated throughout the North, turned public opinion solidly against the previously popular Illinois Democrat. He observed that he could ride all the way from Washington to Chicago by the light of his burning effigy.

Despite the efforts of antislavery senators, who were in the minority, the Kansas-Nebraska bill passed the Senate and became law by the end of May. Many of its northern supporters, placing their trust in the popular sovereignty doctrine, believed slavery would not survive harsh frontier conditions and would be unacceptable to local voters. These senators simply cooperated with the South to maintain national harmony in the face of increasing sectional stresses.

Instead of calming sectional tensions, the Kansas-Nebraska Act intensified them. The measure led directly to the creation of the Republican Party, constituted from Free-Soil Democrats and Antislavery Whigs. In the elections of 1854, the Illinois legislature, in a slap at Douglas for his support of that act, placed Republican Lyman Trumbull in the state's other Senate seat. So rapid was the rise of this new party that in the 1855 session it won a majority in the House and provided fifteen of the Senate's sixty members.

CANING OF CHARLES SUMNER. A Kansas statehood bill sharply divided the Senate during the early months of 1856. Douglas reported from his Committee on Territories a bill affirming the constitutional right of local residents to make the decisions. Republicans responded by seeking Kansas's admission as a free state. Charles Sumner led the free-soil onslaught against Douglas, whom he called "a brutal vulgar man without delicacy or scholarship /who/ looks as if he needs clean linen and should be put under a shower bath." On May 19, 1856, Sumner delivered a scathing denunciation of the Douglas view on the admission of Kansas. His "Crime Against Kansas" speech specifically maligned Sen. Andrew P. Butler (D-SC). (*See Reading No. 34.*)

One of the onlookers in the crowded Senate gallery that day was South Carolina Representative Preston Brooks, a relative of Butler's. Later he said, "I felt it to be my duty to relieve Butler and avenge the insult to my state." When the Senate adjourned at 12:45 p.m. on May 22, 1856, Brooks approached Sumner as the senator sat affixing his postal frank to copies of the Kansas speech. Quickly, Brooks slammed his gold-topped cane onto the unsuspecting Sumner's head. Repeatedly he struck the Republican senator who blindly lurched about the Senate Chamber in a futile effort to protect himself from the ceaseless torrent of blows. Bleeding profusely, Sumner was carried to an adjacent room and then taken to his boarding-house. Brooks and two House members who had accompanied him as bodyguards cooly walked out of the chamber without being detained by the shocked onlookers. Days later the House failed to pass a censure resolution against Brooks, who subsequently resigned and was immediately reelected by approving South Carolinians.

This incident, perhaps the most dramatic in the Senate's history, immediately intensified sectional animosities. Overnight, Sumner and Brooks had become heroes within their respective regions. Later that year, Republicans selected as their first presidential candidate former Senator John C. Fremont, Thomas Hart Benton's son-in-law. Democrats chose James Buchanan, another former senator, to head their ticket. Buchanan easily defeated Fremont amidst growing talk of secession in South Carolina and Virginia.

ROAD TO DISUNION. Early in 1857 the U.S. Supreme Court sought to settle the territorial dispute with its ruling in the *Dred Scott v. Sanford* case. The court found that the Missouri Compromise was unconstitutional on the grounds that Congress could not deny rights in the territories that were enjoyed in the states. This decision held that blacks were not citizens and had no rights under the Constitution. When Kansas proslavery settlers submitted a state constiution directly to Congress, in violation of the popular sovereignty doctrine that Douglas had employed to ease sectional tensions, Douglas, sensing betrayal, turned on his southern supporters. This prompted a breach within the Senate's Democratic majority, twenty-five of whose thirty-seven members were from southern states. Over Douglas's vigorous objections, his Committee on Territories reported a bill to accept the proslavery constitution. On March 23, 1858, the Senate approved the measure. Ultimately the House and Senate agreed to a compromise requiring the constitution to be submitted to the voters of Kansas. In April those voters decisively rejected that document.

Later that year Douglas campaigned for reelection by the Illinois legislature. In a series of momentous debates, his Republican opponent, former Representative Abraham Lincoln, forced Douglas to adopt positions that further alienated him from northern Republicans and southern Democrats. This undermined his influence as he returned to the Senate, following reelection. When the Senate's Democratic caucus met in

December 1858 to select committee chairmen, its members took the unprecedented step of removing Douglas, despite his seniority, as chairman of the Committee on Territories.

The nation's rapid territorial expansion led to the admission of five new states between 1845 and 1850. In the latter years Congress appropriated funds for construction of new chambers in wings to be located at the northern and southern ends of the Capitol. On January 4, 1859, the Senate's large new chamber was ready. Senator John Crittenden of Kentucky brought tears to the eyes of members in the old chamber as they prepared to proceed to their new quarters. "This place which has known us for so long is to know us no more forever as a Senate," he said. His fellow Kentuckian, Vice President John Breckinridge, expressing hope that the Senate would endure the gathering storm of disunion, led the assembled senators out of the worn chamber and forty-five paces down the hall to an uncertain future.

CHAPTER 5

WAR AND RECONSTRUCTION: 1859–1889

In entering its bright new chamber, the Senate took a long stride toward the nation's darkest era. Events of the coming three decades would tear at the fabric of the Constitution and try the Senate's institutional strength as never before. In January 1859, however, senators briefly set aside preoccupation with thickening storm clouds to survey their spacious quarters.

The new hall, measuring 113 feet by 82 feet, included a large gallery along all four walls. The ceiling, 35 feet above the room, featured stained glass panels decorated with symbols of national progress and plenty. Natural light illuminated the room by day, and gas by night. Desks for the sixty-four senators were arranged in three semicircular rows with members of the new Republican Party sitting to the presiding officer's left, while Democrats sat on his right. (*See Reading No. 35.*)

The elections of 1858, reflecting grave economic conditions and public anger over the Dred Scott decision, returned the Republican party to control of the House of Representatives and increased its ranks in the Senate by six. This left the party balance in the upper chamber at thirty-eight Democrats, twenty-six Republicans, with two others. Battle lines between the North and South became more evident as southern senators blocked legislation providing for a transcontinental railroad, cheap land for homesteaders, a higher tariff, and river and harbor improvements. Northern members retaliated by frustrating the South's desire to establish a protectorate over northern Mexico and to secure a new slave state by purchasing Cuba from Spain. Several days before the Senate convened for its regular session in December 1859, John Brown was executed for his efforts to spark a slave insurrection. The wife of a southern senator captured the ominous climate in which the Senate met, noting, ''We are dancing over a powder keg.''

SECESSION. Sectional crises and the breakdown of old

53

political coalitions led to a stalemate in the Senate through the remaining months of the indecisive James Buchanan's presidential term. Following the November 1860 election of Republican Abraham Lincoln and the resulting decision by South Carolina on December 20, 1860, to leave the Union, the Senate that day established a Committee of Thirteen to examine a variety of hastily offered proposals designed to save the Union. Under the chairmanship of Kentucky's venerable John Crittenden the committee recommended extending the 1820 Missouri Compromise line to the Pacific, prohibiting slavery to the north and allowing it south of that line. Congress would be forbidden to interfere with the slave trade and to abolish slavery in the District of Columbia. These proposals struck at the heart of the Republican Party's organizing attraction and they were defeated in January 1861 by a two-vote margin.

On January 9, 1861, Mississippi voted to follow South Carolina in seceding from the Union. Mississippi's Jefferson Davis urged the Senate to allow the other southern states that were separating in rapid order to leave in peace. He asked, ''Is there wisdom, is there patriotism in the land? If so,'' he concluded, ''easy must be the solution to this question. If not, then Mississippi's gallant sons will stand like a wall of fire around their state.'' On January 21 five senators from Florida, Alabama, and Mississippi, led by Davis, bade the Senate a sad farewell. (*See Reading No. 36.*) To the sound of muffled weeping in the packed chamber, senators and spectators stood quietly as the five silently withdrew. In the remaining days of that session senators from all eleven seceding southern states departed.

On March 4, following brief inauguration ceremonies for the first Republican president, the newly organized Senate adjourned. Within six weeks, Fort Sumter in the harbor of Charleston, South Carolina, had fallen and President Lincoln had proclaimed a state of insurrection. As a siege atmosphere gripped the city of Washington, the empty Senate Chamber took on new life as a hospital for a regiment of Massachusetts troops that had sustained casualties passing through hostile Baltimore. With the aroma of cooking bread and bacon filling the air, the soldiers recovered from their wounds under the watchful eyes of Patent Office clerk Clara Barton and other Washington women pressed into nursing service. While one angry soldier sought unsuccessfully to demolish the desk assigned to the departed Jefferson Davis, most passed the time by holding mock sessions and sending home postage-free letters on Senate stationery.

The arrival of fresh troops reinforced government hopes that the insurrection could be quickly quelled. To provide the necessary authority and funds to conduct operations, President Lincoln convened the new Congress on Independence Day. For the first time in its history, the Senate had passed to Republican control, with its Democratic members outnumbered by a 31-10 margin. Ironically, the large new chamber, built to accommodate the senators of a rapidly expanding nation, had fewer occupants than had the old chamber at the time of its reopening four decades earlier.

EXPULSIONS. Throughout its two-century history the Senate has expelled only fifteen members. Other than William Blount in 1797, all expulsions occurred in the early days of the Civil War. As the Senate got down to business in July 1861 it confronted the issue of the status of its departed southern members. Some members' terms had expired and others formally resigned. Many, however, took no formal action. The majority of remaining senators resisted arguments that the seats no longer existed as the states had withdrawn from the Union. This would have supported a state's right to secede. Instead, the Senate adopted a more punitive approach by expelling, with the required two-thirds vote, ten southern members and declaring their seats vacant. John Breckinridge, who two years earlier, as vice president, had led the Senate to its new chamber, returned to the Senate as a member from Kentucky in 1861. In vain, he had hoped to persuade the South to abandon secession. In the fall of 1861, realizing the futility of this course and remaining committed to the South, Breckinridge resigned and joined the Confederate army as a general. On December 4, 1861, the Senate by a 36-0 vote, expelled the Kentucky senator, declaring that "Breckinridge, the traitor, had joined with the enemies of the government."

The following January, the Senate by similar unanimous

votes, expelled Missouri's senators Waldo Johnson and Trusten Polk. Although that border state had remained in the Union, the Judiciary Committee determined that both senators had sworn allegiance to the Confederacy. In February 1862, Indiana's Jesse Bright became the final Civil War-era member to be expelled. A senior and partisan proslavery Democrat, Bright sought unsuccessfully to defend himself against charges of treason in connection with a March 1861 letter of introduction, on behalf of an arms merchant, to Jefferson Davis. Although the Judiciary Committee had voted to dismiss charges against Bright, the Senate removed him by a vote of 32-14.

WAR. Secession decimated the ranks of senior Senate Democrats, and transferred leadership from a coalition of southern and western Democrats to New England Republicans. Republicans from that region controlled the Senate's major committees, including Foreign Relations (Charles Sumner, Massachusetts); Finance (William P. Fessenden, Maine); Military Affairs (Henry Wilson, Massachusetts); and Naval Affairs (John P. Hale, New Hampshire). From July 4 to August 6, 1861, Congress passed sixty-seven public laws designed to address the war emergency. Following the Union defeat at the Battle of Bull Run on July 21, senators revised their view that the rebellion would be easily surpressed.

When the Senate convened in December 1861, the loss at Bull Run had been compounded weeks earlier by a humiliating and pointless Union disaster nearby at the Battle of Ball's Bluff. That engagement resulted in 200 Union dead, including Oregon's Senator Edward D. Baker, a close friend of the president. Radical Republican senators grew impatient with Lincoln's indecision and acted to gain the initiative in the war effort. They organized the Joint Committee on the Conduct of the War. Under the chairmanship of Ohio Radical Republican Benjamin Wade, the committee became the most powerful legislative panel involved in war policies. Brought into being by frustration over corruption, inefficiency, and indecisiveness connected with military operations, the committee expanded the war's objectives beyond preservation of the Union to encompass abolition of slavery. Although its critics viewed the committee as a troublesome inquisitor and an abuse of congressional investigative powers, the panel publicized enemy atrocities and the need for firmer political direction of the military effort.

The Senate in the early war years participated in an outpouring of legislation made possible in part by the extraordinary circumstances occasioned by the departure of southern members. Among the most enduring legislative accomplishment of the period were the Homestead Act, providing cheap land to promote western settlement; the Pacific Railway Act, to build a transcontinental rail connection; the Legal Tender Act, to centralize the nation's banking and currency system; and the Land Grant College Act, to underwrite establishment of colleges promoting "agricultural and mechanical arts."

By the end of 1862, continuing military reverses spurred Radical Republican senators to seek further involvement in the war's conduct. Late in December, Republican senators voted to ask the president to reorganize his cabinet to deal more effectively with such pressing issues as planning for slave emancipation and appointment of Army commanders. Maine's Senator William Fessenden complained, "I am heartsick when I think of the mismanagement of our army. The simple truth is there never was such a shambling, half and half set of incapables collected in one government before or since the world began."

Radical senators sought to remove what they considered to be the negative influence of Secretary of State William Seward. To do it they sent a delegation to meet with Lincoln. Realizing that he could not yield to such direct pressure in the midst of a national crisis, the president derailed this senatorial initiative by subtly exposing the machinations of Treasury Secretary Salmon Chase, a friend of the Radicals. Obtaining the offered resignations of Seward and Chase, Lincoln brought his cabinet and the Senate delegation together, making clear his independence of undue cabinet influence in setting war policy. If the radicals wanted to get rid of Seward, they would have to sacrifice their valued ally Chase. The president thereby defused the crisis and kept both advisers as well as his independence of senatorial dictation.

RECONSTRUCTION. When the Senate reconvened in

December 1863, the military situation had improved following major Union victories at Gettysburg and Vicksburg. With the legislative apparatus to support the war effort firmly in place, the Senate turned to the issue of how the departed southern states would be restored. At the start of that session, Lincoln unveiled his plan for reconstruction of the shattered Union. He would grant amnesty to those who took a loyalty oath. Further he would recognize governments in states where 10 percent of those qualified to vote in 1860 took the oath and where those states agreed to free the slaves.

Radical Senate Republicans such as Ben Wade argued that the president lacked the authority to set reconstruction terms. Noting that 10 percent did not constitute a majority, Wade introduced his own plan requiring 50 percent of voters in seceded states to take an oath before a new government could be formed. Fearing a renewal of Democratic dominance with the return of the southern states Wade and his Senate allies assumed that the president would have no choice but to agree to their tougher plan. Lincoln, however, turned aside arguments of congressional supremacy in such matters by observing, ''I conceive that I may in an emergency do things on military grounds which can not be done constitutionally by Congress.'' To the Radicals' consternation, Lincoln vetoed the so-called Wade-Davis reconstruction bill on July 4, 1864, the final day of the year's legislative session. This produced a blistering manifesto from Wade and Representative Henry Davis asserting congressional prerogative. (*See Reading No. 37.*)

The final session of the Civil War Senate occurred between December 5, 1864, and March 3, 1865. During that period the Senate passed a constitutional amendment abolishing slavery, established a Freedmen's Bureau to assist newly emancipated blacks, and authorized additional funding to relieve the war's enormous financial burdens. Ominously, however, they reached no conclusion over the pressing matter of reconstruction.

The Senate and House, in dealing with the issues of reconstruction, faced challenges of a magnitude unforeseen by the Constitution's framers. The situation grew increasingly complex a month after Congress adjourned, with the South's surrender at Appomattox, Lincoln's assassination several days later, and the resulting elevation of Andrew Johnson to the presidency. Johnson quickly shattered the Radicals' hope that he would follow their program for a wholesale reconstruction of the southern political and social order when, in May 1865, he set forth a lenient amnesty program. As southern states defiantly elected former Confederates to positions of power, including seats in the Senate, dissension intensified between congressional radicals and Johnson.

By the end of December 1865, the Senate and House had established the Joint Committee of Fifteen on Reconstruction. This panel included six senators and was chaired by Senator William Fessenden (R-ME). It brought together Radicals and moderates from both houses and served to rally the growing number of members who perceived that Johnson was abandoning the Republican party in favor of southern Democrats. Its extensive hearings revealed the need for a new constitutional amendment to protect blacks and to require southern loyalty.

Both moderate and Radical senators reacted angrily when the president, in February 1866, vetoed legislation expanding the powers of the Freedmen's Bureau. Johnson contended that the measure was unconstitutional because none of the eleven southern states that it would affect had representatives in Congress at the time of its passage. By vetoing the bill the president was suggesting that the Senate and House lacked their cherished absolute right to determine qualifications of their members and that all legislation passed in the absence of southern members was unconstitutional. When Senate Republicans failed to override the president's veto, Fessenden declared that Johnson had ''broken the faith, betrayed his trust, and must sink from detestation to contempt.'' Revulsion at the president's actions prompted Charles Sumner to rejoice in the Senate and its rules ''as the very temple of constitutional liberty.'' (*See Reading No. 38.*)

The 1866 midterm congressional elections expanded the ranks of Radical Republicans in both houses and signalled a repudiation of Johnson's truculent attitude toward Congress. Months later, in March 1867, Congress passed the Tenure of Office Act to stop Johnson from removing office holders sympathetic to congressional reconstruction goals. The mea-

sure contained a provision requiring Senate permission before
the president could fire civil officials including cabinet officers. This was designed to protect the position of Secretary of
War Edwin Stanton who had been cooperating with the
Radicals. Johnson then removed Stanton and tried to replace
him with Gen. Ulysses Grant. When Grant declined the post,
unwilling to offend allies in Congress, Stanton resumed his
duties, refusing to yield the office to a subsequent appointee.
This, in part, led the House to impeach the president on eleven
counts including violation of the Tenure of Office Act, which
had passed over his veto.

JOHNSON'S IMPEACHMENT TRIAL. The Johnson
impeachment trial began on March 4, 1868, and lasted eleven
weeks. It represented a monumental constitutional confrontation between Congress and the executive over the initiation and
management of national policy. Johnson would surely have
been removed from office, but for his willingness to assume a
more moderate and responsible demeanor in his dealings with
the Senate. In the absence of a vice president, Senate President
Pro Tempore Ben Wade would become president if Johnson
were removed. Senate Republican moderates greatly distrusted
Wade. Additionally, many feared that the Constitution's delicate balance would be destroyed with a precedent allowing
removal of a chief executive unpopular with Congress. With
Johnson remaining out of view in the Executive Mansion, the
Senate on May 16 voted on the major article. (*See Reading No.
39.*) By a margin of 35-19 in favor of conviction, with seven
Republicans joining twelve Democrats in favor of acquittal,
the Senate fell one vote short of the necessary two-thirds
majority for removal.[1]

GILDED AGE. At the beginning of Ulysses Grant's presidency in 1869 Republicans controlled the Senate by a 56-11
margin. Vermont's Senator Justin Morrill cogently expressed
the sense of power attached to Senate membership in those

[1]In March 1875 Andrew Johnson became the only former president to serve in
the Senate. Johnson's death on July 31, 1875, ended his brief tenure.

years. In declining the offer of a cabinet post, he remarked, "There is no gift, no office to which I could be appointed, that I would accept in preference to a seat in the United States Senate. I consider that the highest honor that could be bestowed on me, and its duties the highest function I could perform." At the outset of the Grant administration, senators expected that relations with this political novice would be more cordial than with his contentious predecessor. They hoped that he would be content to take direction from Congress, "leaving the people the duty of correcting any errors committed by their representatives in Congress." Despite their initial optimism, Senate Republican leaders became dismayed at the president's political style. He submitted his cabinet nominees, an undistinguished or inappropriate lot, without previously consulting Senate committee chairmen. Several nominees withdrew in the face of the resulting Senate hostility and most of the rest were gone within a year and a half of their appointments.

BLACK SENATORS. During the Grant years (1869–1877), the Senate turned to vital matters of currency reform, the financial crisis that had been sweeping the nation since 1873, and enforcement of reconstruction measures in the South. In 1870 the Reconstruction legislature of Mississippi elected Hiram Revels, the Senate's first black member. Despite heated opposition from some border-state Democratic members who questioned the validity of his election by a government still under military control, the Senate overwhelmingly accepted Revels's credentials. Elected to fill out an unexpired term, Revels served only until 1871. Four years later Mississippi again sent a black man to the Senate. Blanche K. Bruce served a single six-year term.[2]

REPUBLICAN SPLITS. Unity among Senate Republicans, imposed by wartime necessity, dissolved in the decade following Appomattox. Sen. Charles Sumner (R-MA) emerged as a leader of anti-administration Republicans. In

[2]Eighty years would pass before Edward Brooke (R-MA, 1967–1979) would become the Senate's third black member.

1870, as chairman of the Senate Foreign Relations Committee, Sumner killed Grant's proposal to annex Santo Domingo as a settling place for newly freed blacks. The president retaliated by firing the American ambassador to Great Britain, a close friend of the Massachusetts senator. Grant's forces, led by New York's flamboyant Republican Roscoe Conkling, obtained confirmation for a new ambassador over Sumner's spirited opposition. They punished Sumner further in 1871 by blocking his reappointment as chairman of the prestigious Foreign Relations Committee. This humiliating defeat for a senior member intensified partisan divisions that would remain among Senate Republicans for the rest of the century.

SCANDAL. The Senate's public image, corroded by bitter internal struggles over removal of a president and a committee chairman, suffered greater damage as a consequence of the so-called "Crédit Mobilier" scandals of 1872–1873. During the 1872 election campaign, stories emerged of widespread corruption by Republican officeholders in connection with construction of the recently completed Union Pacific Railroad. To divert profits to themselves, railroad promoters had organized a construction company called Crédit Mobilier of America. The railroad's directors awarded highly profitable contracts to the company, while the railroad approached bankruptcy. Attention centered on a House member who was charged with bribing colleagues to assist the Union Pacific. Among those implicated were Vice President Schuyler Colfax, fifteen House members, and six senators.

The Senate investigated these charges, but the 1873 session ended before it could take specific action. At the same time, the Senate explored allegations that both Kansas senators, Samuel Pomeroy and Alexander Caldwell, had secured their seats through bribery. Pomeroy was spared Senate disciplinary action by the poor credibility of witnesses against him and by the action of the Kansas legislature in refusing to reelect him. Caldwell had bragged to friends that his Senate seat had cost him $60,000. He arrogantly told a Senate investigating committee that bribery of state legislators was not a federal offense and that the Senate could not discipline a member for conduct prior to his election. Caldwell then resigned in the face of certain expulsion. Throughout this period the Senate left no doubt that it possessed the authority to judge its members' conduct, both before and during their terms. The application of this authority, however, proved to be uneven and dictated by strongly partisan considerations. Whenever possible, unless the offense appeared to be a direct assault on its dignity and prerogatives, the Senate preferred to allow the electorate to take the ultimate disciplinary actions.

The Senate further contributed to its declining image by agreeing to raise congressional salaries from $5,000 to $7,500 per year, retroactive for the entire two-year period of the session that was about to expire. The public outcry against this "Salary Grab" act led to the defeat of several senators and to the measure's repeal during the next session. A politically sensitive issue since the time of the Constitutional Convention, congressional pay remained at the $5,000 level until 1907, and has been only reluctantly and modestly increased in the years since.

Senate Republicans found themselves in a tenuous political situation as the Grant administration drew to an end in 1877. The salary grab and the Grant scandals had reduced their majorities. The 1876 presidential election resulted in a stale-mate that was resolved in favor of Republican Rutherford B. Hayes by a single-vote margin within a special electoral commission. Hayes brought to the presidency a commitment to address prevalent abuses in awarding federal jobs and con-tracts. Control of government patronage for positions such as customs collectors and postmasters had long been the province of certain powerful members of Congress. Among those in the Senate were Pennsylvania's Simon Cameron, Michigan's Zachariah Chandler, Indiana's Oliver Morton, and New York's Roscoe Conkling. Each of these men controlled vast organizations of ward heelers and political hacks that sold every form of political favor.

Shortly after taking office, Hayes launched an investigation of the New York custom house, an organization at the very heart of Roscoe Conkling's political machine. The inquiry uncovered a record of monumental corruption and focused attention on the misconduct of Conkling's New York protégés Chester Arthur and Alonzo Cornell. Hayes sought Arthur's and Cornell's resignations and sent to the Senate the names of two moderate Republicans to replace the Conkling henchmen. Late in 1877 Conkling bitterly worked to engineer Senate rejection of these nominations. Correctly sensing that public opinion was on his side, Hayes in mid-1878, while the Senate was out of session, suspended Arthur and Cornell and made interim appointments to their posts. When the Senate finally got the opportunity to vote on the replacements early in 1879, it reversed its earlier action and confirmed both anti-Conkling appointees. This intense political battle split Senate Republicans into three hostile camps, which included administration supporters, Conkling's "Stalwarts," and the "Half-Breeds" who stood between them. This schism, along with the incumbents' inability to deal with the economic crisis that had persisted since 1873, brought disaster to Senate Republicans in the 1878 midterm elections. For the first time in eighteen years, the Democrats regained control of the Senate.

DEADLOCK. Two years later, in the elections of 1880, Senate Democrats lost their comfortable ten-vote margin. For the first and only time in Senate history the two major parties were evenly divided at 37 to 37, with two independents. When the Senate convened in March 1881 for a brief "executive" session to consider newly elected President James Garfield's cabinet nominations, Democrats believed they could continue to control the body. The two independents had promised their support on organizational matters. Without this two-vote advantage, the Democrats would have lost to the Republicans who could count on the tie-breaking vote of Vice President Chester Arthur. At the last minute, however, the Republicans convinced one Independent, William Mahone of Virginia, to vote with them on the election of committee chairmen. Consequently that party, with a 38-38 margin and the vice president's vote in their pocket, took control of the major committees, leaving a few minor ones for the Democrats as had been the practice over the years. As his price for cooperating, Mahone secured an important chairmanship, the right to select key Senate officials, and a pledge that the Republican Party would not run a candidate to contest his reelection as a Virginia independent.

The Republicans' elation ended abruptly. Several of their members were chosen for cabinet posts, while others were frequently absent due to illness or conflicting business. As a result, they were unable to maintain a quorum. This allowed the Democrats to block their efforts to appoint key Senate officers and to distribute other patronage positions. In the midst of the resulting deadlock, President Garfield took the politically explosive action of replacing the Port of New York customs collector, a position Conkling believed was his to control. The New York senator argued that this was an attack on the right of "senatorial courtesy" under which presidents consulted with senators of their party before making major appointments in their states.

To delay proceedings further and to send a message to the president, Conkling and his New York colleague Thomas Platt, in a dramatic move, resigned from the Senate on May 16, 1881. Both men expected that the state legislature would quickly reelect them. The legislature, however, was frustrated with Conkling's antics. As it deliberated through the summer, a deranged patronage seeker, claiming to be a supporter of Conkling, shot and mortally wounded Garfield. When the legislature, in a wave of revulsion for Conkling's Stalwarts, selected two others to fill the Senate seats, Garfield murmured from his deathbed, "Thank God!" Garfield's death on September 19 effectively ended the reign in the Senate of Conkling's "Stalwarts." With Conkling out of the way, Senate Republicans no longer felt bound to support his patronage candidates and they readily confirmed Garfield's earlier choices. The New York resignations gave the Democrats a two-vote majority. In the interest of wrapping up a deadlocked session, that party's leaders decided not to reopen the issue of committee control. In return, Republicans agreed that Democrats could keep the same officers and patronage positions that they had held as majority party in the previous Congress.

The elections of 1882 returned the Republicans to their accustomed control of the Senate. The Senate in these years produced little by way of substantive legislation. The exceptions were measures to institute civil service reform, in the wake of Garfield's death; to regulate interstate commerce, ending widespread railroad abuses; and to deal with corrupt management of Indian affairs.

In one of the dirtiest presidential campaigns in American history, Democrat Grover Cleveland in 1884 defeated Republican James G. Blaine and became the first Democrat to occupy the executive mansion in a quarter century. The greatest financial problem before the Senate was how to eliminate the treasury's growing surplus, as a result of the 1883 tariff, estimated to exceed $150 million. Republicans wished to spend the surplus on military pensions, public works, harbor improvements, and fortifications. Cleveland, however, sought to cut the surplus by reducing taxes and tariff rates on imports.

In 1885, twenty-eight-year-old Woodrow Wilson received his doctorate in history from The Johns Hopkins University. Although he had never visited the U.S. Congress, he completed his dissertation on the topic of "Congressional Government." Regarding the Senate of that era, Wilson concluded, "that though it may not be as good as could be wished, the Senate is as good as it can be under the circumstances. It contains the most perfect product of our politics, whatever that product may be." (*See Reading No. 40.*)

The 1888 election returned the presidency to the Republicans, although Democrat Grover Cleveland received more popular votes than the successful Republican candidate, former Senator Benjamin Harrison. As the Senate prepared to begin its second century in 1889, a new generation of leaders moved to the fore as did new issues and new proposed solutions.

CHAPTER 6

ORIGINS OF THE MODERN SENATE: 1889–1921

The three decades that followed the Senate's 1889 centennial produced a fundamental transformation in that body's operation. More clearly defined party structures brought new cohesion and strength to the institution. With the Republicans firmly in control of the government by 1897, William Allison (R-IA), the Senate's senior majority member, became chairman of his party's caucus. More than any other Senate leader of his time, Allison strengthened partisan control of the Senate's agenda. To do so, he took on the chairmanship of the powerful Republican Steering Committee, a post not previously held by a caucus leader. That panel determined committee assignments and decided which bills would reach the Senate floor and in what order they would be considered. Allison ended the practice of rotating membership of the Steering Committee at the end of each Congress and appointed the same men, all party regulars, each session. He and his closest party associates hand-picked committee members so as to control those who by seniority would eventually chair the key committees. (*See Reading No. 41.*)

Allison himself chaired the Appropriations Committee and ranked as number-two member of the influential Finance Committee. Other major committees such as Rules, Commerce, Judiciary, and Naval Affairs were firmly in the hands of party leaders. On the other side of the aisle Arthur Gorman (D-MD), as his party's leader, instituted practices similar to those of Allison. He chaired the Democratic caucus and the steering committee, whose members he had personally selected. By 1902 the success of the caucus as the Senate's governing agency, moved one disappointed European observer to conclude that the Senate was no longer the "august assembly" that Tocqueville had observed in the 1830s. He believed that the caucus, with power so rigidly centralized, was "one of the principal, if not the principal agent of this fall." (*See Reading No. 42.*)

PROGRESSIVE ERA. Shortly after the start of the twentieth century, the nation unexpectedly got a new president. Theodore Roosevelt (R) had become vice president at the start of William McKinley's second term in March 1901. When McKinley fell victim to an assassin's bullet in September of that year, Roosevelt moved to the White House. This transition began the modern presidency and one of the greatest periods of reform in the nation's history. The new president viewed himself as a mediator between the old-guard preservers of the status quo and insurgent reformers. In the Senate these antagonistic forces were represented on the conservative side by Allison, Nelson Aldrich (R-RI), Orville Platt (R-CT), and John Spooner (R-WI). These men, working closely together, effectively crushed Roosevelt's plans for tariff revision. When the president decided to place his prestige behind efforts to end railroad rate abuses that discriminated against small shippers, he had to compromise with the Senate's conservative hierarchy. His success as a political leader came because he was able to maintain a tough public image as a progressive reformer, while negotiating quietly with the congressional old guard.

DIRECT ELECTION OF SENATORS. Delegates to the 1787 constitutional convention spent relatively little time discussing the manner in which senators were to be elected. Selection by state legislatures worked reasonably well for the Senate's first half century. Eventually, however, disputes arose as more legislatures adopted the practice of making the selection in joint, rather than separate, sessions. This gave greater numerical influence to the larger of a state's two legislative bodies. In those states where different parties controlled each house, deadlocks often resulted. In 1857, for example, closely divided parties within Indiana's upper house were unable to organize for a vote on filling a Senate vacancy. Consequently, that body's Democrats adjourned to the state house chamber, where their party held a solid majority. In joint assembly, the legislature elected two Democratic senators— one to fill a vacancy and one for a new term. The following year, Indiana's rapidly growing Republican party won majorities in both houses of the state legislature. That new majority promptly sent two Republican senators-elect to Washington.

The Senate, under Democratic control, rejected the Republican challengers by a strict party vote.

In the remaining years of the century, as corruption in state legislatures increased, the number of deadlocks in Senate elections multiplied. In 1895 the Delaware legislature took 217 ballots over a period of 114 days without electing a senator. Delaware and other states frequently went without full representation in the Senate for two years or more. (*See Reading No. 43.*)

By the start of the twentieth century, direct popular election of senators had become a major objective for progressive reformers who sought to remove control of government from the influence of special interests. Several western states devised election systems that included a popular referendum for senators and a pledge by state legislative candidates that they would be bound by the referendum's results. Between 1893 and 1902 the House of Representatives, by large margins, passed constitutional amendments providing for direct popular election. The Senate's conservative hierarchy, however, consistently killed those initiatives.

During its first century the Senate had to resolve numerous cases relating to the validity of new members' credentials— both for elected and appointed senators. The Constitution provided that governors could fill Senate vacancies when their state legislatures were not in session. This proved to be a significant power, particularly in those states where the legislature met only for a few months in every two-year period. In 1797 the Senate, acting in its capacity to judge the "elections, qualifications and returns" of its members, ruled that a governor could not make an appointment if a session of the legislature had been held since the vacancy was created. In 1809 the Senate affirmed that an appointed senator could keep his seat—not only until the next meeting of the state legislature—as originally planned, but until a successor had been elected and had presented his credentials.

TREASON OF THE SENATE. The campaign for direct election took on a new force in 1906. At that time two senators had recently been convicted on fraud and corruption charges. Each had taken fees for interceding with federal agencies on behalf of clients. This led publisher William Randolph Hearst to commission a series of articles in his *Cosmopolitan* magazine. Novelist David Graham Philips directed his vitriolic pen at twenty-one current members, eighteen of whom were wealthy Republicans close to the Senate's power center. The resulting nine articles comprising the "Treason of the Senate" series appeared from March through November. Laced with innuendo and exaggeration, the articles initially attracted a wide audience and made the point that large corporations and corrupt state legislators played too large a role in selection of senators. Ultimately, the author went too far. He felt the sting of attacks from other reformers and from President Roosevelt, who coined the expression "muckraker" to describe this kind of overstated and sensationalist journalism. (*See Reading No. 44.*)

Southern senators sought to derail the direct election initiative, fearing that it would favor candidates sympathetic to concerns of their states' black populations. In 1911 the House passed a direct election amendment by a 296-11 margin. In the Senate, after much complex maneuvering, Idaho's William Borah in May 1912 guided the measure to enactment. Within a year three quarters of the states had ratified the new Seventeenth Amendment to the Constitution. (*See Reading No. 45.*) Arkansas Senator Joseph Robinson became the last senator elected by a state legislature and Maryland's Blair Lee, on January 29, 1914, became the first under the new amendment.

It is doubtful that this amendment had a major impact on the quality or character of persons who subsequently became senators. (*See Reading No. 46.*) The old guard, symbolized by William Allison and Nelson Aldrich, was already giving way to men who were more responsive to the needs of a broader segment of a rapidly industrializing society. By 1912 twenty-nine states had senatorial primaries, which successfully bound their legislatures to accept popular sentiment in the choice of specific senators. Turnover among members had reached unusually high rates with 73 percent of senators in 1913 serving their first six-year terms. This turnover had a corrosive effect on old ways and old beliefs. Finally, the election of 1912, which found Republicans hopelessly divided, swept

Democrat Woodrow Wilson into the White House. The election also returned the Senate to Democratic control for the first time in eighteen years.

WOODROW WILSON. Passage of the direct election amendment coincided with a burst of legislative activity at the outset of Wilson's presidency. Unlike Roosevelt, or his own immediate predecessor William Howard Taft, Wilson believed in strong presidential leadership of Congress. An admirer of the British parliamentary system, the president looked to Senate Majority Leader John W. Kern as his "prime minister." Kern recognized that his party controlled the Senate and executive branch only because of the split within Republican ranks. Accordingly, he strove for Democratic party discipline to achieve the major goals of the president's legislative agenda.

To assist his Senate leader, Wilson appeared before a special session of Congress on April 8, 1913. In so doing, he became the first president since John Adams to address both houses in person. This dramatic gesture focused the nation's attention on Congress and Congress' attention on Wilson. The president called for legislation to eliminate the system of privileged tariff protection that the Republicans had nurtured since the Civil War. The new Underwood Tariff easily passed the House, but it ran into intense opposition in the Senate. There, lobbyists from affected manufacturing industries pressured senators to kill the measure.

In an effort to embarrass the Democratic leadership, Senate Republicans called for an investigation of members' ties to the affected industries. In the resulting inquiry, all senators felt obliged to disclose their financial holdings and in so doing, they undercut the opposition and passed the tariff. With this initial effort at public reporting of members' private finances, the Senate handed the president his first major legislative victory. On the heels of this accomplishment, Wilson drove the Senate's leadership to secure passage of the Federal Reserve Act to reform the nation's banking and currency system. In mid-1914, the Senate approved the last of the major economic reform measures of the Progressive Era—the Federal Trade Commission Act and the Clayton Antitrust Act.

"A LITTLE GROUP OF WILLFUL MEN." The onset of world war in April 1914 shifted the Senate's attention away from domestic reform to foreign policy matters. Wilson tried to maintain neutrality in U.S. relations with the combatants and in 1916 he won a second term on the slogan, "He kept us out of war." The elections of 1914 and 1916 kept the Senate in Democratic control, while the Republicans regained the House. On January 22, 1917, for the first time in the nation's history, the president addressed a session of the Senate.

The idealistic tones of Wilson's "Peace Without Victory" speech within a few days turned discordant when the Germans resumed unrestricted submarine warfare and sank an unarmed American merchant ship. The House readily approved the president's urgent plea to arm U.S. trading vessels. In the Senate, however, that request ran into the determined opposition of a dozen noninterventionists. Led by Progressive Republicans Robert La Follette and George Norris, these opponents launched a historic filibuster on March 2, 1917. With public opinion whipped to near hysteria against the Germans, the Senate had less than two days remaining in its session. As the filibuster lumbered into the early morning hours of the final day, George Norris quoted from Wilson's 1885 doctoral dissertation: "It is the proper duty of a representative to look diligently into every affair of government and to talk much about what he sees."

At noon on March 4, the Senate session expired without action on the armed ship bill and Wilson took his oath on the Capitol steps for a second term. Shortly afterwards, the furious president attacked the dissidents as "a little group of willful men, representing no opinion but their own /who/ have rendered the government of the United States helpless and contemptible." Not since the days of the 1794 Jay Treaty had a group of senators been so heatedly attacked throughout the nation. Wilson angrily called the Senate into special session on March 5 and demanded a change in its rules to permit cutting off debate. In the past the Senate had easily turned aside such filibuster-limiting "cloture" provisions as being inconsistent with its constitutional obligation to provide full airing of minority views. Under conditions verging on panic, the Senate speedily adopted the cloture rule. Known as "Rule 22," it limited debate to one hour per member when two-thirds of the senators present and voting agreed to a cloture petition submitted by at least sixteen senators. (*See Reading No. 47.*) Three weeks later Congress declared war on Germany.

The Senate and House set aside political considerations and quickly passed vital war-related legislation, mcuh as they had at the outset of the Civil War. As the 1918 congressional elections approached, however, the president killed the prevailing spirit of bipartisanship by calling for the election of a solidly Democratic Congress as essential to the war effort. This infuriated the Republicans and many voters who subsequently repudiated the president by giving that party control of both houses, including a two-vote margin in the Senate.

LEAGUE OF NATIONS FIGHT. Senate Republican leader Henry Cabot Lodge (R-MA) had already begun to break with Wilson over the president's views of the war's objectives. The two men shared a deeply rooted distrust of each other. The patrician Lodge had received the first doctorate in political science awarded by Harvard University in 1876. Wilson received his doctorate in history from Johns Hopkins a decade later. Each man considered himself as the nation's preeminent scholar in poltics. By 1918 Lodge had served in the Senate a quarter century. In August of that year he would become the Senate's most senior member and Republican floor leader. As the senior Republican on the Senate Foreign Relations Committee, Lodge justly prided himself in his extensive knowledge of international affairs. His intense convictions were based on broad reading and experience, as well as on an understanding of the Senate's unique constitutional role in foreign policy.

In January 1918 Wilson addressed both houses of Congress, setting forth his ''Fourteen Points'' as the basis for a moral peace that would be ''just and holy.'' Lodge and others disagreed with the president's idealistic approach and demanded a peace based on Germany's unconditional surrender. Wilson further antagonized Lodge and other senators by refusing to include senators among the negotiators accompanying him to the Paris Peace Conference. Upon his return, the president addressed a rally in Lodge's hometown, Boston, thereby abandoning an earlier pledge to discuss conference

results with senators before making them public. This fully
alienated Lodge, who became determined to block the proposed Treaty of Versailles and its convenant for a League of
Nations. Lodge argued that the League would place the United
States in the position of guaranteeing the territorial integrity
and independence of every country in the world. In the closing
hours of the March 1919 session, as Wilson was about to
return to Paris, Lodge presented a resolution signed by
thirty-nine Republican senators urging the separation of the
peace treaty from the League convenant. This gesture was
designed to warn the president and the European negotiators of
the intensity of Senate opposition. The Senate intended that all
parties, including Wilson, remember its special obligations in
treaty making.

Wilson retaliated by calling Lodge and his allies "contemptible, narrow, selfish, poor little minds that never get anywhere
but run around in a circle and think they are going some-
where." Nonetheless, he obtained several changes that Lodge
had desired. On July 10, 1919, Wilson arrived in the Senate
chamber carrying a bulky copy of the treaty. He was escorted
by Lodge, who with the return of the Senate to Republican
control in the 1918 elections, held the dual posts of majority
leader and chairman of the Foreign Relations Committee. In a
dramatic speech to the Senate, Wilson urged quick consent to
the treaty's ratification. He expected no changes and assumed
that the Senate, which had never before rejected a treaty,
would grant its approval.

Following protracted hearings, Lodge presented the treaty to
the Senate with four "reservations" to the League's convenant
and forty-five amendments to the treaty itself. Democratic
senators and a group of fifteen "mild reservationists" among
the Republicans voted down all amendments and returned the
treaty to the Foreign Relations Committee for further consideration. Meanwhile, Wilson set out on a 9,000-mile journey
across the nation to bring popular pressure on the Senate to
approve the treaty without change. In declining health, Wilson
suffered a stroke on October 2, 1919, and returned to the
capital. With a stricken president more determined than ever to
hold out against the Senate, Lodge brought the treaty before
the Senate in early November. It contained fourteen "reserva-

tions,'' but no amendments. In the face of Wilson's continued refusal to accept modifications, the Senate on November 19, 1919, in a dramatic moment, decisively rejected the treaty. Again on March 19, 1920, the Senate rebuffed the president as the treaty failed to receive the necessary two-thirds margin. Lost in his illusions of parliamentary government, Wilson paid a heavy price for ignoring the Senate's collateral role in treaty making.

COMMITTEE REFORM. Shortly after the Senate disposed of the Treaty of Versailles, it restructured its committee system. By 1914 the Senate had created seventy-four committees. Fewer than twenty conducted significant business. The most singificant among them were the committees on Finance, Appropriations, District of Columbia, Pensions, Claims, Foreign Relations, and Judiciary. The remaining panels, including Revolutionary War Claims, Five Civilized Tribes of Indians, and Transportation and Sale of Meat Products, existed only to provide office space and a staff member to their chairmen. The Senate had continued its practice of allowing minority party members to chair several of these insignificant committees. The opening in 1909 of the first permanent Senate Office Building, today known as the Richard Russell Building, reduced the demands of members for space previously only available to those who chaired committees. With the war over, the Senate agreed in 1920 to abolish forty-one standing committees. It limited membership on each of the ten major committees to fifteen members. Seniority was henceforth to be determined by a member's standing within a committee, rather than within the entire Senate. This was intended to place a premium on subject specialization. In the future a member who switched committees would have to give up seniority and thus any hope of soon becoming chairman. With party and committee machinery in good working order, the Senate set out to confront the challenges of the post-World War I era.

CHAPTER 7

ERA OF INVESTIGATIONS: 1921–1945

Throughout the nation's history both the Senate and the House have been associated with "good" and "bad" investigations. *The New York Times* reporter William S. White once wrote: "The most controversial and least clearly defined of all the powers of the Senate, the power to conduct investigations, has many times in history far overshadowed the Senate's basic functions." When White made these observations in the early 1950s, at the time of investigative excesses by Sen. Joseph McCarthy, he concluded that two practices of the Senate—investigations and filibusters—had severely undermined the "essential dignity of the Institution." Viewed from the perspective of the "Watergate" and "Abscam" inquiries of the 1970s and 1980s, the Senate's use of its investigative powers could have supported a more positive conclusion. During the twenty-five years following 1921, the Senate defined and effectively employed its investigative powers as never before.

REPUBLICAN ASCENDANCY. The election of 1920 produced a Republican landslide. This came partly in repudiation of Wilson's leadership and as an expression of dissatisfaction with postwar inflation and labor unrest. Warren Harding, promising a "return to normalcy," became the first person in history to win election to the presidency directly from a seat in the Senate.[1] The election also yielded an overwhelming Republican majority (59-37) in the Senate. Not a single Democrat from a state outside the South won a Senate election that year. Despite the large number of Republicans, there were deep divisions within that party's ranks. On the conservative flank stood such stalwarts as Henry Cabot Lodge (MA), Boies Penrose (PA), Reed Smoot (UT), George Moses (NH), and James Watson (IN). Among the most prominent senators

---

[1] In 1960 John F. Kennedy became the second person to move directly from the Senate to the White House.

representing the party's fading progressive wing were Robert
La Follette (WI), William Borah (ID), Hiram Johnson (CA),
and George Norris (NE).

The new Republican administration and its congressional
allies, operating under the assumption that "the business of
America is business," quickly responded to industry's demands to shift tax burdens away from large corporations and to
erect protective tariff barriers. Private interests sought to gain
control of government lands for their timber and mineral
resources. The Interior Department, under the control of
former New Mexico Senator Albert Fall, secretly leased to
commercial interests the naval oil reserves at Teapot Dome in
Wyoming. Senator Robert La Follette, suspecting irregularities, convinced Sen. Thomas Walsh (D-MT) to launch an
investigation. Walsh, a skillful former prosecutor, tenaciously
pursued the complex case, earning great public scorn for what
appeared to be a partisan effort to embarrass a popular
president. Finally, his persistence was rewarded as details of
Secretary Fall's bribe-taking emerged. A second Senate inquiry, conducted by Montana's other senator, Burton K.
Wheeler, led to the resignation of Attorney General Harry
Daugherty. Fall eventually became the first former cabinet
officer to serve a prison term. Daugherty was spared a similar
humiliation only because of poor health. Both cases produced
Supreme Court decisions that greatly strengthened the Senate's
investigative powers. In *McGrain v. Daugherty* (1927), the
Court ruled that the Senate had the right to compel private
citizens to testify before its committees. (*See Reading No. 48.*)

Frustrated with the "do-nothing administration" of Calvin
Coolidge, who moved to the White House in 1923 following
Harding's death, Sen. Robert La Follette mobilized progressive Republicans in a third-party bid during the 1924 presidential campaign. He selected Sen. Burton Wheeler as his running
mate in this ill-fated contest. With the overwhelming election
of Coolidge, the Senate's old-guard Republican majority
sought to strip La Follette of his committee assignments. They
also prevented him from becoming chairman of the Interstate
Commerce Committee, despite his seniority, through the
extraordinary move of voting to give that post to Democratic
Sen. Ellison Smith (SC). Exhausted from the abortive cam-

paign, La Follette died in June 1925. Wisconsin voters quickly reaffirmed their progressive inclination by electing thirty-year-old Robert La Follette, Jr. to take his father's seat.

"Young Bob" La Follette and other Republican progressives sought in vain to lead the mainstream members of their party toward a revival of the previous decade's reform programs. The election in 1928 of former Commerce Secretary Herbert Hoover as president promised little change. After the disastrous stock market crash of October 1929, Senate Republicans pushed ahead with legislation that proved ill-suited to alleviate the nation's economic crises. The prime example of this was the Smoot-Hawley Tariff, which raised rates on imported goods to their highest levels in history. Agrarian and industrial representatives in Congress, to the president's frustration, agreed to support each other's demands for steep rates to protect against cheap foreign competition. La Follette condemned the measure as the product of a series of deals, "conceived in secret, but executed in public with a brazen affrontery that is without parallel in the annals of the Senate."

ETHICS. Progressive era efforts to reduce corruption in political campaigns resulted in statutes limiting the amount of congressional campaign contributions. In the 1918 Michigan Senate race, industrialist Truman Newberry defeated auto magnate Henry Ford. Newberry acknowledged spending the enormous sum of $200,000 in that bitter campaign. Although the Senate seated Newberry in 1919, it launched a thorough investigation of his conduct and concluded that, although duly elected, he showed poor judgment. On November 29, 1919, he was indicted on charges of conspiracy to violate the Federal Corrupt Practices Act through excessive campaign expenditures. Four months later he was convicted and sentenced to two years in prison. In May 1921 the Supreme Court overturned his conviction on the grounds that Congress could not regulate primary elections. In the face of Senate moves to expel him, Newberry resigned in 1922. Against continuing revelations of Harding administration scandals, the Senate in 1925 agreed to a revision of the Federal Corrupt Practices Act. This statute set specific reporting requirements, prohibited solicitation of contributions from federal employees, and severely limited corporations' contributions. In 1941 the Supreme Court reversed its earlier ruling, finding that as primary elections were "a step in the exercise by the people of their choice of representatives in Congress," they were subject to congressional regulation.

Soon the Senate again became embroiled in two protracted and sensational election cases. They stemmed from the 1926 campaigns of William Vare (R-PA) and Frank Smith (R-IL), each of whom won his respective contest. Smith reportedly received $125,000 from public utilities tycoon Samuel Insull, while retaining a seat on his state's powerful Commerce Commission. Pennsylvania Governor Gifford Pinchot wrote the Senate that "The stealing of votes for Mr. Vare and the amount and sources of money spent on his behalf make it clear to me that the election returns do not in fact represent the will of the sovereign voters of Pennsylvania." After extended inquiry, the Senate refused to seat both men. Shortly afterwards, in 1929, the Senate censured Connecticut's Hiram Bingham for placing a lobbyist on his Senate payroll. Observing that his actions were "not the result of corrupt motives," the Senate concluded they were "contrary to good morals and senatorial ethics and tend to bring the Senate into disfavor and disrepute."

While the Senate remained alert to the appearance of corruption and diligent in its efforts to remain the sole judge of its members' ethics, it reacted harshly to those who questioned its collective ethical posture. Early in 1933, Senate Sergeant at Arms David Barry, a Republican whose term of office was soon to end with the arrival a Democratic majority, published an article in which he assessed the contemporary state of congressional morality. Barry observed that "there are not many senators or representatives who sell their votes for money, and it is pretty well known who those few are." For this indiscretion, he was brought before the Senate and summarily fired.

WOMEN SENATORS. In 1918 Rep. Jeannette Rankin (MT) became the first woman to run for the Senate. In a field of three candidates, she received 23 percent of the vote. Four years later the governor of Georgia appointed Rebecca Latimer Felton (D) to serve the remaining months of an unexpired term.

She was sworn in on November 21, 1922, and on the following day stepped aside for Walter George (D), her duly elected replacement. She thus became the first woman senator and the person holding the shortest Senate term. At the age of 87, she was also the oldest person ever to enter Senate service. Hattie Caraway (D-AR) in 1932 became the first woman ever elected to the Senate. A year earlier she had been appointed to fill the vacancy caused by the death of her husband, Sen. Thaddeus Caraway (D-AR). During the first one hundred Congresses the Senate has had sixteen women members.

EXECUTIVE SESSIONS. In 1929 the Senate launched another investigation related to the maintenance of its prerogatives. An Associated Press reporter had obtained information on a vote taken in secret session on the nomination of a former senator to a judicial post. As a result of this inquiry, the Senate reversed its 140-year-old policy of conducting nomination and treaty debates behind closed doors. As early as 1831, observers had joked that the Senate had followed the closed-door practice only to maintain press interest. One senator at that time noted that ''if a desire was felt that every subject should be bruited about in every corner of the United States, should become a topic of universal conversation, nothing more was necessary than to close the doors of the Senate Chamber and make it the object of a secret, confidential deliberation.''

THE GREAT DEPRESSION. The election of 1930, amidst the gloom of a deepening depression, returned the House to Democratic control and erased the Republicans' Senate majority. With a margin of forty-eight Republicans, forty-seven Democrats, and one Independent, President Hoover bitterly noted that the Democrats should organize the Senate, as well as the House, so that he could deal with a unified and responsible opposition. This he preferred to a Democratic ''opposition in the Senate conspiring in the cloakrooms to use every proposal of mine for demagoguery.'' Hoover, following Abraham Lincoln's 1861 practice of keeping Congress out of town during an emergency, decided not to call Congress into special session in March 1931 to deal with the worsening economic situation. Instead, he waited until the regular session in December.[2] That session produced a number of reform efforts such as the Reconstruction Finance Corporation, which provided federal loans to banks and railroads to restore employment and purchasing power. The Glass-Steagall Act made available $750 million of government gold supplies for industrial and business investment needs. Finally, the Federal Home Loan Bank Act sought to reduce the number of home mortgage foreclosures and stimulate residential construction. These measures, proved inadequate for the nation's relief needs. In November 1932, the voters sent Democrat Franklin Roosevelt to the White House and gave Democrats overwhelming control (60-D, 35-R, 1-I) of the Senate.

PECORA INVESTIGATION. In the waning months of the Hoover administration the Senate Banking Committee, chaired by Republican Progressive Peter Norbeck (ND), began an investigation of Wall Street trading practices. Originally supported by the president to uncover Democratic efforts to embarrass his administration, this investigation quickly took on a life of its own. In the tradition established by the earlier Teapot Dome inquiry, the Senate used its newly strengthened investigative powers to fashion imaginative new legislation. Under the brilliant leadership of chief counsel Ferdinand Pecora, the committee produced the Securities Act of 1933, the Banking Act of 1933, and the Securities Exchange Act of 1934.

FIRST HUNDRED DAYS. When the Senate convened on

[2]The Constitution provided that Congress was to meet annually on the first Monday in December. A statute established March 4 as the beginning of both presidential and congressional terms. The president was empowered to convene special congressional sessions as he deemed necessary. The Senate customarily met for a few days in March once every four years to consider nominations received at the start of a new presidential term. Then it adjourned until the regular December session. The Twentieth Amendment to the Constitutuion changed this by setting January 3 as the beginning of the congressional term, starting in 1934, and January 20 for the president, as of 1937.

March 9, 1933, it faced a new president determined to restore national confidence with bold new legislative initiatives. That session of the 73rd Congress lasted exactly 100 days. On the first day the House passed the President's Emergency Banking Relief Act after only thirty-eight minutes of debate and without reference to a printed copy of the bill. The Senate gave its approval later in the day and Roosevelt signed the act that evening. This extraordinary responsiveness prompted Raymond Moley, unofficial leader of Roosevelt's ''Brain Trust,'' to observe that ''capitalism was saved in eight days.''

The remainder of that session stands as a monument to the ability of Congress and the president to cooperate in times of grave national emergency. Many of the initiatives bore a uniquely senatorial stamp as with Sen. Arthur Vandenberg's (R-MI) Federal Deposit Insurance Corporation and George Norris's (R-NE) Tennessee Valley Authority. Sen. Robert Wagner (D-NY) left his imprint on two of the New Deal's most important legislative monuments. The Social Security Act established a national old-age pension program and provided federal grants-in-aid to states to assist dependent mothers and children. The National Labor Relations Act, known as the ''Wagner Act,'' was almost entirely the New York senator's brainchild. Roosevelt remained neutral on this sensitive issue and watched as Wagner overcame the virtually insurmountable hurdles that business interests set in his path. The bill passed the Senate by a 63-12 margin in May 1933. It supported the right of workers to join labor unions and to bargain collectively through representatives of their own choosing. This measure profoundly changed the entire nature of labor-management relations.

The elections of 1936 served as a popular mandate for the sweeping legislative accomplishments of President Roosevelt's first term. As Senate Democratic Leader Robert C. Byrd (WV) wistfully noted nearly a half-century later, Roosevelt's ''broad coat-tails carried Democrats into office seemingly by the truckload.'' With a margin of seventy-six Democrats to sixteen Republicans, freshmen Democrats spilled over into the back-row desks on the Republican side of the Senate chamber. Not since the period of Civil War and Reconstruction had one party enjoyed such dominance in the Senate.

COURT-PACKING. At the moment of his greatest electoral triumph, Roosevelt committed the greatest political blunder of his presidency. With the legislative branch securely under his control, the chief executive turned to the troublesome judiciary. Roosevelt feared that the Supreme Court, dominated by conservative Republican appointees, would continue to hack away at the gains of his New Deal. This they had done in ruling unconstitutional the Agricultural Adjustment Act and the National Recovery Act. The president sent to the Senate a proposal that would allow him to appoint one justice for each member of the Court over the age of seventy, for a maximum of fifteen members. Occurring on the 150th anniversary of the Constitution's adoption, Roosevelt's action unleashed a furious torrent of criticism across the country and within the Senate. While Senate Republicans looked on in delighted amusement, southern conservatives joined with western progressives in opposition. Senate debate began on July 6, 1937, in an unair-conditioned Senate chamber during a brutally hot summer. Majority Leader Joseph Robinson (D-AR), bravely tried to marshal the president's beleaguered forces. On July 14, at the height of the battle, tension, heat, and illness overtook Robinson. Early that morning he was found dead in his apartment a block from the Supreme Court. The loss of this talented legislative leader doomed the president's plan. Several days later the Senate unceremoniously returned it to the Judiciary Committee for suitable burial.

The battle over Roosevelt's Court bill marked a turning point in the Senate's modern history. It forged a conservative coalition of southern and western members that endured for the next two decades. That coalition blocked every measure that came before the special session the president called in November 1937. Consequently, Roosevelt decided to ''purge'' the Democratic Party of its conservative leaders in the 1938 elections. His campaign against Senators Walter George (GA) and Millard Tydings (MD) ended in failure and they returned determined to use the Senate to frustrate the president's future initatives. From that time through the end of his presidency in 1945, Roosevelt's domestic program took a back seat to foreign policy necessities as the flames of war swept across Europe.

THE ISOLATIONISTS. In the two decades since the Senate had rejected the Treaty of Versailles and the League of Nations, a spirit of "isolationism" dominated Senate foreign policy debates. Among the most fervent and effective of those senators wishing to remain free of foreign economic and military entanglements were Wiliam Borah, Hiram Johnson, Burton Wheeler, George Norris, Robert La Follette, Jr., Arthur Vandenberg, and Robert Taft. Throughout the 1920s and 1930s Senate isolationists supported a short-sighted policy of high protective tariffs against foreign goods and rigorous repayment of war debts from America's struggling European allies. William Borah became one of the most effective among the Senate's isolationists. As chairman of the Foreign Relations Committee between 1924 and 1933, and as that panel's senior minority member until his death in 1940, Borah sought to block U.S. involvement in major international alliances. When he attached five "reservations" to U.S. participation in the World Court, the League of Nations refused to accept them and President Coolidge declared the nation's participation at an end. Borah also followed his isolationist instincts in developing a sixty-two nation agreement to outlaw war and in opposing U.S. intervention in Nicaragua.

Borah was particularly suspicious of munitions manufacturers, whom he called "international racketeers." His efforts led in 1934 to the formation of a special Senate committee to investigate the munitions industry. Sen. Gerald Nye (ND), a progressive Republican isolationist, had become closely identified with the issue. As a measure of the respect in which the Senate's Democratic majority held him, they elected Nye chairman. He expressed widely held isolationist views in predicting that "when the Senate investigation is over, we shall see that war and preparation for war is not a matter of national honor and defense, but a matter of profit for few."

The Nye Committee, holding ninety-three hearings over the next two years, focused on the activities of American shipbuilders. (*See Reading No. 49.*) Although it found little hard evidence to support its thesis, the committee confirmed the popular opinion that greedy munitions interests had lured the United States into World War I. Based on the committee's work the Senate and House passed three neutrality acts between 1935 and 1937 in response to growing hostilities in Europe. Nye, however, went too far in attacking the memory of Woodrow Wilson, suggesting that the former president had "falsified" about his knowledge of secret treaties. This unleashed a furious counterattack by Senate Democrats Tom Connally (TX) and Carter Glass (VA). Before a packed Senate chamber, Glass slammed his fist onto his desk until blood dripped from his knuckles. As Democrats cheered, Glass lambasted the "man who thus insults the memory of Woodrow Wilson." After this incident, the Democratic majority refused to provide additional funding and the Nye Committee perished.

WAR. On September 1, 1939, Germany invaded Poland and soon Europe was again at war. In October Congress repealed an arms embargo and the president told the country, "This nation will remain a neutral nation, but I can not ask that every American remain neutral in thought as well." On January 16, 1940, William Borah died. At his funeral service in the Senate chamber, every desk but his was filled. No one delivered a eulogy, for no one could match his eloquence. Isolationist sentiment slowly eroded as events dragged the nation closer to war. On March 8, the Senate approved (60-31) the president's "Lend-Lease" plan providing war materiel for Great Britain. On December 7, 1941, Japan attacked the American base at Pearl Harbor and destroyed Senator Borah's earlier assurance that the United States was safe from military assault. Thus ended two decades of Senate debate over the role of the nation in the broader world.

On December 8, following the president's "Day of Infamy" speech to a joint session of Congress, Sen. Arthur Vandenberg, a leader of the isolationists, dramatically reversed his position. He told the Senate "I have fought every trend which I thought would lead to needless war; but when war comes to us—and particularly when it comes like a thug in the night—I stand with my Commander in Chief for the swiftest and most invincible reply of which our total strength may be capable." Following the Republican leader's brief address, the Senate voted unanimously to declare war.

During the ensuring war, Congress gave extraordinary powers to the president, much as it had during the Civil War.

There was little for the Senate to do but to pass essential authorizations and appropriations. With solid Democratic majorities, it loyally supported the president's emergency programs. Sen. Alben Barkley (D-KY) had become majority leader in 1937 following Joseph Robinson's death. Over the years he had functioned more as a messenger to the Senate from the president than a leader in his own right. Frustration at this subordinate role grew within Barkley as it did within the Senate at large. The inevitable explosion occurred on February 23, 1944, following Roosevelt's veto of a tax bill that the president ridiculed as providing "relief not for the needy but for the greedy." In his veto message, the president had charged Congress with unnecessary delay and obfuscation in his plan to simplify the nation's tax code.

Barkley had urged the chief executive not to veto the bill. In anger, Barkley resigned his post as majority leader before a packed Senate chamber. (*See Reading No. 50.*) He charged that Roosevelt's characterization of the bill as tax relief for the greedy was a "calculated and deliberate assault on the legislative integrity of every member of Congress." Following his forty-five-minute speech, the Senate gave Barkley a boisterous standing ovation. Within minutes of receiving his formal resignation, the caucus of Democratic senators unanimously reelected their leader. At that moment he took on the new role as the Senate's representative to the White House and no longer the president's emissary to the Senate. Shortly thereafter, both houses decisively overrode the president's veto. These two events signaled the Senate's determination to regain its traditional independence from executive domination.

THE TRUMAN COMMITTEE. The 1920s witnessed the Teapot Dome inquiry. In the 1930s the Senate sponsored three significant investigations including the Nye munitions probe, the Pecora stock market study, and Robert La Follette's civil liberties inquiry. The latter, undertaken between 1936 and 1940, focused on violations stemming from interference with labor's right to organize that had been guaranteed by the 1935 Wagner Act.

The investigation, however, that produced the most dramatic consequences for its chairman began in March 1941 when the Senate created the Special Committee to Investigate the National Defense Program. This enterprise was the brain-child of Harry S. Truman, a relatively obscure Missouri member who had begun his Senate service in 1935. Truman had become convinced that waste and corruption were stran-gling the nation's efforts to mobilize itself for the war in Europe. During the three years of his chairmanship, the committee held hundreds of hearings, both public and private, heard from thousands of witnesses, and traveled many miles to conduct field inspections. Truman became widely known for the thoroughness and effectiveness of his work. Along the way, he developed working experience with business, labor, agriculture, and executive agencies that would serve him well in later years. Truman's widely respected fairness and deter-mination erased his earlier public image as a minion of Kansas City politicos. In 1944, when Democratic party leaders sought a replacement for controversial Vice President Henry Wallace, they settled on Truman as an ideal compromise choice.

Vice President Truman's service as the Senate's presiding officer lasted just eighty-three days. In common with other senators who had become vice president, he found the job unchallenging. On April 12, 1945, while presiding, he wrote to his mother, ''I have to sit up here and make parliamentary rulings, some of which are common sense and some of which are not.'' As the session adjourned, Truman walked over to the House side of the Capitol for a drink with Speaker Rayburn and other congressional leaders. Before the vice president arrived, the White House press secretary had phoned Rayburn to ask that Truman call him at once. Truman made the call, turned pale, raced back to his office, and sped to the Executive Mansion. There, first lady Eleanor Roosevelt quietly told him, ''Harry, the president is dead.''

CHAPTER 8

THE POSTWAR SENATE: 1945–1963

In the two decades that separated World War II from the conflict in Vietnam, the Senate moved swiftly away from executive branch domination into an era of relative independence. Until the end of the 1950s, power resided with a small coterie of well-entrenched conservative southern leaders. After the elections of 1958, a new cadre of moderate and liberal senators began to chip away at that centralization. By 1963 Senate floor leader Mike Mansfield (D-MT) personified a new era in which members of a strengthened Democratic majority would divide power and authority on a more equitable basis. The Senate of the mid-1960s stood in dramatic contrast to its predecessors of ten, twenty, or thirty years earlier. Only the determined hand of President Lyndon Johnson and deepening U.S. entanglement in southeast Asia restrained the expansion of this new spirit.

LEGISLATIVE REORGANIZATION ACT. In World War II, the United States fought German and Italian dictatorships. On the home front, members of the Senate had become increasingly concerned about an executive branch dictatorship. Throughout the war years, reform advocates toyed with proposals to strengthen congressional resources in the recognition that an effective legislature stood as the best protection against tyranny, both foreign and domestic. As early as 1941, Sen. A. B. Chandler (D-KY) proposed that the Senate permit each member to hire one "research expert." At that time, a senator who did not chair one of the Senate's thirty-four committees was entitled to hire one clerk at $3,900, one at $2,400, one at $2,200, two at $1,800, and one at $1,500. If he represented one of the fourteen states with a population exceeding three million, he could add another $1,500 per year clerk. Senior members who chaired committees objected to any plan that would add subject specialists to the clerical ranks, fearing that it might establish a cadre of "political assistants" who would eventually be in a position to compete for their bosses' jobs. Consequently, executive agencies and outside lobbyists continued as the Senate's principal source of bill drafting and specialized technical assistance.

In September 1942, President Roosevelt unwittingly increased Congress' frustration at its second-class position when he delivered a stern message to both houses. Angered over their delay in enacting key administration proposals, he threatened, "In the event that Congress fails to act, and act adequately, I shall accept the responsibility, and I shall act." Sen. Robert La Follette responded that it was "time for the American people to take stock of the situation, war or no war." To relieve the crushing burden of members' multiple committee assignments, the Wisconsin senator proposed reducing the number of committees as well as the number of members assigned to each. La Follette made the cause of congressional reform his personal crusade, achieving victory in mid-1946 at the cost of losing his Senate seat to Joseph R. McCarthy.

The Legislative Reorganization Act became the single most important institutional reform measure of the Senate's history. It reduced the number of Senate committees from thirty-three to fifteen and limited senators to service on two major committees. The act permitted each committee to hire up to four professional and six clerical staff members. To mimize autocratic control by chairmen, it set regular committee meeting days, spelled out committee jurisdiction in the Senate rules, and required public sessions unless a majority of a committee voted to close them. All committees were required to keep transcripts of hearings and to send permanently valuable records to the National Archives. The measure established the Legislative Reference Service as a separate division within the Library of Congress. The Service was to include subject specialists paid at levels comparable to the most senior experts working within the executive branch. The House refused to go along with the Senate's plan to provide an administrative assistant for each member and to establish party legislative policy committees. Consequently, the Senate independently adopted those proposals for itself.

EIGHTIETH CONGRESS. On the day after Harry Truman suddenly became president, he returned to the Capitol for a private luncheon with his former Senate colleagues. Despite his cordial relations with well-placed Senate leaders, the new president's relations with Congress in 1945 quickly soured. Political and economic pressures accompanying the end of World War II forced heated confrontations between the legislative and executive branches. For example, administration refusal to remove wartime price controls resulted in cattle producers withholding meat supplies from the marketplace on the eve of the 1946 congressional elections. Voters responded to this and other problems of postwar conversion by increasing the number of Republicans in the Senate from thirty-eight to fifty-one, giving that party a majority for the first time since the election of 1930.

With Republicans in control, the Eightieth Congress (1947–1949) faced major foreign and domestic policy challenges. Senate Foreign Relations Committee chairman Arthur Vandenberg led his once-isolationist party colleagues into a new bipartisan foreign policy alliance with Senate Democrats. His "Vandenberg Resolution," which the Senate adopted 64-4, led to the creation of the North Atlantic Treaty Organization. In contrast to the Senate's refusal in 1919 to approve participation in the League of Nations, in 1945 it had readily agreed to the United Nations Charter. In 1947 the Senate approved the "Truman Doctrine" proposals for massive aid to Greece and Turkey. A year later it passed the "Marshall Plan" providing financial aid to speed European recovery. President Truman was far less successful, however, in achieving his domestic agenda. This situation so enraged him that he labeled the Eightieth Congress the "Do-Nothing Congress." The Taft-Hartley Labor-Management Relations Act proved to be the one notable domestic accomplishment of that Congress. The handiwork of Sen. Robert Taft (R-OH), the measure outlawed the "closed shop," which required workers to join a labor union as a condition of employment. Although Truman quickly vetoed the measure, the Senate and House achieved the necessary two-thirds margin to pass the act over the president's objections.

CLASS OF 1948. Leaders within the national Democratic

party sought the strongest possible challengers to take on
Republican Senate incumbents in the 1948 elections. Fearing
that the increasingly unpopular Truman would lose the White
House to Republican Thomas Dewey, they reasoned that the
Senate should become their party's outpost in the government.
On election day, however, voters defied pollsters' predictions
and gave a surprise victory to Truman. They also returned the
Senate to Democratic control, with a gain of nine seats.
Among the new members of the Senate "Class of 1948" were
Lyndon Johnson (D-TX), Hubert Humphrey (D-MN), Russell
Long (D-LA), Clinton Anderson (D-NM), Paul Douglas (D-
IL), Estes Kefauver (D-TN), Robert Kerr (D-OK), and
Margaret Chase Smith (R-ME). Smith became the first woman
elected to the Senate without being preceded by her husband
and the first to serve in both houses of Congress.[1]

Despite the addition of a number of administration supporters to the Senate's membership, the president's "Fair Deal"
program failed to advance beyond limited gains in public
housing assistance, Social Security expansion, and an increase
in the minimum wage. Southern and western senators formed
a potent coalition in which the South supported western water
projects and commodity supports in return for the West's
cooperation in blocking civil rights legislation. The administration lost its battles to repeal the antilabor Taft-Hartley Act,
and to enact major education and health insurance legislation.
The Senate became preoccupied with foreign policy issues
growing out of the 1949 Communist take-over of China and the
Soviet Union's development of the atomic bomb. These events
led Sen. Joseph R. McCarthy to charge on February 9, 1950,
in Wheeling, WV, that there were a large number of Communist working in the State Department.

MCCARTHYISM. Sen. McCarthy provided the spark that
ignited a four-year-long national conflagration. As Senate
Democratic Leader Robert Byrd observed three decades later,
"There was never quite anyone like McCarthy in the Senate

---

[1]In 1986 Barbara Mikulski (D-MD) became the first Democratic woman
elected to the Senate in her own right.

before or after; nor has this chamber ever gone through a more painful period."[2] A man of restless and compulsive energy, McCarthy exploited a national mood of anxiety over Communist advances throughout Europe and Asia. At the time of McCarthy's initial attack, Sen. Patrick McCarran (D-NV), chairman of the Senate Judiciary Committee, had been considering legislation to protect American society from what he considered subversive infiltration by undesirable foreign nationals. McCarran also chaired his committee's Subcommittee on Internal Security. From 1950 through 1953 that committee, in an example of Senate investigations at their worst, conducted dramatic inquiries into individuals and groups accused of Communist party sympathies or activities. In 1950 Congress enacted, over Truman's veto, the Internal Security Act, McCarran's measure requiring registration of Communist-front organizations and providing for internment of Communists during national emergencies.

On February 20, 1950, eleven days after his Wheeling speech, McCarthy held the Senate floor for eight hours, detailing his case against "81 loyalty risks." (*See Reading No. 51.*) The Senate's Democratic leadership responded by establishing a special subcommittee of the Foreign Relations Committee to examine McCarthy's charges. Chaired by Sen. Millard Tydings (D-MD), the panel conducted extensive hearings. In July it concluded that McCarthy had perpetrated a "fraud and a hoax" on the Senate and the American public. In the midst of the Tydings subcommittee's investigation, Sen. Margaret Chase Smith delivered in the Senate her eloquent "Declaration of Conscience" speech. (*See Reading No. 52.*) In a lightly veiled attack on McCarthy, she charged that the Senate's reputation as the world's greatest deliberative body was being "debased to the level of a forum of hate and

---

[2]In March 1980 Sen. Robert C. Byrd (D-WV) launched an unprecedented and extensive series of addresses to the Senate on its history and traditions. That series continued through the One Hundredth Congress (1987–1988) and included one hundred separate lectures on all areas of the Senate's historical development. It offers a unique perspective on the Senate by a senior member who served both as majority and minority floor leader.

character assassination.'' McCarthy retaliated by supporting Tydings's opponent in the 1950 election. The urbane Maryland senator, who had survived President Roosevelt's 1938 effort to ''purge'' him from the Senate, fell before the McCarthy onslaught.

KEFAUVER CRIME COMMITTEE. The 1950 election also claimed another prominent Democrat, as Illinois Republican Everett Dirksen defeated Senate Majority Leader Scott Lucas (D-IL). Lucas had held the post for only two years. Unlike Alben Barkley, who had served as Senate Democratic leader from the death of Joseph Robinson in 1937 until his own election as vice president in 1948, Lucas failed to exercise strong party leadership. Already in trouble with the voters, Lucas's undoing came when fellow Senate Democrat Estes Kefauver allowed his celebrated investigating committee, on the eve of the election, to look into corruption charges involving Lucas associates.

From mid-1950 through May 1951, the freshman senator had skillfully used his chairmanship of the Senate Select Committee to Investigate Organized Crime in Interstate Commerce to gain national prominence. Earlier, when the Senate Commerce and Judiciary committees were unable to agree as to which of them had jurisdiction over organized crime, they created this ''select'' committee composed of members from both their panels. As Kefauver had proposed the investigation, he was named chairman. Employing the new medium of television to broadcast his sensational hearings, Kefauver turned the spotlight of national attention onto alleged gangsters and Mafia bosses, whom he claimed were working in league with law enforcement officials in major U.S. cities. Overnight, Kefauver became a leading candidate for his party's 1952 presidential nomination.

MCCARTHY'S CENSURE. Sen. McCarthy grew bolder with each successive confrontation. On June 14, 1951, in a Senate floor speech, he accused Gen. George Marshall, one of the nation's most respected individuals, of ''whimpering appeasement.'' Sen. William Benton (R-CT) introduced a resolution to consider McCarthy's expulsion from the Senate.

The Wisconsin senator, in a departure from the Senate tradition of courteous behavior even toward one's most detested colleague, responded, "Benton has established himself as a hero of every Communist and crook in and out of government."

In 1952, Dwight Eisenhower's presidential election victory wiped out the Democrats' narrow Senate margin and gave the Republicans control by one vote (48-47-1). Robert Taft (R-OH), who had earlier preferred to exercise party leadership as chairman of the Republican Policy Committee, became Senate Majority Leader. On the Democratic side, forty-four-year-old Lyndon Johnson, after only four years in the Senate, became the youngest person ever to serve as his party's floor leader. Deeply concerned at McCarthy's antics, Taft believed that appointment of William Jenner (R-IN) to chair the Internal Security Subcommittee would effectively block the troublesome senator from using that platform to continue his anti-Communist crusade. McCarthy had other ideas. As chairman of the Committee on Government Operations, he exercised his prerogative to preside over that panel's Permanent Subcommittee on Investigations, a successor to the Truman defense committee. The new chairman built a staff of ambitious investigators, including young Robert F. Kennedy. Over the next two years the subcommittee conducted 445 "preliminary inquiries" and 157 investigations.

McCarthy finally went too far, however, when he decided to attack the Army. An extended series of hearings on possible security breaches ended in a confrontation between the chairman and Army Secretary Robert Stevens. From April through June 1954, the nation watched the committee's televised hearings. McCarthy had temporarily stepped down as chairman to engage the enemy directly. In the process, he wildly maligned all who stood in his way, including numerous senators. By midyear, he had totally discredited himself. His Senate colleagues were no longer willing to tolerate his gross abuse of members and the institution. On December 2, 1954, the Senate agreed (67-22) to a resolution stating that his conduct was "contrary to senatorial traditions and is hereby condemned." (*See Reading No. 53.*) McCarthy, a pathetic and repudiated figure, remained in the Senate for several more years until alcoholism brought about his death in 1957.

BRICKER AMENDMENT. The Eisenhower administration, in its earliest years, suffered frustration at the hands of another Senate Republican—Ohio's John Bricker. During the Truman presidency in 1951, Bricker began a vigorous campaign for passage of a constitutional amendment allowing Congress to "regulate all executive and other agreements with any foreign power or international organization." Citing the alleged American "sell-out" in the 1945 Yalta Agreement, Bricker feared that U.S. involvement in the United Nations might lead to other such pacts that would undermine the country's freedoms. By 1953 he had obtained sixty-two Senate cosponsors. President Eisenhower saw the Bricker Amendment as a Senate attempt to limit his powers over foreign policy. Democratic Leader Lyndon Johnson gladly seized the opportunity to save the administration from the isolationists within its own party. With Walter George (D-GA), senior minority member of the Foreign Relations Committee, he drafted a substitute that stated, "An international agreement other than a treaty shall become effective as internal law in the United States only by act of Congress." Eisenhower's lobbying had weakened Senate support for Bricker's version, but the Johnson substitute fell short of Senate adoption, in February 1954, by a dramatic one-vote margin. Although this killed the amendment, it did nothing to still the Senate's continuing frustration over the use of executive agreements to circumvent its responsibilities in the treaty ratification process.

LYNDON JOHNSON. As soon as he arrived in the Senate in 1949, Lyndon Johnson cultivated the affection and support of Georgia's Richard Russell, a leader of the Senate's fabled "Inner Club." The young Texan secured a prize assignment on the Armed Services Committee and, after the outbreak of the conflict in Korea, convinced Russell to create a special Defense Preparedness Subcommittee that he could chair. Johnson fully recalled the value of a similar war investigating committee in propelling Harry Truman to higher office. In 1951, after only two years in the Senate, Johnson became his party's deputy floor leader. He quickly transformed this largely honorific whip's post to one of real influence. Two years later, when Majority Leader Ernest McFarland lost his reelection bid to Republican Barry Goldwater, Johnson became Democratic floor leader at the start of the 1953 session.

The mid-1953 death of Republican Leader Robert Taft created within the Senate an extraordinary political reversal. When the Ohio governor appointed a Democratic successor to Taft, Johnson's party suddenly found itself with a majority of the Senate's members (48-D, 47-R, 1-I). This led the new Republican leader, William Knowland (CA) to complain of the burdens of having to deliver a legislative program without the requisite numerical power to do so. To this, Johnson responded, "The Senator from California frequently refers to himself as a majority leader with a minority; and he has made reference to all the problems that go with that situation. If anyone has more problems than a majority leader with a minority," Johnson concluded, "it is a minority leader with a majority!" Lyndon Johnson endeared himself to freshmen Democrats, in 1953 and for his remaining eight years in the Senate, by devising a system of committee assignments that provided each new member a seat on a major committee before more senior senators could select their second key assignment. Later the Republicans, under Everett Dirksen's leadership, would adopt the same system. This became a major step toward limiting senior members' monopoly on control of Senate operations. The 1954 elections, occurring as the Senate moved to censure Joseph McCarthy, restored the Democrats to control of the chamber.

DEMOCRATIC ASCENDANCY. Johnson developed a cordial relationship with Eisenhower, who preferred to work with the Democratic leader rather than with his own party leader, William Knowland. The closeness of Senate party divisions between 1953 and 1958 and the relative strength of southern Democrats, placed a great premium on Johnson's behind-the-scenes political style. His success in guiding passage of a major civil rights act in 1957 demonstrated his skill in uniting sectional and partisan blocs in the national interest. The elections of 1958 dramatically changed the Senate's political composition. An economic recession, White House influence-peddling scandals, and concerns over Soviet breakthroughs in outer space produced the largest transfer of seats from one party to another in the Senate's history. The Democrats gained thirteen Republican seats, giving them a 62-34 majority. With the addition of four seats from the newly admitted states of Alaska and Hawaii, their 65-35 margin was greater than at any time since the election of 1940.

Among senators who had arrived since the mid-1950s were a growing number who began to challenge both the institution's traditional ways and the freewheeling style of its majority leader. (*See Reading No. 54.*) Following the 1958 election, Eisenhower turned sharply conservative, vetoing measures that he regarded as too costly. Relations between the Senate and president reached an all-time low in mid-1959 when the Senate rejected the nomination of former Atomic Energy Commission chairman Lewis Strauss to be secretary of commerce. This was the first rejection of a cabinet nomination since 1925 and only the eighth in history. The Strauss defeat was directly attributable to the nominee's arrogant disdain for the Senate's right to oversee executive operations. Eisenhower called the rejection "one of the most depressing official disappointments I experienced during my eight years in the White House."

The Strauss defeat foreshadowed a long-term realignment in executive-legislative power relationships. For nearly four decades Congress had delegated large blocks of legislative authority to the presidency. With the 1960 elections on the horizon, Senate Democrats felt compelled to seek issues on which they could conspicuously oppose the president. As a result, the 1959–1960 session accomplished little. Johnson had expected to obtain the Democratic presidential nomination. When that prize went instead to Senator John F. Kennedy (D-MA), the Texas Democrat accepted the vice presidential bid to give the ticket a broader geographical and ideological appeal. When the Senate reconvened in the brief period between the conventions and the November elections, visitors who jammed the Senate's galleries knew they would be seeing a president. Vice President Richard Nixon, the Republican nominee, presided over the Senate while Kennedy accustomed himself to his new role as "the majority leader's leader."

The Kennedy-Johnson ticket won in November by the barest of margins. As the 1961 session convened, Democrats caucused and elected Mike Mansfield as their new floor leader.

The mild-mannered Mansfield immediately invited Johnson, who had presided over that meeting, to continue to do so as vice president. This ignited a firestorm of resentment among Democrats, who feared that Johnson would use his customary strong-arm tactics to impose the executive's will on the Senate. The Texan bitterly declined Mansfield's offer. That dramatic incident marked a major transition in the style of leadership that senators would be willing to accept.

KENNEDY'S ONE THOUSAND DAYS. Mansfield and Kennedy both began their Senate service in 1953. Within a few years Mansfield decided to pursue a Senate leadership role, while Kennedy set his sights on the White House. By 1961, each had achieved his goal. Tired of the Lyndon Johnson activist leadership style, Senate Democrats deliberately opted for moderation and a diffusion of power by selecting the self-effacing Mansfield. Although Democrats controlled the Senate at the start of the Kennedy administration by a nearly two-to-one majority, the party was deeply divided between conservative, moderate, and liberal factions. Preoccupied with massive civil rights demonstrations and foreign policy crises in Cuba, Berlin, and Southeast Asia, Kennedy's "New Frontier" program failed to achieve significant legislative endorsement. Bold new proposals in education, housing, medical care, and civil rights generally remained bottled up in committees under the chairmanship of such deeply conservative southerners as Allen Ellender (Agriculture), Richard Russell (Armed Services), A. Willis Robertson (Banking), Harry F. Byrd (Finance), and James O. Eastland (Judiciary). The major foreign policy breakthrough of the Kennedy years came on September 24, 1963, when the Senate consented to the ratification of a Limited Nuclear Test Ban Treaty.

In the Senate, under Mansfield's leadership, subcommittees proliferated, providing platforms for less senior and less conservative Democrats. In issue areas where the administration had little interest in shaping policy, these chairmen seized the initiative. With their own party in control of the administration for the first time in eight years, they expressed profound frustration over the lack of Johnson-style legislative leadership. Mansfield reacted bitterly, deeply resenting the comparison with Johnson. He had planned, on November 22, 1963, to deliver a vigorous defense of his stewardship. However, a gunman in Dallas, Texas, that day took deadly aim at the president and, in a blood-spattered instant, propelled Lyndon Johnson to the White House.

CHAPTER 9

THE MODERN SENATE

The final quarter century of the Senate's first two hundred years intensified the conflict between tradition and innovation that has characterized the institution's entire history. Throughout this period the Senate continued to operate under rules last substantially changed in 1884. Yet new precedents interpreting those rules for contemporary conditions accumulated in the late 1970s to fill a volume of over 1,300 pages. In 1963 many Senate committees continued to meet in secret and floor proceedings were closed to radio and television coverage. By 1986 those restrictions had been abandoned, except in the most unusual circumstances. The hallowed right to fillibuster remained intact, but procedures for limiting debate, although difficult and cumbersome to apply, had become more readily available.

Old structures trembled under the weight of a dramatically increased workload. Senators, once accustomed to specializing in a limited number of state-related issues, came under greater pressure to perform in all major areas of national concern. Staff grew during this period from 2,500 to over 7,000, necessitating addition of a third office building in 1982. In a move that diminished the power of committee chairmen, the minority party was given control of one-third of all committee staff resources and individual senators received funding to hire aides as personal representatives within these committees. Finally, increased demands on members' time stimulated significant reform efforts. In the mid-1980s frustrated senators banded together in an informal "Quality of Life Caucus" to seek relief from fragmented schedules and staggering workloads.

DIFFUSION OF POWER. Sen. Mike Mansfield served as majority leader from 1961 to 1977, longer than any other floor leader in the Senate's history. Mansfield believed that each senator should be allowed maximum latitude to conduct his business with minimum interference from party leadership.

When pressures for action coincided with pressures for continued deliberation, he favored the latter. Mansfield strongly supported the Senate's historic role as protector against the "tyranny of the majority"—as a forum where reasonable delay and constructive deliberation had at least equal standing with efficiency and action. (*See Reading No. 55.*) The Democratic leader, to a much greater degree than his predecessor Lyndon Johnson, carefully cultivated Republican floor leader Everett Dirksen (IL), who served until 1969, and then Hugh Scott (PA), who retired with Mansfield in 1977.

Senate Democrats in 1977 elected Robert C. Byrd (WV) as majority leader. Byrd, a member of the class of 1958 and Democratic Whip since 1971, had earned a reputation for diligent hard work and mastery of the Senate's complex body of rules and precedents. When the Republicans won control of the Senate in 1981, Byrd became minority leader and former minority leader Howard Baker (TN) assumed the majority leader's post. Baker retired in 1985 and was succeeded by Robert Dole (KS). In 1987, with the return of the Democrats to power, Byrd resumed the majority leader's post and Dole became minority leader. Each of these floor leaders, in his own way, followed in the Mansfield tradition of allowing maximum possible latitude to each senator.

CLOTURE. For two centuries the Senate has carefully guarded its constitutional and historical role as forum for the protection of minority views through the device of unlimited debate. Although the emergencies surrounding World War I forced adoption of a procedure to close off discussion in due course, that "cloture" rule was successfully applied on only six occasions between 1917 and 1964. On June 10, 1964, the Senate, by a margin of four votes, invoked cloture for the first time on a civil rights measure. Passage of the 1964 Civil Rights Act marked the end of successful efforts by southern senators to bottle up such legislation. It also heralded the increased use of cloture to speed up consideration of controversial bills.

During the two decades following 1964, the Senate achieved cloture on sixty-one occasions. This occurred for two reasons. First, senators increasingly used the filibuster, or the threat of it, on routine matters. Second, after years of trying to reduce the number of votes necessary to invoke cloture, the Senate in 1975 adopted a rules change that dropped the requirement of two-thirds present and voting (67 if all were present) to 60 percent of the full Senate (60 if there were no vacancies). In 1979 the Senate, under Majority Leader Robert Byrd, successfully limited the so-called "post-cloture" filibuster used by some members to further delay proceedings after cloture had been invoked.

Yet, the ability of members to offer nongermane amendments and to devise other dilatory tactics continued a situation that prompted Sen. Thomas Eagleton to observe, "No other legislative body in the world, not even the St. Louis Board of Aldermen, permits that kind of shenanigans." The introduction of television in 1986 promised to turn the spotlight of adverse national publicity on those who persisted, without apparent reason, in unduly delaying the Senate's proceedings. New and less visible devices emerged to slow consideration of legislation. The most significant of these was the so-called "hold." To speed consideration of routine legislation, the Senate in modern times has made greater use of "unanimous consent" agreements, in which differences are ironed out before a measure is taken up on the floor. These agreements worked only in the absence of objection. Thus members, for any reason and without being publicly identified, could delay action by threatening to object pending opportunity for further study.

RELATIONS WITH THE PRESIDENCY. In 1964 the Senate, following several decades of relative independence from the White House, cooperated closely with the administration of Lyndon Johnson. On the domestic front the next two years produced an outpouring of constructive legislation under the "Great Society" label. In foreign affairs, the Senate supported the increasing military involvement in southeast Asia, passing in August 1964, the "Gulf of Tonkin Resolution" by a margin of 88-2. Later, Johnson would refer to this as the equivalent of a congressional declaration of war. By 1970, as Congress moved to repeal that resolution, President Richard Nixon widened the war with an invasion of Cambodia. In an effort to reassert senatorial prerogatives, Senators John

Sherman Cooper (R-KY) and Frank Church (D-ID) successfully engineered adoption of a resolution restricting use of U.S.
ground forces in Cambodia. Finally, in 1973 Congress passed
the War Powers Resolution limiting the president's power to
commit U.S. troops without congressional approval.

A year later the Senate joined the House in imposing greater
legislative control over government spending. The Congressional Budget and Impoundment Control Act curtailed the
president's ability to ''impound'' congressionally appropriated
funds as a means of killing programs he was otherwise unable
to block. More importantly, it established a budget mechanism
designed to bring greater coordination between individual
spending decisions and an overall budget limitation. A similar
measure had been enacted as part of the 1946 Legislative
Reorganization Act. The earlier provision failed after only
three years. The 1974 budget act, considered one of the most
important postwar pieces of legislation governing congressional operations, produced a record of mixed success during
the first decade of its existence. The resurgence of congressional dominance over the executive culminated in August
1974 with President Nixon's resignation.

WATERGATE. Throughout its history, the Senate has
effectively expanded its investigative function. Building on the
earlier accomplishments of the Walsh, Nye, La Follette,
Truman, Kefauver, and McCarthy probes, the Senate in 1973
conducted a searching examination of ethical misconduct
associated with the 1972 presidential campaign. The Senate
Select Committee on Presidential Campaign Activities,
chaired by Sen. Sam Ervin (D-NC), tested the limits of
''executive privilege'' in its efforts to force President Nixon's
cooperation. When the committee learned, on July 23, 1973,
of the existence of tape recorded conversations between the
president and his aides, it initiated a legal battle to secure the
recordings. The panel failed to obtain the tapes, as a federal
judge ruled that such an effort exceeded its proper legislative
function and might prejudice the forthcoming criminal investigation of the president's action. Although the Ervin Committee ended its public hearings early in 1974, its actions triggered

the House impeachment proceedings that prompted Nixon's August 1974 resignation.

IMPEACHMENT. Among its constitutionally mandated investigative functions, none surpasses the Senate's responsibility as a court of impeachment. Exercising those responsibilities for the first time in fifty years, the Senate on October 9, 1986, removed from office Federal District Judge Harry E. Claiborne on charges of bringing the judiciary into disrepute by filing false income tax returns. This marked only the fifth occasion in the Senate's history that it had acted in this manner. From the time that the House of Representatives brought impeachment charges against Sen. William Blount in 1798, the Senate had considered twelve impeachment cases. Among those impeached were a president, a Supreme Court justice, a cabinet officer, and nine federal judges. The five removals came exclusively from the ranks of federal judges. Over the course of the twentieth century, the Senate expressed increasing frustration at the requirement to take time from more pressing national concerns to evaluate the often complex issues surrounding the impeachment charges.

In the 1986 Claiborne case, the Senate established a special Impeachment Committee to receive evidence. This avoided a time-consuming trial before the full Senate, while giving the impeached judge opportunity for an extended presentation of his case. When the full Senate convened as a court of impeachment, the prosecutors from the House, and Claiborne with his counsel, summarized their respective positions. On October 9, there occurred a rare moment of high drama. With nearly every senator at his or her desk, members in turn rose to announce their verdicts as to the judge's guilt or innocence. When the balloting ended, the Senate had convicted Claiborne on three articles by overwhelming margins. Occurring in the final days of a lengthy session, the trial seriously delayed the Senate's work on major government funding bills. With several other possible impeachment cases on the horizon, Senate reformers looked for ways to relieve the Senate from the reponsibilities of this two-hundred-year-old constitutional requirement. (*See Reading No. 56.*)

COMMITTEES. Proliferation of subcommittees, democratization of procedure, and rapid staff expansion characterized the development of Senate committees in the decades following the 1946 reorganization. In 1947 the fifteen Senate committees had a total of 44 subcommittees. By 1976 that number had more than tripled to 140. This pushed the number of subcommittee assignments per senator from two to fourteen. In 1975, to curb the powers of autocratic chairmen, the Senate adopted reforms requiring open hearings and business meetings, except in rare cases. Between 1970 and 1975 the total number of closed congressional hearings dropped from 41 to 7 percent. Senators were permitted to hire one staff aide for each of three committees to which they were assigned. Previously, a committee's chairman and the ranking minority member controlled staff hiring and administration. This served to decentralize and fragment committee operations.

That fragmentation accelerated in 1977 when the Senate acknowledged the right of the minority to hire one-third of all committee staff. The number of committee staff grew from 232 in 1946 to 948 in 1974. Following the 1975 additions, that number reached an all-time high of 1,277. By 1987 approximately 1,200 persons worked for Senate committees. The volume of legislation considered by Senate committees also increased significantly. As part of its 1977 committee reforms, the Senate reduced the number of subcommittees and sought to lighten the burden on individual members. Again in 1981 and 1985 the Senate considered changes to reduce fragmentation of members' time and attention.

COMMUNICATIONS WITH THE PUBLIC. The single most dramatic institutional change in the final twenty-five years of the Senate's first two centuries has occurred in its communications with the public. In earlier times, members customarily returned to their states during the three or four annual recesses. Transcontinental jets enabled western senators to shuttle routinely across the continent for weekend meetings in their states. Their constituents, similarly, made the trip to the nation's capital with greater ease and less expense than would have been dreamed possible several decades earlier. Introduction of videotape and television satellite communications technology vastly expanded regional and local news coverage of senators' activities. In 1986, after extended debate on whether television would compromise its deliberate manner of doing business, the Senate began live radio and television coverage of its daily sessions. (*See Reading No. 57.*)

In the 1970s the Senate provided members with office automation systems to faciliatate handling of constituent correspondence. By the 1980s senators from large states routinely received as many as 15,000 pieces of mail each week. Through the use of computers, senators' offices were able to reduce response times from several weeks to as little as forty-eight hours. They were also able to develop automated mailing lists of great assistance in sending follow-up letters related to constituents' earlier inquiries. Many members transferred their constituent service operations from Washington back to their home states, using low-cost leased telephone lines for improved access to citizens and federal agencies.

CAMPAIGNS. Since the mid-1950s Senate candidates have taken advantage of television to project their personalities and programs to statewide audiences. The advent of videotape technology in the early 1980s enhanced their ability to reach voters on almost a daily basis with updated messages. This changed the traditional site of a candidate's activity from the speaker's rostrum to the television studio. As Senate candidates came to rely on political action committees (PACs) for funding and media consultants for packaging, the power and value of traditional political party organizations declined dramatically. Campaign costs soared. In 1984 Sen. Jesse Helms (R-NC) spent a record $15 million to secure his reelection. This came in sharp contrast to the days prior to the 1913 adoption of the direct election amendment, when Senate candidates needed only to convince a plurality of a state legislature to win election. As the Senate approached its third century, there were renewed calls for partial public funding of congressional campaigns to reduce the influence of large corporate donors.

ETHICS AND DISCIPLINE. In the years since the end of World War II the Senate has grappled with difficult issues of ethical conduct for its members. A 1951 Subcommittee on Ethical Standards, chaired by Sen. Paul Douglas (D-IL), recommended that the Senate develop a voluntary code of conduct to clarify new or complex situations where the application of basic moral principles was far from obvious, and to keep well-intentioned members from blundering into error. The Douglas Committee issued one of the earliest calls for mandatory disclosure, by public officials, of income, assets, and financial transactions. The Senate, however, continued without a formal and binding code of conduct until 1963. At that time Sen. Jacob Javits (R-NY) declared that it was "completely incongruous for Senate committees to question executive appointees vigorously on their financial affairs when those of us in Congress and our staffs are not subject to similar standards and requirements." Within days of his statement, the Senate confronted charges of corruption and influence ped- dling lodged against one of its top staff aides, Majority Secretary Robert G. "Bobby" Baker. A protégé of former Senate barons Lyndon Johnson and Robert Kerr, Baker re- signed his post as the Senate Rules Committee prepared to launch a broad probe of Senate employees' financial activities. That investigation focused on the conditions that permitted Baker to amass a large personal fortune and it resulted in a call for limited financial disclosure by Senate officers and senior employees. In July 1964 the Senate established a bipartisan Select Committee on Standards and Conduct.

Shortly after its creation, the select committee launched an investigation in response to newspaper charges that Sen. Thomas Dodd (D-CT) had improperly exchanged favors with a public relations representative of West German interests, that he had used campaign funds to meet personal expenses, and that he had double-billed the government for travel expenses. In mid-1967 the Senate voted 92-5 to censure Dodd for using campaign funds for personal purposes, noting that his con- duct, "which is contrary to accepted morals, derogates from the public trust expected of a Senator and tends to bring the Senate into disfavor and disrepute." A year later, the Senate adopted its first formal code of ethical conduct. It set limits on outside employment for members and staffs, required disclo- sure of campaign contributions and set restrictions on their use, and obligated members and senior staff to file annual financial reports.

In the decade that followed adoption of these codes, one president, two senators, and fifteen House members were subject to congressional or judicial investigation for ethical misconduct. Hostile public reaction to the apparent tendency within Congress to ignore these cases of wrongdoing led both houses in 1977 to toughen their codes of conduct and to strengthen the powers of their respective ethics committees. In 1979 the Senate "denounced" Sen. Herman Talmadge (D-GA) for financial misconduct. Although this verdict was intended to be slightly less severe than a "censure," it added the Georgia Democrat to the list of six others who had been treated in this way over the course of the Senate's history. Three years later, in 1982, the Senate moved to expel convicted Sen. Harrison Williams (D-NJ) for accepting mining stock in return for his promise to get government contracts for the mine's output. In the face of certain expulsion, Williams resigned.

The Senate's approach to matters of ethics and discipline provides a useful example of its uncommon ability to reconcile protection of its members and procedures with overriding requirements for justice and institutional integrity. This has been accomplished without rigid rules of conduct and central-ized enforcement mechanisms. Although characteristically fluid and protracted, the process of setting and applying standards of conduct, as with the broader legislative process, has functioned to achieve creditable results.

A VISION REALIZED. The United States Senate is the one institution within the federal government that the framers of the Constitutuion, after two centuries, would immediately recognize. They would understand its passion for deliberation, its untidiness, its aloofness from the House of Representatives, and its suspicion of the presidency. They would probably not comprehend the role of legislative political parties. They would wonder why its proceedings had been opened to the public, both in person and through the medium of radio and television. The framers would certainly be aghast at the three ornate office buildings and the 7,000 staff members who fill them, yet they would understand the Senate's capacity for meeting the changing circumstances inherent in the nation's twentieth-century rise to world-power status. They would sympathize with continuing calls for reform of Senate procedures just as they would acknowledge the force of precedent and tradition that make those changes so difficult. Above all, they would be delighted that the Senate, and the Constitution that created it, had endured for two centuries.

PART II

READINGS

READING NO. 1

JAMES MADISON ON THE ROLE OF THE SENATE, JUNE 26, 1787[1]

Here from James Madison's secret notes of proceedings during the Constitutional Convention are his views, in the third person, on the Senate's distinctive role. At this point in the convention, he advocated a nine-year term of office for senators. This is a classic description of his intended distinction between the Senate and the House of Representatives.

γ   γ   γ

MR. MADISON. In order to judge of the form to be given to this institution, it will be proper to take a view of the ends to be served by it. These were first to protect the people against their rulers: secondly to protect the people against the transient impressions into which they themselves might be led. A people deliberating in a temperate moment, and with the experience of other nations before them, on the plan of Government most likely to secure their happiness, would first be aware, that those charged with the public happiness, might betray their trust. An obvious precaution against this danger would be to divide the trust between different bodies of men, who might watch and check each other. In this they would be governed by the same prudence which has prevailed in organizing the subordinate departments of Government, where all business liable to abuses is made to pass through separate hands, the one being a check on the other. It would next occur to such a people, that they themselves were liable to temporary errors, through want of information as to their true interest, and that men chosen for a short term, and employed but a small portion of that in public affairs, might err from the same cause. This reflection would naturally suggest that the Government be so constituted, as that one of its branches might have an oppor-

[1]Wilbourn E. Benton, ed., *1787, Drafting the U.S. Constitution* (College Station, TX, 1986), vol. 1, pp. 480–482.

tunity of acquiring a competent knowledge of the public interests. Another reflection equally becoming a people on such an occasion, would be that they themselves, as well as a numerous body of Representatives, were liable to err also, from fickleness and passion. A necessary fence against this danger would be to select a portion of enlightened citizens, whose limited number, and firmness might seasonably interpose against impetuous councils. It ought finally to occur to a people deliberating on a Government for themselves, that as different interests necessarily result from the liberty meant to be secured, the major interest might under sudden impulses be tempted to commit injustice on the minority. In all civilized Countries the people fall into different classes having a real or supposed difference of interests. There will be creditors and debtors, farmers, merchants and manufacturers. There will be particularly the distinction of rich and poor. It was true as had been observed [by Mr. Pinkney] we had not among us those hereditary distinctions, of rank which were a great source of the contests in the ancient Governments as well as the modern States of Europe, nor those extremes of wealth or poverty which characterize the latter. We cannot however be regarded even at this time, as one homogeneous mass, in which every thing that affects a part will affect in the same manner the whole. In framing a system which we wish to last for ages, we should not lose sight of the changes which ages will produce. An increase of population will of necessity increase the proportion of those who will labour under all the hardships of life, and secretly sigh for a more equal distribution of its blessings. These may in time outnumber those who are placed above the feelings of indigence. According to the equal laws of suffrage, the power will slide into the hands of the former. No agrarian attempts have yet been made in this Country, but symtoms, of a leveling spirit, as we have understood, have sufficiently appeared in a certain quarters to give notice of the future danger. How is this danger to be guarded against on republican principles? How is the danger in all cases of interested coalitions to oppress the minority to be guarded against? Among other means by the establishment of a body in the Government sufficiently respectable for its wisdom and virtue, to aid on such emergences, the preponderance of justice by throwing its weight into that scale. Such being the objects of the second branch in the proposed Government he thought a considerable duration ought to be given to it. He did not conceive that the term of nine years could threaten any real danger; but in pursuing his particular ideas on this subject, he should require that the long term allowed to the second branch should not commence till such a period of life, as would render a perpetual disqualification to be re-elected little inconvenient either in a public or private view. He observed that as it was more than probable we were now digesting a plan which in its operation would decide for ever the fate of Republican Government we ought not only to provide every guard to liberty that its preservation could require, but be equally careful to supply the defects which our own experience had particularly pointed out.

READING NO. 2

JOHN DICKINSON'S "LETTERS OF FABIUS," 1788[2]

John Dickinson played an active role in the Constitutional Convention as a delegate from Delaware. Twenty years earlier he published his famed Letters of a Farmer in Pennsylvania to the Inhabitants of the British Colonies, *in which he suggested force, but urged conciliation, as a rememdy for colonial difficulties with Great Britain. This excerpt from his "Letters of Fabius" was first published in a Delaware newspaper during the 1788 debates on the Constitution's ratification.*

γ　　　　　γ　　　　　γ

Can this limited, fluctuating senate, placed amidst such powers, if it should become willing, ever become able, to make America pass under its yoke? The senators will generally be inhabitants of places very distant one from another. They can scarcely be acquainted till they meet. Few of them can ever act together for any length of time, unless their good conduct recommends them to a re-election; and then there will be frequent changes in a body dependant upon the acts of other bodies, the legislatures of the several states, that are altering every year. Machiavel and Cæsar Borgia together could not form a conspiracy in such a senate, destructive to any but themselves and their accomplices.

It is essential to every good government, that there should be some council, permanent enough to get a due knowledge of affairs internal and external; so constituted, that by some deaths or removals, the current of information should not be impeded or disturbed; and so regulated, as to be responsible to, and controulable by the people. Where can the authority for combining these advantages, be more safely, beneficially, or satisfactorily lodged, than in the senate, to be formed accord-

[2]Arthur Taylor Prescott, ed., *Drafting the Federal Constitution* (Baton Rouge, LA, 1941), pp. 172–173.

ing to the plan proposed? Shall parts of the trust be committed to the president, with counsellors who shall subscribe their advices? If assaults upon liberty are to be guarded against, and surely they ought to be with sleepless vigilance, why should we depend more on the commander in chief of the army and navy of The United States, and of the militia of the several states, and on his counsellors, whom he may secretly influence, than of the senate to be appointed by the persons exercising the sovereign authority of the several states? In truth, the objections against the powers of the senate originated from a desire to have them, or at least some of them, vested in a body, in which the several states should be represented, in proportion to the number of inhabitants, as in the house of representatives. This method is *unattainable,* and the wish for it should be dismissed from every mind, that desires the existence of a confederation.

What assurance can be given, or what probability be assigned, that a board of counsellors would continue honest, longer than the senate? Or, that they would possess more useful information, respecting all the states, than the senators of all the states? It appears needless to pursue this argument any further.

READING NO. 3

THE CONSTITUTION OF THE UNITED STATES, 1787[3]

Included here are those portions of the U.S. Constitution that specifically set forth the Senate's structure and authority.

γ   γ   γ

THE CONSTITUTION OF THE UNITED STATES

Article I

Section 1. All legislative Powers herein granted shall be vested in a Congress of the United States, which shall consist of a Senate and House of Representatives.

Section 3. The Senate of the United States shall be composed of two Senators from each State, chosen by the Legislature thereof, for six Years; and each Senator shall have one Vote.

Immediately after they shall be assembled in Consequence of the first Election, they shall be divided as equally as may be into three Classes. The Seats of the Senators of the first Class shall be vacated at the Expiration of the second Year, of the second Class at the Expiration of the fourth Year, and of the third Class at the Expiration of the sixth Year, so that one third may be chosen every second Year; and if Vacancies happen by Resignation, or otherwise, during the Recess of the Legislature of any State, the Executive thereof may make temporary Appointments until the next Meeting of the Legislature, which shall then fill such Vacancies.

No Person shall be a Senator who shall not have attained to the Age of thirty Years, and been nine Years a Citizen of the

---

[3]*Constitution of the United States,* Article I, sections 1, 3-7; Article II, section 2.

United States, and who shall not, when elected, be an Inhabitant of that State for which he shall be chosen.

The Vice President of the United States shall be President of the Senate, but shall have no vote, unless they be equally divided.

The Senate shall chuse their other Officers, and also a President pro tempore, in the Absence of the Vice President, or when he shall exercise the Office of President of the United States.

The Senate shall have the sole Power to try all Impeachments. When sitting for that Purpose, they shall be on Oath or Affirmation. When the President of the United States is tried, the Chief Justice shall preside: And no Person shall be convicted without the concurrence of two thirds of the Members present. Judgment in Cases of Impeachment shall not extend further than to removal from Office, and disqualification to hold and enjoy any Office of honor, Trust or Profit under the United States: but the Party convicted shall nevertheless be liable and subject to Indictment, Trial, Judgment and Punishment, according to law.

Section 4. The Times, Places and Manner of holding Elections for Senators and Representatives, shall be prescribed in each State by the Legislature thereof; but the Congress may at any time by Law make or alter such Regulations, except as to the Places of chusing Senators.

The Congress shall assemble at least once in every Year, and such Meeting shall be on the first Monday in December, unless they shall by Law appoint a different Day.

Section 5. Each House shall be the Judge of the Elections, Returns and Qualifications of its own Members, and a Majority of each shall constitute a Quorum to do business; but a smaller Number may adjourn from day to day, and may be authorized to compel the Attendance of absent Members, in such Manner, and under such Penalties as each House may provide.

Each House may determine the Rules of its Proceedings, punish its Members for disorderly Behaviour, and, with the Concurrence of two thirds, expel a Member.

Each House shall keep a Journal of its Proceedings, and from time to time publish the same, excepting such Parts as may in their Judgment require Secrecy; and the yeas and Nays of the Members of either House on any question shall, at the Desire of one fifth of those Present, be entered on the Journal.

Neither House, during the Session of Congress, shall, without the Consent of the other, adjourn for more than three days, nor to any other place than that in which the two Houses shall be sitting.

Section 6. The Senators and Representatives shall receive a Compensation for their Services, to be ascertained by Law, and paid out of the Treasury of the United States. They shall in all Cases, except Treason, Felony and Breach of the Peace, be privileged from Arrest during their Attendance at the Session of their respective Houses, and in going to and returning from the same; and for any Speech or Debate in either House, they shall not be questioned in any other Place.

No Senator or Representative shall, during the Time for which he was elected, be appointed to any civil Office under the Authority of the United States, which shall have been created, or the Emoluments whereof shall have been encreased during such time; and no Person holding any Office under the United States, shall be a Member of either House during his Continuance in Office.

Section 7. All Bills for raising Revenue shall originate in the House of Representatives; but the Senate may propose or concur with Amendments as on other Bills.

Every Bill which shall have passed the House of Representatives and the Senate, shall, before it become a Law, be presented to the President of the United States; If he approve he shall sign it, but if not he shall return it, with his Objections to that House in which it shall have originated, who shall enter the Objections at large on their Journal, and proceed to reconsider it. If after such Reconsideration two thirds of that House shall agree to pass the Bill, it shall be sent, together with the Objections, to the other House, by which it shall likewise be reconsidered, and if approved by two thirds of that House, it shall become a Law. But in all such Cases the Votes of both

Houses shall be determined by yeas and Nays, and the Names of the Persons voting for and against the Bill shall be entered on the Journal of each House respectively. If any Bill shall not be returned by the President within ten Days (Sundays excepted) after it shall have been presented to him, the Same shall be a Law, in like Manner as if he had signed it, unless the Congress by their Adjournment prevent its Return, in which Case it shall not be a Law.

Every Order, Resolution, or Vote to which the Concurrence of the Senate and House of Representatives may be necessary (except on a question of Adjournment) shall be presented to the President of the United States; and before the Same shall take Effect, shall be approved by him, or being disapproved by him, shall be repassed by two thirds of the Senate and House of Representatives, according to the Rules and Limitations prescribed in the Case of a Bill.

Article II

Section 2. The President shall . . . have Power, by and with the Advice and Consent of the Senate, to make Treaties, provided two thirds of the Senators present concur; and he shall nominate, and by and with the Advice and Consent of the Senate, shall appoint Ambassadors, other public Ministers and Consuls, Judges of the supreme Court, and all other Officers of the United States, whose Appointments are not herein otherwise provided for, and which shall be established by Law: but the Congress may by Law vest the Appointment of such inferior Officers, as they think proper, in the President alone, in the Courts of Law, or in the Heads of Departments.

The President shall have Power to fill up all Vacancies that may happen during the Recess of the Senate, by granting Commissions which shall expire at the End of their next Session.

READING NO. 4

GEORGE MASON'S OBJECTIONS TO THE SENATE, OCTOBER 7, 1787[4]

A delegate from Virginia to the Constitutional Convention, George Mason became a leading opponent of the document and refused to sign it. On October 7, 1787, he wrote to George Washington to explain his opposition in their state's ratifying convention.

γ   γ   γ

The Senate have the power of altering all money-bills, and of originating appropriations of money, and the salaries of the officers of their appointment, in conjunction with the President of the United States—Although they are not the representatives of the people, or amenable to them. These, with their other great powers, (viz. their powers in the appointment of ambassadors, and all public officers, in making treaties, and in trying all impeachments) their influence upon, and connection with, the supreme executive from these causes, their duration of office, and their being a constant existing body, almost continually sitting, joined with their being one complete branch of the legislature, will destroy any balance in the government, and enable them to accomplish what usurpations they please, upon the rights and liberties of the people.

[4] Arthur Taylor Prescott, ed., *Drafting the Federal Constitution* (Baton Rouge, LA, 1941), p. 329.

READING NO. 5

ELBRIDGE GERRY'S OPPOSITION[5]

Active in the nation's affairs from 1772 until his death in 1814, Elbridge Gerry of Massachusetts set forth his objections to the Constitution during the 1787–1788 ratification debates.

γ　　　　　γ　　　　　γ

A Senate chosen for six years will, in most instances, be an appointment for life, as the influence of such a body over the minds of the people will be coequal to the extensive powers with which they are vested, and they will not only forget, but be forgotten by their constituents—a branch of the Supreme Legislature thus set beyond all responsibility is totally repugnant to every principle of a free government.

[5]Paul Leicester Ford, ed., *Pamphlets on the Constitution of the United States* (Brooklyn, NY, 1888), p. 12.

READING NO. 6

TRISTRAM DALTON TO CALEB STRONG, JANUARY 1, 1789[6]

Late in 1788 the Massachusetts legislature elected Tristram Dalton and Caleb Strong as that state's first two members of the U.S. Senate. Dalton, who began his Senate service with the disability of a broken jaw, drew a two-year term and failed to be reelected in 1791. Strong, who had served as a delegate to the Constitutional Convention, began with a four-year term, was reelected in 1792, and resigned in 1796.

γ   γ   γ

Newburyport Jany 1st 1789

I thank you, my Dear Sir, for your favor of the 15 of the last month—and am greatly disappointed in not being able to meet you immediately on your arrival in Boston, which you expect may be about the 9th Inst.

I have been confined to my chamber for more than three weeks, by an ulcer tooth—and a fractured Jaw, occasioned by the extraction of it—this is the first day that I could read or write—and how much longer I shall be kept close is as yet uncertain.

Considering the necessity of now arranging all my domestic business—and the shortness of the time to do it, this detention is a great Evil, for which I was not prepared, having for near forty years enjoyed so much health as not to have been obliged to keep my bed one day.

I hope to see you in Boston—but, as I cannot at your first arrival, you'll excuse me in saying that you may expect applications in favor of a number of Persons who want Places in the federal Revenue and some will be so modest as to insist on an absolute promise to favor them—perhaps adding that I have promised—for they have already said you have, in a case

---

[6]Caleb Strong Papers, Massachusetts Historical Society, Boston.

where I suppose no application has been made to you. To the most importunate I have been obliged to answer—that I will promise no man until I am at Congress—when that person who shall appear to me will Serve his Country best in the Station proposed, shall have my interest—whether he be my friend or foe—

Be assured, Dr. Sir, that I have not promised my interest to any man—neither will I untill at Congress—

Applications to me have been so many & some of them so curious I thought it friendly, and a mark of that Confidence I ever wish to cultivate, to hand you this intelligence in Season lest by false report of my Conduct you be em[baras]sed

> With Compliments of the Season
> I am, Dear Sir, your
> real friend & most
> hble Servant
> Tristam Dalton

Honble Caleb Strong

READING NO. 7

THE SENATE'S FIRST STANDING RULES, APRIL 1789[7]

On April 7, 1789, the day after its first quorum had been attained, the Senate appointed a special five-man committee to draft rules of Senate procedure. All committee members were lawyers; two had served in the Continental Congress; three had been delegates to the Constitutional Convention. The Senate adopted the first nineteen rules on April 16, 1789, and the twentieth on April 18.

γ   γ   γ

I

The President having taken the Chair and a quorum being present the Journal of the preceding day shall be read, to the end that any mistake may be corrected that shall have been made in the entries.

II

No member shall speak to another, or otherwise interrupt the business of the Senate, or read any printed paper while the Journals or public papers are reading, or when any member is speaking in any debate.

III

Every member when he speaks shall address the Chair standing in his place, and when he has finished shall sit down.

---

[7]Linda Grant De Pauw, ed., *Senate Legislative Journal* /1789/, (Baltimore, 1972), vol. 1, pp. 18–20.

IV

No member shall speak more than twice in any one debate on the same day, without leave of the Senate.

V

When two members rise at the same time, the President shall name the person to speak; but in all cases the member first rising shall speak first.

VI

No motion shall be debated until the same shall be seconded.

VII

When a motion shall be made and seconded, it shall be reduced to writing, if desired by the President, or any member, delivered in at the table, and read by the President before the same shall be debated.

VIII

While a question is before the Senate, no motion shall be received unless for an amendment, for the previous question; or for postponing the main question, or to commit it, or to adjourn.

IX

The previous question being moved and seconded, the question from the Chair shall be—"Shall the main question be now put?"—And if the nays prevail, the main question shall not then be put.

X

If a question in debate contain several points, any member may have the same divided.

XI

When the yeas and nays shall be called for by one fifth of the members present, each member called upon shall, unless for special reasons he be excused by the Senate, declare openly and without debate, his assent or dissent to the question—In taking the yeas and nays, and upon the call of the House, the names of the members shall be taken alphabetically.

XII

One day's notice at least shall be given of an intended motion for leave to bring in a bill.

XIII

Every bill shall receive three readings previous to its being passed; and the President shall give notice at each, whether it be the first, second, or third; which readings shall be on three different days, unless the Senate unanimously direct otherwise.

XIV

No bill shall be committed or amended until it shall have been twice read, after which it may be referred to a Committee.

XV

All Committees shall be appointed by BALLOT, and a plurality of votes shall make a choice.

XVI

When a member shall be called to order, he shall sit down until the President shall have determined whether he is in order or not; and every question of order shall be decided by the President without debate: but if there be a doubt in his mind, he may call for the sense of the Senate.

XVII

If a member be called to order for words spoken, the exceptionable words shall be immediately taken down in writing, that the President may be better enabled to judge of the matter.

XVIII

When a blank is to be filled, and different sums shall be proposed, the question shall be taken on the highest sum first.

XIX

No member shall absent himself from the service of the Senate without leave of the Senate first obtained.

XX

Before any petition or memorial, addressed to the Senate, shall be received and read at the table, whether the same shall be introduced by the President, or a member, a brief statement of the contents of the petition or memorial shall verbally be made by the introducer.

READING NO. 8

PROTOCOL FOR PRESENTATION OF A BILL, APRIL 23, 1789[8]

Perhaps this proposal, which the House refused to accept, reflected senators' expectation that the flow of most legislation would be from the House to the Senate. Indeed, during the first session of the First Congress the Senate initiated only 15 percent of all bills. The plan certainly reflected an attitude of institutional superiority.

γ γ γ

The Committee appointed on the 16th of April, to report a mode of communication to be observed between the Senate and House of Representatives, with respect to papers, bills and messages, and to confer thereon with such Committee as may be appointed, by the House of Representatives for that purpose, have conferred with a Committee of the House, and have agreed to the following REPORT:

When a bill or other message shall be sent from the Senate to the House of Representatives, it shall be carried by the Secretary, who shall make one obeisance to the Chair on entering the door of the House of Representatives, and another, on delivering it at the table into the hands of the Speaker— After he shall have delivered it, he shall make an obeisance to the Speaker, and repeat it as he retires from the House.

When a bill shall be sent up by the House of Representatives to the Senate, it shall be carried by two members, who, at the bar of the Senate, shall make their obeisance to the President, and thence advancing to the Chair, make a second obeisance, and deliver it into the hands of the President—After having delivered the bill, they shall make their obeisance to the President, and repeat it as they retire from the bar: The Senate

---

[8]Linda Grant De Pauw, ed., *Senate Legislative Journal* /1789/, (Baltimore, 1972), vol. 1. pp. 23–24.

shall rise on the entrance of the members within the bar, and continue standing until they retire.

All other messages from the House of Representatives, shall be carried by one member, who shall make his obeisance as above mentioned—but the President of the Senate, alone, shall rise.

READING NO. 9

VICE PRESIDENT ADAMS'S INAUGURAL ADDRESS, APRIL 21, 1789[9]

This represents the first effort by the first vice president to define his relationship, in a constitutionally powerless office, to the body over which he was obligated to preside.

γ   γ   γ

GENTLEMEN OF THE SENATE,

INVITED to this respectable situation by the suffrages of our fellow-citizens, according to the Constitution, I have thought it my duty cheerfully and readily to accept it. Unaccustomed to refuse any public service, however dangerous to my reputation, or disproportioned to my talents, it would have been inconsistent to have adopted another maxim of conduct, at this time, when the prosperity of the country, and the liberties of the people, require perhaps, as much as ever, the attention of those who possess any share of the public confidence.

I should be destitute of sensibility, if, upon my arrival in this city, and presentation to this Legislature, and especially to this Senate, I could see, without emotion, so many of those characters, of whose virtuous exertions I have so often been a witness—from whose countenances and examples I have ever derived encouragement and animation—whose disinterested friendship has supported me, in many intricate conjunctures of public affairs, at home and abroad:—Those celebrated defenders of the liberties of this country, whom menaces could not intimidate, corruption seduce, nor flattery allure: Those intrepid assertors of the rights of mankind, whose philosophy and policy, have enlightened the world, in twenty years, more than it was ever before enlightened in many centuries, by ancient schools, or modern universities.

I must have been inattentive to the course of events, if I were

[9]Linda Grant De Pauw, ed., *Senate Legislative Journal* /1789/ (Baltimore, 1972), vol. 1, pp. 21–22.

either ignorant of the same, or insensible to the merit of those other characters in the Senate, to whom it has been my misfortune to have been, hitherto, personally unknown.

It is with satisfaction, that I congratulate the people of America on the formation of a national Constitution, and the fair prospect of a consistent administration of a government of laws. On the acquisition of an House of Representatives, chosen by themselves; of a Senate thus composed by their own State Legislatures; and on the prospect of an executive authority, in the hands of one whose portrait I shall not presume to draw—Were I blessed with powers to do justice to his character, it would be impossible to increase the confidence or affection of his country, or make the smallest addition to his glory. This can only be effected by a discharge of the present exalted trust on the same principles, with the same abilities and virtues, which have uniformly appeared in all his former conduct, public or private. May I nevertheless, be indulged to enquire, if we look over the catalogue of the first magistrates of nations, whether they have been denominated Presidents or Consuls, Kings or Princes, where shall we find one, whose commanding talents and virtues, whose over-ruling good fortune have so completely united all hearts and voices in his favor? who enjoyed the esteem and admiration of foreign nations and fellow-citizens with equal unanimity? Qualities so uncommon, are no common blessings to the country that possesses them. By those great qualities, and their benign effects, has Providence marked out the head of this nation, with an hand so distinctly visible, as to have been seen by all men, and mistaken by none.

It is not for me to interrupt your deliberations by any general observations on the state of the nation, or by recommending, or proposing any particular measures. It would be superfluous, to gentlemen of your great experience, to urge the necessity of order.—It is only necessary to make an apology for myself. Not wholly without experience in public assemblies, I have been more accustomed to take a share in their debates, than to preside in their deliberations. It shall be my constant endeavor to behave towards every member of this MOST HONORABLE body with all that consideration, delicacy, and decorum which becomes the dignity of his station and character: But, if from inexperience, or inadvertency, any thing should ever escape me, inconsistent with propriety, I must entreat you, by imputing it to its true cause, and not to any want of respect, to pardon and excuse it.

A trust of the greatest magnitude is committed to this Legislature—and the eyes of the world are upon you. Your country expects, from the results of your deliberations, in concurrence with the other branches of government, consideration abroad, and contentment at home—prosperity, order, justice, peace, and liberty:—And may God Almighty's providence assist you to answer their just expectations.

READING NO. 10

THE SENATE RECEIVES GEORGE WASHINGTON, APRIL 30, 1789[10]

The acerbic Sen. William Maclay of Pennsylvania kept the only informal journal of the Senate's closed-door proceedings during the precedent-setting First Congress. Here he describes, with gleeful disgust, the Senate's role in inaugurating the nation's first president.

γ   γ   γ

30th April, Thursday.—This is a great, important day. Goddess of etiquette, assist me while I describe it. The Senate stood adjourned to half after eleven o'clock. About ten dressed in my best clothes; went for Mr. Morris' lodgings, but met his son, who told me that his father would not be in town until Saturday. Turned into the Hall. The crowd already great. The Senate met. The Vice-President rose in the most solemn manner. This son of *Adam* seemed impressed with deeper gravity, yet what shall I think of him? He often, in the midst of his most important airs—I believe when he is at loss for expressions (and this he often is, wrapped up, I suppose, in the contemplation of his own importance)—suffers an unmeaning kind of vacant laugh to escape him. This was the case to-day, and really to me bore the air of ridiculing the farce he was acting. "Gentlemen, I wish for the direction of the Senate. The President will, I suppose, address the Congress. How shall I behave? How shall we receive it? Shall it be standing or sitting?"

Here followed a considerable deal of talk from him which I could make nothing of. Mr. Lee began with the House of Commons (as is usual with him), then the House of Lords, then the King, and then back again. The result of his information was, that the Lords sat and the Commons stood on the delivery

[10]Edgar S. Maclay, ed., *Journal of William Maclay* (New York, 1890), pp. 7–9.

of the King's speech. Mr. Izard got up and told how often he had been in the Houses of Parliament. He said a great deal of what he had seen there. [He] made, however, this sagacious discovery, that the Commons stood because they had no seats to sit on, being arrived at the bar of the House of Lords. It was discovered after some time that the King sat, too, and had his robes and crown on.

Mr. Adams got up again and said he had been very often indeed at the Parliament on those occasions, but there always was such a crowd, and *ladies along,* that for his part he could not say how it was. Mr. Carrol got up to declare that he thought it of no consequence how it was in Great Britain; they were no rule to us, etc. But all at once the Secretary, who had been out, whispered to the Chair that the Clerk from the Representatives was at the door with a communication. Gentlemen of the Senate, how shall he be received? A silly kind of resolution of the committee on that business had been laid on the table some days ago. The amount of it was that each House should communicate to the other what and how they chose; it concluded, however, something in this way: That everything should be done with all the *propriety* that was *proper.* The question was, Shall this be adopted, that we may know how to receive the Clerk? It was objected [that] this will throw no light on the subject; it will leave you where you are. Mr. Lee brought the House of Commons before us again. He reprobated the rule; declared that the Clerk should not come within the bar of the House; that the proper mode was for the Sergeant-at-Arms, with the mace on his shoulder, to meet the Clerk at the door and receive his communication; we are not, however, provided for this ceremonious way of doing business, having neither mace nor sergeant nor Masters in Chancery, who carry down bills from the English Lords.

Mr. Izard got up and labored unintelligibly to show the great distinction between a communication and a delivery of a thing, but he was not minded. Mr. Elsworth showed plainly enough that if the Clerk was not permitted to deliver the communication, the Speaker might as well send it inclosed. Repeated accounts came [that] the Speaker and Representatives were at the door. Confusion ensued; the members left their seats. Mr. Read rose and called the attention of the Senate to the neglect that had been shown Mr. Thompson, late Secretary. Mr. Lee rose to answer him, but I could not hear one word he said. The Speaker was introduced, followed by the Representatives. Here we sat an hour and ten minutes before the President arrived—this delay was owing to Lee, Izard, and Dalton, who had stayed with us while the Speaker came in, instead of going to attend the President. The President advanced between the Senate and Representatives, bowing to each. He was placed in the chair by the Vice-President; the Senate with their president on the right, the Speaker and the Representatives on his left. The Vice-President rose and addressed a short sentence to him. The import of it was that he should now take the oath of office as President. He seemed to have forgot half what he was to say, for he made a dead pause and stood for some time, to appearance, in a vacant mood. He finished with a formal bow, and the President was conducted out of the middle window into the gallery, and the oath was administered by the Chancellor. Notice that the business done was communicated to the crowd by proclamation, etc., who gave three cheers, and repeated it on the President's bowing to them.

As the company returned into the Senate chamber, the President took the chair and the Senators and Representatives, their seats. He rose, and all arose also, and addressed them (see the address). This great man was agitated and embarassed more than ever he was by the leveled cannon or pointed musket. He trembled, and several times could scarce make out to read, though it must be supposed he had often read it before. He put part of the fingers of his left hand into the side of what I think the tailors call the fall of the breeches [corresponding to the modern side-pocket], changing the paper into his left [right] hand. After some time he then did the same with some of the fingers of his right hand. When he came to the words *all the world,* he made a flourish with his right hand, which left rather an ungainly impression. I sincerely, for my part, wished all set ceremony in the hands of the dancing-masters, and that this first of men had read off his address in the plainest manner, without ever taking his eyes from the paper, for I felt hurt that he was not first in everything. He was dressed in deep brown, with metal buttons, with an eagle on them, white stockings, a bag, and sword.

READING NO. 11

THE SENATE THANKS THE PRESIDENT, MAY 16, 1789[11]

Ever sensitive to precedent and protocol, the Senate consumed more than two weeks preparing this response to Washington's inaugural address. It traveled as a body to the president's residence, where John Adams stiffly read the message to an equally uncomfortable chief executive.

γ   γ   γ

SIR,

WE, the Senate of the United States, return you our sincere thanks for your excellent speech delivered to both Houses of Congress; congratulate you on the complete organization of the federal government, and felicitate ourselves and our fellow citizens on your elevation to the office of President; an office highly important by the powers constitutionally annexed to it, and extremely honorable from the manner in which the appointment is made. The unanimous suffrage of the elective body in your favor is peculiarly expressive of the gratitude, confidence and affection of the citizens of America, and is the highest testimonial at once of your merit and their esteem. We are sensible, Sir, that nothing but the voice of your fellow citizens could have called you from a retreat, chosen with the fondest predilection, endeared by habit, and consecrated to the repose of declining years. We rejoice, and with us all America, that, in obedience to the call of our common country, you have returned once more to public life. In you all parties confide; in you all interests unite; and we have no doubt that your past services, great as they have been, will be equalled by your future exertions; and that your prudence and sagacity as a statesman will tend to avert the dangers to which we were exposed, to give stability to the present government, and

[11]Linda Grant De Pauw, ed., *Senate Legislative Journal* /1789/ (Baltimore, 1972), vol. 1, pp. 38–39.

dignity and splendor to that country, which your skill and valor as a soldier, so eminently contributed to raise to independence and empire.

When we contemplate the coincidence of circumstances, and wonderful combination of causes, which gradually prepared the people of this country for independence; when we contemplate the rise, progress and termination of the late war, which gave them a name among the nations of the earth, we are, with you, unavoidably led to acknowledge and adore the great arbiter of the universe, by whom empires rise and fall. A review of the many signal instances of divine interposition in favor of this country claims our most pious gratitude:—and permit us, Sir, to observe, that among the great events, which have led to the formation and establishment of a federal government, we esteem your acceptance of the office of President as one of the most propitious and important.

In the execution of the trust reposed in us, we shall endeavor to pursue that enlarged and liberal policy, to which your speech so happily directs. We are conscious, that the prosperity of each State is inseparably connected with the welfare of all, and that in promoting the latter, we shall effectually advance the former. In full persuasion of this truth, it shall be our invariable aim to divest ourselves of local prejudices and attachments, and to view the great assemblage of communities and interests committed to our charge with an equal eye. We feel, Sir, the force, and acknowledge the justness of the observation, that the foundation of our national policy should be laid in private morality; if individuals be not influenced by moral principles, it is in vain to look for public virtue; it is, therefore, the duty of Legislators to enforce, both by precept and example, the utility as well as the necessity of a strict adherence to the rules of distributive justice. We beg you to be assured, that the Senate will, at all times, cheerfully co-operate in every measure, which may strengthen the union, conduce to the happiness, or secure and perpetuate the liberties of this great confederated republic.

We commend you, Sir, to the protection of Almighty God, earnestly beseeching him long to perserve a life so valuable and dear to the people of the United States, and that your administration may be prosperous to the nation and glorious to yourself.

READING NO. 12

THE SENATE IN SESSION, ca. 1796[12]

William McKoy, as a young man, visited the Senate chamber in Philadelphia shortly after it opened its doors to the public in the mid-1790s. He published the following recollection in the late 1820s.

γ   γ   γ

Among the thirty Senators of that day there was observed constantly during the debate the most delightful silence, the most beautiful order, gravity, and personal dignity of manner. They all appeared every morning full-powdered and dressed, as age or fancy might suggest, in the richest material. The very atmosphere of the place seemed to inspire wisdom, mildness, and condescension. Should any of them so far forget for a moment as to be the cause of a protracted whisper while another was addressing the Vice-President, three gentle taps with his silver pencilcase upon the table by Mr. Adams immediately restored everything to repose and the most respectful attention, presenting in their courtesy a most striking contrast to the independent loquacity of the Representatives below stairs, some few of whom persisted in wearing, while in their seats and during the debate, their ample *cocked* hats, placed ''fore and aft'' upon their heads.

---

[12]Quoted in Roy Swanstrom, *The United States Senate, 1787–1801*, Sen. Doc. 99-19, (Washington, 1985), p. 197.

READING NO. 13

JEFFERSON'S MANUAL OF PARLIAMENTARY PRACTICE[13]

Presiding over the Senate from 1797 to 1801, Vice President Thomas Jefferson prepared a legislative manual to guide future presiding officers. The following excerpt is taken from the opening section.

γ γ γ

SEC. I.—IMPORTANCE OF ADHERING TO RULES.

Mr. Onslow, the ablest among the Speakers of the House of Commons, used to say, "It was a maxim he had often heard when he was a young man, from old and experienced Members, that nothing tended more to throw power into the hands of administration, and those who acted with the majority of the House of Commons, than a neglect of, or departure from, the rules of proceeding; that these forms, as instituted by our ancestors, operated as a check and control on the actions of the majority, and that they were, in many instances, a shelter and protection to the minority, against the attempts of power." So far the maxim is certainly true, and is founded in good sense, that as it is always in the power of the majority, by their numbers, to stop any improper measures proposed on the part of their opponents, the only weapons by which the minority can defend themselves against similar attempts from those in power are the forms and rules of proceeding which have been adopted as they were found necessary, from time to time, and are become the law of the House, by a strict adherence to which the weaker party can only be protected from those irregularities and abuses which these forms were intended to check, and which the wantonness of power is but too often apt

---

[13]Reprinted in U.S. House of Representatives, *Constitution, Jefferson's Manual and Rules of the House of Representatives*, House Doc. 97-271, (Washington, 1983), pp. 111–114.

to suggest to large and successful majorities, *2 Hats., 171, 172.*

And whether these forms be in all cases the most rational or not is really not of so great importance. It is much more material that there should be a rule to go by than what that rule is; that there may be a uniformity of proceeding in business not subject to the caprice of the Speaker or captiousness of the members. It is very material that order, decency, and regularity be preserved in a dignified public body. *2 Hats., 149.*

READING NO. 14

SEN. JOHN QUINCY ADAMS TO HIS FATHER, MARCH 8, 1805[14]

John Quincy Adams served as a senator from Massachusetts from 1803 to 1808. Here he gives to former Federalist President John Adams an insider's account of Republican administration efforts in the Senate to undercut the Federalist-dominated judiciary.

γ   γ   γ

DEAR SIR:

During the last days of the session of Congress which has just expired, I found it impossible to continue the correspondence which I had previously maintained even so far as to enclose from day to day the public documents as they were printed. From ten o'clock in the morning until seven in the evening the Senate was constantly in session, with the interval of only half an hour each day for a slight collation, which the members took at the Capitol itself; and this, together with a walk of an hour to reach that place, and a walk of an hour to return from it, scarcely left me the hours of the night for repose. The scene has now closed. On Sunday evening last, the 3rd instant, at half past nine o'clock, the two Houses adjourned without day, and thus terminated a session which it was high time to bring to an end; a session which has been the parent of several legislative acts, important in themselves and promising still more important consequences. The attention both of Congress and of the public to these has, however, been almost swallowed up in the interest and anxiety with which every step of the judicial transactions, which have engrossed so large a portion of our time, has been followed and scrutinized. On the subject of Mr. Chase's impeachment, until the sentence was pronounced, I felt myself under an obligation to impose

---

[14]Allan Nevins, ed., *The Diary of John Quincy Adams, 1794–1845* (New York, 1951), pp. 106–109.

absolute silence upon my pen, and, as far as human infirmity
would admit, upon my tongue. Even now, it is a subject upon
which it would perhaps be most discreet for those who were
called to decide upon the articles to observe a dignified and
unaffected silence. The questions of guilt or innocence as they
affect the man are probably at rest; but the spirit which
impelled to the prosecution, and in which its highest importance consisted, is so far from being subdued or abashed, that
you will perceive it has burst forth with redoubled violence
from its defeat, and finding itself baffled by an unexpected
resistance to the stroke it aimed at judicial independence, has
not only taken a more pointed and deadly aim at that, but
coupled it with another blow directed at the Senate itself.
These will probably be the subject of future contestation, and
may perhaps bring to the test the validity of some principles
upon which our constitutions stand, and which have never yet
been tried by the touchstone of experience.

The attack by *impeachment* upon the judicial department of
our national government began two years ago, and has been
conducted with great address as well as with persevering
violence. The impeachment and conviction of Mr. Pickering,
of a man notoriously and confessedly insane, for acts committed in that state, and during the whole course of the impeachment remaining in it, was but a preparatory step to the assault
upon Judge Chase, as this in its turn was unquestionably
intended to pave the way for another prosecution, which would
have swept the supreme judicial bench clean at a stroke. As the
experiment in the case Mr. Pickering was completely successful, I confess I have been disappointed, agreeably disappointed, in the issue of the succeeding step. It was impossible
to establish by a stronger case than that, the principle that
criminality was not an essential ingredient of impeachable
offenses. And upon the score of *humanity* it would have been
certainly a much less odious transaction to convict and remove
a man of the first parts, after a full and solemn trial for
peccadilloes of temper stretched into crimes and misdemean-
ors, than to pass a like degrading and defaming sentence upon
one visited with the heaviest of human calamities, and to make
that awful visitation of God itself the basis of the prosecution.
I can, indeed, never reflect upon the proceedings and judg-

ments in that cruel affair without dejection of heart and humiliation of spirit. I feel for the honor of the body to which I belong, and for the honor of my country, sullied as they are by a sentence of *guilt,* inflicted upon a man for being among the most miserable of the human race, for being bereft by the hand of heaven of that attribute, which by rendering man rational would render him accountable. Nor can I satisfactorily explain to myself how it has happened, that the same men, who would be prevailed upon to sanction by a judgment pronounced under oath what to my mind appears so flagrant a violation of all justice and decency, should now stop and make an effectual stand in support of fair and honorable principle against *this* inroad of turbulent ambition. There is indeed one way of solving the difficulty which sometimes presents itself to my mind as probable, and which, if just, may be a foundation for substantial hope in future. The trial of Pickering did not sufficiently develop the intentions of those by whom it was managed. It did not disclose the full extent of their views. But when it was seen that on the very day of his conviction the impeachment of Mr. Chase was voted, and when the application of those absurd doctrines upon which he had been construed into a criminal was instantly extended to a judge of the Supreme Court, with undisguised intimations that it would soon be spread over the whole of that Bench, some of those whose weakness had yielded to the torrent of popular prejudice in the first instance, had the integrity to reflect, rallied all their energy to assist them, and took a stand which has arrested for a time that factious impetuosity that threatens to bury all our national institutions in one common ruin.

READING NO. 15

SENATE CHAMBER, MARCH 2, 1805[15]

Dr. Samuel Mitchill served as a senator from New York from 1804 to 1809. Shortly after arriving in the Senate he reported the following dramatic scene to his wife.

γ　　　　γ　　　　γ

I am here in a situation full of remarkable events. Yesterday the Senate passed judgment on one of the justices of the Supreme Court, as I wrote you.

This day I have witnessed one of the most affecting scenes of my life. Colonel Burr, whose situation and misfortunes you well know, after having presided in the Senate during almost the whole session, came in, as is customary, and took the chair today. He went on with the public business as usual until about two o'clock. Then, the Senate-chamber happening to be cleared for the purpose of considering some matters of an executive nature, he rose from the chair, and very unexpectedly pronounced to the Senate his farewell address. He did not speak to them, perhaps, longer than twenty minutes or half an hour, but he did it with so much tenderness, knowledge, and concern that it wrought upon the sympathy of the Senators in a very uncommon manner. Every gentleman was silent, not a whisper was heard, and the deepest concern was manifested. When Mr. Burr had concluded he descended from the chair, and in a dignified manner walked to the door, which resounded as he with some force shut it after him. On this the firmness and resolution of many of the Senators gave way, and they burst into tears. There was a solemn and silent weeping for perhaps five minutes.

For my own part, I never experienced any thing of the kind so affecting as this parting scene of the Vice-President from the Senate in which he had sat six years as a Senator and four years

[15]"Dr. Mitchill's Letters from Washington: 1801–1813," *Harper's New Monthly Magazine*, 58 (April 1879), pp. 749–750.

as presiding officer. My colleague, General Smith, stout and manly as he is, wept as profusely as I did. He laid his head upon his table and did not recover from his emotion for a quarter of an hour or more. And for myself, though it is more than three hours since Burr went away, I have scarcely recovered my habitual calmness. Several gentlemen came up to me to talk about this extraordinary scene, but I was obliged to turn away and decline all conversation.

I have just received a billet from him and have written an answer to it. He is a most uncommon man, and I regret more deeply than ever the sad series of events which removed him from public usefulness and confidence. The Senate passed a bill to give him the privilege of franking letters and parcels during life, but the House of Representatives refused their assent. The Senate has also passed him unanimously a vote of thanks for the ability, impartiality, and dignity with which he has presided in that body. Burr is one of the best officers that ever presided over a deliberative assembly. Where he is going or how he is to get through with his difficulties I know not.

It was not my intention to have written to you to-day, but the occurrence of this remarkable event determined me to give you an account of it while the transaction was fresh and the impression warm.

READING NO. 16

AARON BURR'S FAREWELL TO THE SENATE, MARCH 2, 1805[16]

This address, described in Reading No. 15, is considered one of the most dramatic ever delivered before the Senate. Here, a newspaper reporter assigned to cover the Senate recounts the departing vice president's remarks.

γ   γ   γ

The VICE PRESIDENT took an affectionate leave of the Senate, in substance as follows:

"Mr. BURR began by saying that he had intended pass the day with them, but the increase of a slight indisposition (sore throat) had determined him then to take leave of them. He touched lightly on some of the rules and orders of the House, and recommended, in one or two points, alterations, of which he briefly explained the reasons and principles.

"He said he was sensible he must at times have wounded the feelings of individual members. He had ever avoided entering into explanations at the time, because a moment of irritation was not a moment for explanation; because his position (being in the chair) rendered it impossible to enter into explanations without obvious danger of consequences which might hazard the dignity of the Senate, or prove disagreeable and injurious in more than one point of view; that he had, therefore, preferred to leave to their reflections his justification; that, on his part, he had no injuries to complain of; if any had been done or attempted, he was ignorant of the authors; and if he had ever heard, he had forgotten, for, he thanked God, he had no memory for injuries.

"He doubted not but that they had found occasion to observe, that to be prompt was not therefore to be precipitate; and that to act without delay was not always to act without

[16]*The Debates and Proceedings in the Congress of the United States,* 8th Congress, pp. 71–72.

reflection; that error was often to be preferred to indecision; that his errors, whatever they might have been, were those of rule and principle, and not of caprice; that it could not be deemed arrogance in him to say that, in his official conduct, he had known no party, no cause, no friend; that if, in the opinion of any, the discipline which had been established approached to rigor, they would at least admit that it was uniform and indiscriminate.

"He further remarked, that the ignorant and unthinking affected to treat as unnecessary and fastidious a rigid attention to rules and decorum; but he thought nothing trivial which touched, however remotely, the dignity of that body; and he appealed to their experience for the justice of this sentiment, and urged them in language the most impressive, and in a manner the most commanding, to avoid the smallest relaxation of the habits which he had endeavored to inculcate and establish.

"But he challenged their attention to considerations more momentous than any which regarded merely their personal honor and character—the preservation of law, of liberty, and the Constitution. This House, said he, is a sanctuary; a citadel of law, of order, and of liberty; and it is here—it is here, in this exalted refuge; here, if anywhere, will resistance be made to the storms of political phrensy and the silent arts of corruption; and if the Constitution be destined ever to perish by the sacrilegious hands of the demagogue or the usurper, which God avert, its expiring agonies will be witnessed on this floor.

"He then adverted to those affecting sentiments which attended a final separation—a dissolution, perhaps forever, of those associations which he hoped had been mutually satisfactory. He consoled himself, however, and them, with the reflection, that, though they separated, they would be engaged in the common cause of disseminating principles of freedom and social order. He should always regard the proceedings of that body with interest and with solicitude. He should feel for their honor and the national honor so intimately connected with it, and took his leave with expressions of personal respect, and with prayers, and wishes," &c.

READING NO. 17

SEN. WILLIAM PLUMER ON THE VALUE OF SENATE SPEECHES, MARCH 12, 1806[17]

Sen. William Plumer of New Hampshire kept a daily diary of Senate activities between 1803 and the end of his service in 1807. As with William Maclay's Journal, *this diary provides an invaluable account of life in the early Senate.*

γ   γ   γ

I have for sometime been convinced that speeches in the Senate in most cases have very little influence upon the Vote. I believe that in 19 cases out of 20 they do not change a single vote. For this inefficiency there are various causes. All our documents, communications, reports bills & amendments are printed & laid on our tables & those of us who examine subjects for ourselves & do not vote on the faith of others, reads, & examine & form opinions for ourselves. Having read & examined a subject—we converse with each other & freely exchange our sentiments—This not only confirms or changes the opinion of some, but fixes the vote of others who never give themselves the trouble of examination. Some Senators are implicitly led by the administration—Others have their file leader. When a senator is making a long set speech the chairs are most of them deserted & the vote is often settled in a conversation at the fire side. The conversation is there often so loud as to interrupt the senator who is speaking—for our Vice-President has not the talents requisite for a good presiding officer. Under these circumstances it is often difficult for a man, who knows he is not attended to, to deliver an able & eloquent argument. It is a damper too strong for my nerves— To this add we have no stenographer, & seldom any hearers in the galleries. When the speeches of senators are printed in Newspapers, the speakers are obliged to submit to the drudgery

[17]Everett Somerville Brown, *William Plumer's Memorandum of Proceedings in the United States Senate, 1803–1807* (New York, 1923), pp. 448–450.

of writing them themselves, which is a severe task. I speak none—at least for this & the last session—& yet my influence on many subjects is not confined to my own vote. I am industrious in all private circles—I openly & frankly express my opinions & assign my reasons. And I have frequently plenary evidence that my brother senators, of all parties, have much confidence in my opinion. For I am influenced by no party views.

In the other House it is different—galleries are usually attended, frequently crouded, with spectators—Always one, often two, steongraphers attend, & their speeches are reported in the gazettes. The house is more numerous—several of them absolutely depend upon their file leaders to direct their vote— Yet I believe even in that House there are few votes changed by the public arguments of the members.

READING NO. 18

A SENATOR REPORTS TO HIS CONSTITUTENTS, JUNE 29, 1797[18]

Although elected by state legislatures until the early twentieth century, senators felt the need to report directly to the citizens of their states. In an era of slow and unreliable communication, they often used "circular letters." Printed in batches of up to five hundred, these letters were circulated from person to person and displayed in post offices throughout a member's state. They often served as a source of news beyond that of Senate activities as demonstrated in this letter from Tennessee Sen. William Cocke.

γ   γ   γ

Sir,

My best endeavors to promote the interest, preserve the peace, and secure the happiness of the United States, will, I hope, meet the entire approbation of my fellow-citizens in the State of Tenessee, to whom I hold myself accountable for my public conduct, and whose confidence and esteem, I consider as the highest reward, that can be bestowed on a faithful servant. Grateful, as I am, for the many honors, that my country has, at various times, been pleased to confer on me, I cannot but labor to deserve, as well as to receive a continuation of their confidential regard. It gives me real pleasure to inform you, that there appears a considerable change of sentiment in a number of respectable members of the Senate of the United States, favorable to the State of Tennessee, and friendly to the extinguishment of the claims injurious to our rights. This day, Mr. Blount and myself waited on the President, for the purpose of making known to him the situation, that a number of our citizens were likely to be involved in, should the Commissioners proceed to run the boundary line. The Secretary of War

[18]Noble E. Cunningham, Jr., ed, *Circular Letters of Congressmen to Their Constituents, 1789–1829* (Chapel Hill, NC, 1978), pp. 100–102.

being at the President's, afforded us a favorable opportunity of stating to them, in the fullest manner, every thing relating to the interest of the State respecting the running of the said line. They both seemed fully impressed with the importance and necessity of attending to this subject, and promised to take the same into consideration, and to notify the Commissioners of the result of their deliberation.

The time of Congress has been chiefly occupied in contemplating the different subjects recommended by the President, and the following statement presents to your view, the proceedings of this Session to the present day:

Titles of Acts passed this Session

1. An Act prohibiting, for a limited time, the Exportation of Arms and Ammunition, and for encouraging the Importation thereof. *Approved and signed.*
2. An Act to prevent Citizens of the United States from privateering against Nations in Amity with the United States. *Approved and signed.*
3. An Act to provide for the further Defence of the Ports and Harbours of the United States. *Approved and signed.*
4. An Act authorizing a Detachment of the Militia of the United States. *Approved and signed—and is like the one passed in* 1794.
5. An Act in addition to an Act intitled "An Act concerning the registering and recording Ships and Vessels." *Approved and signed.*
6. An Act directing the appointment of Agents in relation to the sixth article of the British Treaty.
7. An Act providing a Naval Armament. . . .

A treaty of peace has been concluded and ratified, between the United States and Tunis and Tripoli.—The Spanish treaty is not likely at this time to be carried into effect,—the proceedings on this head I communicated, some days past, to governor Sevier; and expect they will be published in the Knoxville papers.

It is now certain, that the Emperor of Germany has made a separate peace, with the Republic of France. The victories obtained by the French arms, under the command of General Buonaparte, as well as those on the Rhine, led to that event:—The generosity of that gallant officer to his enemies has made him more conspicuous, than the glory he has atchieved by arms.—The British Government is in a tottering situation.—Mutinies still continue on board the channel fleet;—the contagion has probably reached the army:—The bank has stopped payment:—The mob, it is said, have assembled in the city of London;—A motion has been made in the House of Commons to censure Pitt, for his administration:—The people have petitioned the king to dismiss him from his council:—Serious discontents pervade every part of the kingdom; and the Irish are in a state of insurrection.—Mr. Hammond set out from London for Vienna, previous to the signing the preliminary articles of peace, between the Republic and the Emperor; but did not arrive, time enough to include England, which was the object of his mission to that court.

Our warmest politicians, who, at the first meeting of Congress, were for raising fleets and armies, assuming the manly tone of Austria, and the erect attitude of Great Britain, begin to exercise their better judgment, and, at this time, I believe, prefer peace. General Pinckney of South Carolina, General Marshall of Virginia, and Mr. Gerry of Massachusetts, are appointed Commissioners to settle our differences with the Republic of France: And I hope their wisdom, prudence and good intentions will produce an accommodation, honorable and advantageous to both countries; and thereby restore that harmony, and good understanding, which once so happily subsisted between them; and which should be the first object of Republicans to strengthen and perpetuate. I am, with every sentiment of esteem, Your obedient servant,

William Cocke.

READING NO. 19

VIEWS OF A FRESHMAN SENATOR, 1804[19]

In 1804 the House of Representatives witnessed a great deal more activity and excitement than the Senate. Here are Samuel Mitchill's observations on giving up a seat in the House for one in the Senate.

γ γ γ

GEORGETOWN, *November 26, 1804.*

On Friday, November 23, I resigned my seat in the House of Representatives. This I was enabled to do from having received from Albany my commission from the Legislature of New York to act as a Senator. Accordingly, I wrote a letter of resignation to Mr. Macon, the Speaker, which was read to the House, and account thereof ordered to be transmitted to Morgan Lewis, Esq., Governor of the State, that he may issue his proclamation for choosing my successor in the district consisting of the counties of Kings, Richmond, and the city and county of New York. I feel no small regret on separating from a body of constituents who have so often given me proofs of their confidence. But it is not a total separation from them, for I still represent them in a body where my vote is greatly more ponderous; for while in the House of Representatives it was only one-seventeenth of the weight of the State, it is now, when shared with General Smith, my colleague, increased to one-half. My credentials having been read in the Senate by Mr. Otis, the Secretary, Mr. Burr, the President, invited me to advance and take the oath prescribed by the Constitution. Having been thus qualified into office, I retired to one of the scarlet chairs lined with morocco leather, and took my seat among the Senators as a member of the Supreme Executive Council.

[19]"Dr. Mitchill's Letters from Washington: 1801–1813," *Harper's New Monthly Magazine*, 58 (April 1879), p. 748.

READING NO. 20

SENATE CHAMBER, 1834[20]

Robert Mills, the nation's first native-born professional architect, provided this description of the Senate Chamber in a Washington guidebook.

γ   γ   γ

This is a large semi-circular room, covered with a dome, richly ornamented with deep sunken panels and circular apertures to admit light from above; across the chord of the semi-circle, a screen of columns stretches on each side of the President's chair, which is placed in a niche on an elevated platform, in front of which below are the Secretary and chief clerk's desk. The columns of this screen are of Grecian Ionic order, and composed of the beautiful variegated marble of the Potomac, with caps of Italian white; these, with its entablature, support a gallery: in front of which is another, but lighter gallery, running around the circle of the room, supported by reeded and gilt iron columns, surmounted by a rich gilt iron balustrade. . . . The walls of the Senate Chamber are hung with fluted drapery, placed between pilasters of marble, which extend up to the spring of the cornice. The principal light of this room comes in from the east; but there is, in addition, a borrowed light from above. The [Vice President's] chair is placed on the line of the diameter of the circle, and from this, as a centre, the Senators' desks describe concentred curves, cut by radii, which form the aisles. These desks are all of mahogany, and single, each with a large arm-chair; they are placed on platforms, gradually rising one above the other. . . .

The Senate Chamber is of the same general form with the Halls of Representatives, but has the advantage of plain walls and few recesses; consequently it is a good speaking and

---

[20]Robert Mills, *Guide to the Capitol of the United States* (Washington, 1834), pp. 43–44.

hearing room. The dome is very flat. The dimensions of the Chamber are as follows: 75 feet in its greatest length, or diameter, 45 feet in its greatest width, and 45 feet high.

READING NO. 21

HENRY CLAY'S ATTACK ON PRESIDENT JACKSON, DECEMBER 26, 1833[21]

Before a crowded and tension-filled Senate chamber, Sen. Henry Clay launched a well-prepared attack on the policies of President Andrew Jackson. This was the opening salvo in opposition attempts to censure and discredit the president. This is considered one of Clay's most significant addresses.

γ   γ   γ

We are, said he, in the midst of a revolution, hitherto bloodless, but rapidly tending towards a total change of the pure republican character of the Government, and to the concentration of all power in the hands of one man. The powers of Congress are paralyzed, except when exerted in conformity with his will, by frequent and an extraordinary exercise of the executive veto, not anticipated by the founders of the constitution, and not practised by any of the predecessors of the present Chief Magistrate. And, to cramp them still more, a new expedient is springing into use, of withholding altogether bills which have received the sanction of both Houses of Congress, thereby cutting off all opportunity of passing them, even if, after their return, the members should be unanimous in their favor. The constitutional participation of the Senate in the appointing power is virtually abolished, by the constant use of the power of removal from office without any known cause, and by the appointment of the same individual to the same office, after his rejection by the Senate. How often have we, Senators, felt that the check of the Senate, instead of being, as the constitution intended, a salutary control, was an idle ceremony? How often, when acting on the case of the nominated successor, have we felt the injustice of the removal? How often have we said to each other, well, what

[21]*Register of Debates in Congress,* 23d Congress, 1st sess., December 26, 1833, pp. 59–60.

can we do? the office cannot remain vacant without prejudice to the public interests; and, if we reject the proposed substitute, we cannot restore the displaced, and perhaps some more unworthy man may be nominated?

The Judiciary has not been exempted from the prevailing rage for innovation. Decisions of the tribunals, deliberately pronounced, have been contemptuously disregarded, and the sancity of numerous treaties openly violated. Our Indian relations, coeval with the existence of the Government, and recognised and established by numerous laws and treaties, have been subverted; the rights of the helpless and unfortunate aborigines trampled in the dust, and they brought under subjection to unknown laws, in which they have no voice, promulgated in an unknown language. The most extensive and most valuable public domain that ever fell to the lot of one nation is threatened with a total sacrifice. The general currency of the country, the life-blood of all its business, is in the most imminent danger of universal disorder and confusion. The power of internal improvement lies crushed beneath the veto. The system of protection of American industry was snatched from impending destruction at the last session; but we are now coolly told by the Secretary of the Treasury, without a blush, "that it is understood to be *conceded on all hands* that a tariff for protection merely is to be finally abandoned." By the 3d of March, 1837, if the progress of innovation continue, there will be scarcely a vestige remaining of the Government and its policy, as they existed prior to the 3d of March, 1829. In a term of years, a little more than equal to that which was required to establish our liberties, the Government will have been transformed into an elective monarchy—the worst of all forms of government.

Such is a melancholy but faithful picture of the present condition of our public affairs. It is not sketched or exhibited to excite, here or elsewhere, irritated feeling: I have no such purpose. I would, on the contrary, implore the Senate and the people to discard all passion and prejudice, and to look calmly but resolutely upon the actual state of the constitution and the country. Although I bring into the Senate the same unabated spirit, and the same firm determination, which have ever guided me in the support of civil liberty, and the defence of our constitution, I contemplate the prospect before us with feelings of deep humiliation and profound mortification.

It is not among the least unfortunate symptoms of the times, that a large proportion of the good and enlightened men of the Union, of all parties, are yielding to sentiments of despondency. There is, unhappily, a feeling of distrust and insecurity pervading the community. Many of our best citizens entertain serious apprehensions that our Union and our institutions are destined to a speedy overthrow. Sir, I trust that the hopes and confidence of the country will revive. There is much occasion for manly independence and patriotic vigor, but none for despair. Thank God, we are yet free; and, if we put on the chains which are forging for us, it will be because we deserve to wear them. We should never despair of the republic. If our ancestors had been capable of surrendering themselves to such ignoble sentiments, our independence and our liberties would never have been achieved. The winter of 1776–'7, was one of the gloomiest periods of our revolution; but on this day, fifty-seven years ago, the father of his country achieved a glorious victory, which diffused joy, and gladness, and animation throughout the States. Let us cherish the hope that, since he has gone from among us, Providence, in the dispensation of his mercies, has near at hand, in reserve for us, though yet unseen by us, some sure and happy deliverance from all impending dangers.

READING NO. 22

WEBSTER'S "SECOND REPLY TO HAYNE," January 27, 1830[22]

Here are reprinted the closing lines of one of the most eloquent speeches in Senate history. In this classic address, Daniel Webster argued that the states are sovereign only so far as their power is not limited by the Constitution. Generations of schoolchildren were required to memorize these lines.

γ   γ   γ

When my eyes shall be turned to behold for the last time the sun in heaven, may I not see him shining on the broken and dishonored fragments of a once glorious Union; on States dissevered, discordant, belligerent; on a land rent with civil feuds, or drenched, it may be, in fraternal blood! Let their last feeble and lingering glance rather behold the gorgeous ensign of the republic, now known and honored throughout the earth, still full high advanced, its arms and trophies streaming in their original lustre, not a stripe erased or polluted, not a single star obscured, bearing for its motto, no such miserable interrogatory as 'What is all this worth?' nor those other words of delusion and folly, Liberty first and Union afterwards; but everywhere, spread all over in characters of living light, blazing on all its ample folds, as they float over the sea and over the land, and in every wind under the whole heavens, that other sentiment, dear to every true American heart,—Liberty *and* Union, now and forever, one and inseparable!

[22]*Register of Debates in Congress,* 21st Congress, 1st sess., January 27, 1830, pp. 81–82.

READING NO. 23

JOHN C. CALHOUN'S DEFENSE OF STATES' RIGHTS, JANUARY 16, 1833[23]

Several days after taking his oath as a senator, John C. Calhoun responded to President Jackson's threat to use force against South Carolina in an address overflowing with anger and passion.

γ   γ   γ

The system of oppression goes on. The weaker side sees it is a hopeless case, and makes resistance. The stronger still adheres to the system. The middle power is then thrown to the stronger side, and the stronger calls in force which puts down reason. This was the process of consolidation. Gentlemen might contend that this was not a question of consolidation; but it is consolidation. And he could see no distinction between a consolidated Government and one which assumed the right of judging of the propriety of interposing military power to coerce a State.

We made no such Government. South Carolina sanctioned no such Government. She entered the confederacy with the understanding that a State, in the last resort, has a right to judge of the expediency of resistance to oppression or secession from the Union. And for so doing it is that we are threatened to have our throats cut, and those of our wives and children. No—I go too far. I did not intend to use language so strong. The Chief Magistrate had not yet recommended so desperate a remedy. The present is a great question, and the liberties of the American people depend upon the decision of it. It was impossible that a consolidated Government could exist in this country; it never can. Did I say in this country? It never can exist in any country. If any man would look into the history of the world, and find any single case in which the

[23]*Register of Debates in Congress,* 22nd Congress, 2d sess., January 16, 1833, pp. 102–103.

government of absolute majority, unchecked by any constitutional restraints, had lasted one century, he would yield the question. For himself, he had been from his earliest life, deeply attached to the Union; and he felt, with a proportionate intensity, the importance of this question. In his early youth he had cherished a deep and enthusiastic admiration of this Union. He had looked on its progress with rapture, and encouraged the most sanguine expectations of its endurance. He still believed that if it could be conformed to the principles of 1798, as they were then construed, it might endure forever. Bring back the Government to those principles, and he would be the last to abandon it, and South Carolina would be amongst its warmest advocates. But depart from these principles, and in the course of ten years we shall degenerate into a military despotism. The cry had been raised, "the Union is in danger." He knew of no other danger but that of military despotism. He would proclaim it on this floor, that this was the greatest danger with which it was menaced—a danger the greatest which any country had to apprehend.

He begged pardon for the warmth with which he had expressed himself. Unbecoming as he knew that warmth to be, he must throw himself on his country and his countrymen for indulgence. Situated as he was, and feeling as he did, he could not have spoken otherwise.

READING NO. 24

DANIEL WEBSTER, FEBRUARY 16, 1833[24]

*Webster began this speech early in the afternoon, paused for
the Senate's customary two-hour break at 3 p.m. and concluded it before a jammed chamber at 8 p.m. Eighty-eight
pages of notes testify to Webster's careful preparation in his
effort to counter Calhoun's defense of nullification.*

γ   γ   γ

Mr. President, if the friends of nullification should be able
to propagate their opinions, and give them practical effect,
they would, in my judgment, prove themselves the most skilful
"architects of ruin," the most effectual extinguishers of
high-raised expectation, the greatest blasters of human hopes,
which any age has produced. They would stand up to proclaim,
in tones which would pierce the ears of half the human race,
that the last great experiment of representative government had
failed. They would send forth sounds, at the hearing of which
the doctrine of the divine right of kings would feel, even in its
grave, a returning sensation of vitality and resuscitation.
Millions of eyes, of those who now feed their inherent love of
liberty on the success of the American example, would turn
away from beholding our dismemberment, and find no place
on earth whereon to rest their gratified sight. Amidst the
incantations and orgies of nullification, secession, disunion,
and revolution, would be celebrated the funeral rites of
constitutional and republican liberty.

But, sir, if the Government do its duty; if it act with firmness
and with moderation, these opinions cannot prevail. Be assured, sir, be assured, that, among the political sentiments of
this people, the love of union is still uppermost. They will
stand fast by the constitution, and by those who defend it. I

---

[24]*Register of Debates in Congress,* 22nd Congress, 2d sess., February 16,
1833, pp. 586–587.

164

rely on no temporary expedients—on no political combination—but I rely on the true American feeling, the genuine patriotism of the people, and the imperative decision of the public voice. Disorder and confusion, indeed, may arise, scenes of commotion and contest are threatened, and perhaps may come. With my whole heart, I pray for the continuance of the domestic peace and quiet of the country. I desire most ardently the restoration of affection and harmony to all its parts. I desire that every citizen of the whole country may look to this Government with no other sentiments but those of grateful respect and attachment. But I cannot yield, even to kind feelings, the cause of the constitution, the true glory of the country, and the great trust which we hold in our hands for succeeding ages. If the constitution cannot be maintained without meeting these scenes of commotion and contest, however unwelcome, they must come. We cannot, we must not, we dare not, omit to do that which, in our judgment, the safety of the Union requires. Not regardless of consequences, we must yet meet consequences; seeing the hazards which surround the discharge of public duty, it must yet be discharged. For myself, sir, I shun no responsibility justly devolving on me, here or elsewhere, in attempting to maintain the cause. I am tied to it by indissoluble bands of affection and duty, and I shall cheerfully partake in its fortunes and its fate. I am ready to perform my own appropriate part whenever and wherever the occasion may call on me, and to take my chance among those upon whom blows may fall first and fall thickest. I shall exert every faculty I possess in aiding to prevent the constitution from being nullified, destroyed, or impaired; and even should I see it fall, I will still, with a voice, feeble, perhaps, but earnest as ever issued from human lips, and with fidelity and zeal which nothing shall extinguish, call on the PEOPLE to come to its rescue.

[The press of the immense concourse, of both sexes, which filled the galleries, the lobbies, and even the floor of the Senate chamber, during the evening sitting, was greater, if possible, than it was during the forenoon. At the conclusion of Mr. W.'s speech, there was a spontaneous burst of applause from the galleries.]

Mr. POINDEXTER moved an adjournment; but the President ordered the galleries to be cleared, and would not receive the motion to adjourn until the order had been executed; when

The Senate adjourned.

READING NO. 25

ALEXIS DE TOCQUEVILLE VIEWS THE SENATE, 1831[25]

During his celebrated tour of the United States in 1831, the French aristocrat Alexis de Tocqueville observed both houses of Congress in session. He concluded that the Senate's "superiority" derived from the indirect manner in which senators were elected.

γ   γ   γ

There are certain laws of a democratic nature which contribute, nevertheless, to correct in some measure these dangerous tendencies of democracy. On entering the House of Representatives at Washington, one is struck by the vulgar demeanor of that great assembly. Often there is not a distinguished man in the whole number. Its members are almost all obscure individuals, whose names bring no associations to mind. They are mostly village lawyers, men in trade, or even persons belonging to the lower classes of society. In a country in which education is very general, it is said that the representatives of the people do not always know how to write correctly.

At a few yards' distance is the door of the Senate, which contains within a small space a large proportion of the celebrated men of America. Scarcely an individual is to be seen in it who has not had an active and illustrious career: the Senate is composed of eloquent advocates, distinguished generals, wise magistrates, and statesmen of note, whose arguments would do honor to the most remarkable parliamentary debates of Europe.

How comes this strange contrast, and why are the ablest citizens found in one assembly rather than in the other? Why is the former body remarkable for its vulgar elements, while the

[25]Alexis de Tocqueville, *Democracy in America* (New York, 1966), vol. 1, pp. 204–205.

latter seems to enjoy a monopoly of intelligence and talent? Both of these assemblies emanate from the people; both are chosen by universal suffrage; and no voice has hitherto been heard to assert in America that the Senate is hostile to the interests of the people. From what cause, then, does so startling a difference arise? The only reason which appears to me adequately to account for it is that the House of Representatives is elected by the people directly, while the Senate is elected by elected bodies. The whole body of the citizens name the legislature of each state, and the Federal Constitution converts these legislatures into so many electoral bodies, which return the members of the Senate. The Senators are elected by an indirect application of the popular vote; for the legislatures which appoint them are not aristocratic or privileged bodies, that elect in their own right, but they are chosen by the totality of the citizens; they are generally elected every year, and enough new members may be chosen every year to determine the senatorial appointments. But this transmission of the popular authority through an assembly of chosen men operates an important change in it by refining its discretion and improving its choice. Men who are chosen in this manner accurately represent the majority of the nation which governs them; but they represent only the elevated thoughts that are current in the community and the generous propensities that prompt its nobler actions rather than the petty passions that disturb or the vices that disgrace it.

The time must come when the American republics will be obliged more frequently to introduce the plan of election by an elected body into their system of representation or run the risk of perishing miserably among the shoals of democracy.

READING NO. 26

THOMAS HART BENTON ON DE TOCQUEVILLE[26]

In his classic two-volume memoir, Sen. Thomas Hart Benton entitled a chapter "Error of De Tocqueville in Relation to the House of Representatives." He disputes the Frenchman's assessment of the value of indirect election, arguing that the best senators had earlier served in the House of Representatives and thus owed their selection directly to the people.

γ   γ   γ

He seems to look upon the members of the two Houses as different orders of beings—different classes—a higher and a lower class; the former placed in the Senate by the wisdom of State legislatures, the latter in the House of Representatives by the folly of the people—when the fact is, that they are not only of the same order and class, but mainly the same individuals. The Senate is almost entirely made up out of the House! and it is quite certain that every senator whom Mons. de Tocqueville had in his eye when he bestowed such encomium on that body had come from the House of Representatives! placed there by the popular vote, and afterwards transferred to the Senate by the legislature; not as new men just discovered by the superior sagacity of that body, but as public men with national reputations, already illustrated by the operation of popular elections. And if Mons. de Tocqueville had chanced to make his visit some years sooner, he would have seen almost every one of these senators, to whom his exclusive praise is directed, actually sitting in the other House.

Admitting that there might be a difference between the appearance of the two Houses, and between their talent, at the time that Mons. de Tocqueville looked in upon them, yet that difference, so far as it might then have existed, was accidental

[26]Thomas Hart Benton, *Thirty Years' View* (New York, 1871), vol. 1, pp. 206–207.

and temporary, and has already vanished. And so far as it may have appeared or may appear in other times, the difference in favor of the Senate may be found in causes very different from those of more or less judgment and virtue in the constituencies which elect the two Houses. The Senate is a smaller body, and therefore may be more decorous; it is composed of older men, and therefore should be graver; its members have usually served in the highest branches of the State governments, and in the House of Representatives, and therefere should be more experienced; its terms of service are longer, and therefore give more time for talent to mature, and for the measures to be carried which confer fame. Finally, the Senate is in great part composed of the pick of the House, and therefore gains double—by brilliant accession to itself and abstraction from the other. These are causes enough to account for any occasional, or general difference which may show itself in the decorum or ability of the two Houses. But there is another cause, which is found in the practice of some of the States— the caucus system and rotation in office—which brings in men unknown to the people, and turns them out as they begin to be useful; to be succeeded by other new beginners, who are in turn turned out to make room for more new ones; all by virtue of arrangements which look to individual interests, and not to the public good. . . . Short service, and not popular election, is the evil of the House of Representatives; and this becomes more apparent by contrast—contrast between the North and the South—the caucus, or rotary system, not prevailing in the South, and useful members being usually continued from that quarter as long as useful; and thus with fewer members, usually showing a greater number of men who have attained a distinction. Monsieur de Tocqueville is profoundly wrong, and does great injury to democratic government, as his theory countenances the monarchial idea of the incapacity of the people for self-government.

READING NO. 27

THE PRESIDENT REFUSES A SENATE REQUEST, DECEMBER 12, 1833[27]

In a classic assertion of executive privilege, President Andrew Jackson declines to submit a document requested by the Senate. This led directly to his censure.

γ   γ   γ

To the Senate of the United States:

I have attentively considered the resolution of the Senate, of the 11th instant, requesting the President of the United States to communicate to the Senate "a copy of the paper which has been published, and which purports to have been read by him to the heads of the executive departments, dated the 18th day of September last, relating to the removal of the deposites of the public money from the Bank of the United States and its offices."

The Executive is a co-ordinate and independent branch of the Government equally with the Senate; and I have yet to learn under what constitutional authority that branch of the Legislature has a right to require of me an account of any communication, either verbally or in writing, made to the heads of departments acting as a cabinet council. As well might I be required to detail to the Senate the free and private conversation I have held with those officers on any subjects relating to their duties and my own.

Feeling my responsibility to the American people, I am willing, upon all occasions, to explain to them the grounds of my conduct; and I am willing, upon all proper occasions, to give to either branch of the Legislature any information in my possession that can be useful in the execution of the appropriate duties confided to them.

Knowing the constitutional rights of the Senate, I shall be

[27]*Register of Debates in Congress,* 23rd Congress, 1st sess., /December 12, 1833/ p. 37.

the last man, under any circumstances, to interfere with them. Knowing those of the Executive, I shall, at all times, endeavor to maintain them, agreeably to the provisions of the constitution, and the solemn oath I have taken to support and defend it.

I am constrained, therefore, by a proper sense of my own self-respect, and of the rights secured by the constitution to the executive branch of the Government, to decline a compliance with your request.

ANDREW JACKSON

READING NO. 28

HENRY CLAY ASSERTS SENATORIAL PREROGATIVE, DECEMBER 26, 1833[28]

In building his case for Jackson's censure, Henry Clay examines the respective roles of Congress and the president under the Constitution.

γ γ γ

Allow me, in a few words, to present to the Senate my ideas of the structure of our Federal Government. It has no power but granted power; and the power granted must be found in the constitution, the instrument granting it. If the question arise, is a specific power granted? the grant must be shown, or the power must be proven to be necessary and proper to carry into effect a granted power. Our executive power, such as it is, must be looked for in the constitution, which has created and modified it, and not in the forms in which executive power practically exists in other countries, nor in the nature which is supposed to belong to it in the writings of Montesquieu, or any other specific author. And so of our legislative and judicial powers.

With respect to each of the three great departments into which Government is divided, we are to look for their respective powers into the constitution itself, and not into the theories of abstract or speculative philosophers. They have neither more nor less power than what is given. As to each, the constitution uses general language, which is to be interpreted not so much by its terms, as by the specific delineations of authority which are subsequently made.

In reference to the general duty assigned to the President to "take care that the laws be faithfully executed," what does this mean? According to the exposition which I am considering, the President would absorb all the powers of Government. For, in

[28]*Register of Debates in Congress,* 23rd Congress, 1st sess., /December 26, 1833/ pp. 68–69.

each particular case of the execution of a law, if his judgment was not satisfied that it was law, he might withhold the requisite executive agency. If a treaty were to be carried into effect; if a law to be executed; or a judicial decision to be enforced, denying that the treaty was valid, the law constitutional, or the decision agreeable to law, he might refuse the necessary means to enforce the execution of them respectively; and the practical result of the whole would be, that nothing under Government could be done but what was agreeable to the President. Such a view of our Government must be rejected.

In my opinion, when the constitution enjoined the President "to take care that the laws be faithfully executed," it required nothing more than this, to employ the means intrusted to him to overcome resistance whenever it might be offered to the laws. Congress, by the fourteenth clause of the eighth section of the first article of the constitution, is invested with power to provide for calling forth the militia to execute the laws of the Union, suppress insurrections, and repel invasions. It might as well be contended that Congress, under this power, deciding what was and what was not law, could direct, by the militia, that only to be executed which Congress deemed to be law. By the second section of the second article of the constitution, the President is made commander-in-chief of the army and navy of the United States, and of the militia when called into actual service; and, by subsequent clause, the injunction in question is given to him. Thus invested with the command and employment of the physical force of the Union, can a doubt remain that the purpose of the direction which the constitution gives to him to take care that the laws be faithfully executed, was that he should, when properly called upon by the civil authority, employ that force to subdue unlawful resistance? Understood in any other sense, those few words become a vortex, into which the whole powers of Government are irresistibly drawn.

We have established a system, in which power has been most carefully separated and distributed between three separate and independent departments. We have been told a thousand times, and all experience assures us, that such a division is indispensable to the existence and preservation of freedom. We have established and designated offices, and appointed officers in each of those departments, to execute the duties respectively allotted to them. The President, it is true, presides over the whole; specific duties are often assigned by particular laws to him alone, or to other officers under his superintendence. His parental eye is presumed to survey the whole extent of the system in all its movements: but has he power to come into Congress, and to say such laws only shall you pass; to go into the courts, and prescribe the decisions which they may pronounce; or even to enter the offices of administration, and, where duties are specifically confided to those officers, to substitute his will to their duty? Or, has he a right, when those functionaires, deliberating upon their own solemn obligations to the people, have moved forward in their assigned spheres, to arrest their lawful progress, because they have dared to act contrary to his pleasure? No, sir; no, sir. His is a high and glorious station, but it is one of observation and superintendence. It is to see that obstructions in the forward movement of Government, unlawfully interposed, shall be abated by legitimate and competent means.

READING NO. 29

JACKSON'S "PROTEST" TO THE SENATE, APRIL 15, 1834[29]

Andrew Jackson responds to his censure by the Senate. The secretary of the Senate read this message in a packed chamber, whose occupants included half the members of the House of Representatives. When cheering broke out in the gallery, the sergeant at arms arrested several spectators for rowdyism.

γ　　　　　γ　　　　　γ

To the Senate of the United States:

It appears by the published Journal of the Senate that on the 26th of December last a resolution was offered by a member of the Senate, which after a protracted debate was on the 28th day of March last modified by the mover and passed by the votes of twenty-six Senators out of forty-six who were present and voted, in the following words viz:

Resolved, That the President, in the late Executive proceedings in relation to the public revenue, has assumed upon himself authority and power not conferred by the Constitution and laws, but in derogation of both.

Having had the honor, through the voluntary suffrages of the American people, to fill the office of President of the United States during the period which may be presumed to have been referred to in this resolution, it is sufficiently evident that the censure it inflicts was intended for myself. Without notice, unheard and untried, I thus find myself charged on the records of the Senate, and in a form hitherto unknown in our history, with the high crime of violating the laws and Constitution of my country.

It can seldom be necessary for any department of the Government, when assailed in conversation or debate or by the strictures of the press or of popular assemblies, to step out of

---

[29]James D. Richardson, *A Compilation of the Messages and Papers of the Presidents, 1789–1897* (Washington, 1896), vol. 3, pp. 69–72.

its ordinary path for the purpose of vindicating its conduct or of pointing out any irregularity or injustice in the manner of the attack; but when the Chief Executive Magistrate is, by one of the most important branches of the Government in its official capacity, in a public manner, and by its recorded sentence, but without precedent, competent authority, or just cause, declared guilty of a breach of the laws and Constitution, it is due to his station, to public opinion, and to a proper self-respect that the officer thus denounced should promptly expose the wrong which has been done. . . .

The duty of defending so far as in him lies the integrity of the Constitution would indeed have resulted from the very nature of his office, but by thus expressing it in the official oath or affirmation, which in this respect differs from that of any other functionary, the founders of our Republic have attested their sense of its importance and have given to it a peculiar solemnity and force. Bound to the performance of this duty by the oath I have taken, by the strongest obligations of gratitude to the American people, and by the ties which unite my every earthly interest with the welfare and glory of my country, and perfectly convinced that the discussion and passage of the above-mentioned resolution were not only unauthorized by the Constitution, but in many respects repugnant to its provisions and subversive of the rights secured by it to other coordinate departments, I deem it an imperative duty to maintain the supremacy of that sacred instrument and the immunities of the department intrusted to my care by all means consistent with my own lawful powers, with the rights of others, and with the genius of our civil institutions. To this end I have caused this my *solemn protest* against the aforesaid proceedings to be placed on the files of the executive department and to be transmitted to the Senate. . . .

The high functions assigned by the Constitution to the Senate are in their nature either legislative, executive, or judicial. It is only in the exercise of its judicial powers, when sitting as a court for the trial of impeachments, that the Senate is expressly authorized and necessarily required to consider and decide upon the conduct of the President or any other public officer. Indirectly, however, as has already been suggested, it may frequently be called on to perform that office.

Cases may occur in the course of its legislative or executive proceedings in which it may be indispensable to the proper exercise of its powers that it should inquire into and decide upon the conduct of the President or other public officers, and in every such case its constitutional right to do so is cheerfully conceded. But to authorize the Senate to enter on such a task in its legislative or executive capacity the inquiry must actually grow out of and tend to some legislative or executive action, and the decision, when expressed, must take the form of some appropriate legislative or executive act.

The resolution in question was introduced, discussed, and passed not as a joint but as a separate resolution. It asserts no legislative power, proposes no legislative action, and neither possesses the form nor any of the attributes of a legislative measure. It does not appear to have been entertained or passed with any view or expectation of its issuing in a law or joint resolution, or in the repeal of any law or joint resolution, or in any other legislative action.

Whilst wanting both the form and substance of a legislative measure, it is equally manifest that the resolution was not justified by any of the executive powers conferred on the Senate. These powers relate exclusively to the consideration of treaties and nominations to office, and they are exercised in secret session and with closed doors. This resolution does not apply to any treaty or nomination, and was passed in a public session.

READING NO. 30

THE SENATE REFUSES TO ACCEPT THE PRESIDENT'S MESSAGE, MAY 1834[30]

As soon as the secretary finished reading Jackson's "Protest," Sen. George Poindexter angrily moved that the Senate not enter the president's message into its journal. He charged that the communication had nothing to do with the chief executive's official duties and that it demonstrated disrespect for the Senate. On May 7 the Senate agreed to Poindexter's motion and refused to print the message.

γ   γ   γ

1. *Resolved,* That the protest communicated to the Senate on the 17th ultimo, by the President of the United States, asserts powers as belonging to the President which are inconsistent with the just authority of the two Houses of Congress, and inconsistent with the constitution of the United States— . . .

2. *Resolved,* That while the Senate is, and ever will be, ready to receive from the President all such messages and communications as the constitution and laws, and the usual course of public business, authorize him to transmit to it, yet it cannot recognize any right in him to make a formal protest against votes and proceedings of the Senate, declaring such votes and proceedings to be illegal and unconstitutional, and requesting the Senate to enter such protest on its journals—. . .

3. *Resolved,* That the aforesaid protest is a breach of the privileges of the Senate, and that it be not entered on the Journals—

4. *Resolved,* That the President of the United States has no right to send a protest to the Senate against any of its proceedings—

[30]U.S. Senate, *Journal of the Senate,* 23rd Congress, 1st sess. /May 7, 1834/ pp. 252–253.

READING NO. 31

A FRAGMENT OF WASHINGTON'S COFFIN[31]

On January 29, 1850 Henry Clay presented to the Senate his program of compromise intended to reconcile the major issues dividing North and South. He employed an unusual prop to make his point.

γ　　　　　γ　　　　　γ

But, sir, I find myself engaged much beyond what I intended, when I came this morning from my lodgings, in the exposition with which I intended these resolutions should go forth to the consideration of the world. I cannot omit, however, before I conclude, relating an incident, a thrilling incident, which occurred prior to my leaving my lodgings this morning.

A man came to my room—the same at whose instance a few days ago I presented a memorial calling upon Congress for the purchase of Mount Vernon for the use of the public—and, without being at all aware of what purpose I entertained in the discharge of my public duty to-day, he said to me: ''Mr. Clay, I heard you make a remark the other day which induces me to suppose that a precious relic in my possession would be acceptable to you.'' He then drew out of his pocket, and presented to me, the object which I now hold in my hand. And what, Mr. President, do you suppose it is? It is a fragment of the coffin of Washington—a fragment of that coffin in which now repose in silence, in sleep, and speechless, all the earthly remains of the venerated Father of his Country. Was it portentous that it should have been thus presented to me? Was it a sad presage of what might happen to that fabric which Washington's virtue, patriotism, and valor established? No, sir, no. It was a warning voice, coming from the grave to the Congress now in session to beware, to pause, to reflect before

---

[31]*The Congressional Globe,* 31st Congress, 1st sess., /January 29, 1850/ p. 246.

they lend themselves to any purposes which shall destroy that Union which was cemented by his exertions and example. Sir, I hope an impression may be made on your mind such as that which was made on mine by the reception of this precious relic.

READING NO. 32

CALHOUN'S LAST FORMAL ADDRESS, MARCH 4, 1850[32]

Terminally ill, John C. Calhoun prepared one of his greatest speeches, a valiant defense of the South. He sat impassively, but alert, as another senator read it for him. His conclusion is reprinted here.

γ   γ   γ

Having now shown what cannot save the Union, I return to the question with which I commenced, How can the Union be saved? There is but one way by which it can with any certainty; and that is, by a full and final settlement, on the principle of justice, of all the questions at issue between the two sections. The South asks for justice, simple justice, and less she ought not to take. She has no compromise to offer, but the constitution; and no concession or surrender to make. She has already surrendered so much that she has little left to surrender. Such a settlement would go to the root of the evil, and remove all cause of discontent, by satisfying the South, she could remain honorably and safely in the Union, and thereby restore the harmony and fraternal feelings between the sections, which existed anterior to the Missouri agitation. Nothing else can, with any certainty, finally and for ever settle the questions at issue, terminate agitation, and save the Union.

But can this be done? Yes, easily; not by the weaker party, for it can of itself do nothing—not even protect itself—but by the stronger. The North has only to will it to accomplish it— to do justice by conceding to the South an equal right in the acquired territory, and to do her duty by causing the stipulations relative to fugitive slaves to be faithfully fulfilled—to cease the agitation of the slave question, and to provide for the insertion of a provision in the constitution, by an amendment,

[32]*The Congressional Globe,* 31st Congress, 1st sess., /March 4, 1850/ pp. 454–455.

which will restore to the South, in substance, the power she possessed of protecting herself, before the equilibrium between the sections was destroyed by the action of this Government. There will be no difficulty in devising such a provision—one that will protect the South, and which, at the same time, will improve and strengthen the Government, instead of impairing and weakening it.

But will the North agree to this? It is for her to answer the question. But, I will say, she cannot refuse, if she has half the love of the Union which she professes to have, or without justly exposing herself to the charge that her love of power and aggrandizement is far greater than her love of the Union. At all events, the responsibility of saving the Union rests on the North, and not on the South. The South cannot save it by any act of hers, and the North may save it without any sacrifice whatever, unless to do justice, and to perform her duties under the constitution, should be regarded by her as a sacrifice.

It is time, Senators, that there should be an open and manly avowal on all sides, as to what is intended to be done. If the question is not now settled, it is uncertain whether it ever can hereafter be; and we, as the representatives of the States of this Union, regarded as governments, should come to a distinct understanding as to our respective views, in order to ascertain whether the great questions at issue can be settled or not. If you, who represent the stronger portion, cannot agree to settle them on the broad principle of justice and duty, say so; and let the States we both represent agree to separate and part in peace. If you are unwilling we should part in peace, tell us so, and we shall know what to do, when you reduce the question to submission or resistance. If you remain silent, you will compel us to infer by your acts what you intend. In that case, California will become the test question. If you admit her, under all the difficulties that oppose her admission, you compel us to infer that you intend to exclude us from the whole of the acquired territories, with the intention of destroying, irretrievably, the equilibrium between the two sections. We would be blind not to perceive in that case, that your real objects are power and aggrandizement, and infatuated not to act accordingly.

I have now, Senators, done my duty in expressing my

opinions fully, freely, and candidly, on this solemn occasion. In doing so, I have been governed by the motives which have governed me in all the stages of the agitation of the slavery question since its commencement. I have exerted myself, during the whole period, to arrest it, with the intention of saving the Union, if it could be done; and if it could not, to save the section where it has pleased Providence to cast my lot, and which I sincerely believe has justice and the constitution on its side. Having faithfully done my duty to the best of my ability, both to the Union and my section, throughout this agitation, I shall have the consolation, let what will come, that I am free from all responsibility.

READING NO. 33

WEBSTER'S "SEVENTH OF MARCH" SPEECH[33]

Three days after John C. Calhoun's address, Daniel Webster delivered his reply. Beginning in a low-key but distinct manner, the Massachusetts senator consumed three hours in presenting his greatest oration.

γ　　　　　γ　　　　　γ

Mr. President, I wish to speak to-day, not as a Massachusetts man, nor as a northern man, but as an American, and a member of the Senate of the United States. It is fortunate that there is a Senate of the United States; a body not yet moved from its propriety, not lost to a just sense of its own dignity, and its own high responsibilities, and a body to which the country looks with confidence, for wise, moderate, patriotic, and healing counsels. It is not to be denied that we live in the midst of strong agitations, and surrounded by very considerable dangers to our institutions of government. The imprisoned winds are let loose. The East, the West, the North, and the stormy South, all combine to throw the whole ocean into commotion, to toss its billows to the skies, and to disclose its profoundest depths. I do not expect, Mr. President, to hold, or to be fit to hold, the helm in this combat of the political elements; but I have a duty to perform, and I mean to perform it with fidelity—not without a sense of the surrounding dangers, but not without hope. I have a part to act, not for my own security or safety, for I am looking out for no fragment upon which to float away from the wreck, if wreck there must be, but for the good of the whole, and the preservation of the whole; and there is that which will keep me to my duty during this struggle, whether the sun and the stars shall appear, or shall not appear, for many days. I speak to-day for the preservation of the Union. "Hear me for my cause." I speak

---

[33]*The Congressional Globe,* 31st Cong., 1st sess., /March 7, 1850/ p. 476.

185

to-day, out of a solicitous and anxious heart, for the restoration to the country of that quiet and that harmony which make the blessings of this Union so rich and so dear to us all. These are the topics that I propose to myself to discuss; these are the motives, and the sole motives, that influence me in the wish to communicate my opinions to the Senate and the country; and if I can do anything, however little, for the promotion of these ends, I shall have accomplished all that I desire.

READING NO. 34

SUMNER'S "CRIME AGAINST KANSAS" SPEECH, MAY 19, 1856[34]

One of the most savage addresses ever delivered on the Senate floor, this speech greatly inflamed tensions between the North and South and caused Rep. Preston Brooks to assault Charles Sumner three days later.

γ　　　　γ　　　　γ

Mr. President, you are now called to redress a great transgression. Seldom in the history of nations has such a question been presented. . . .

But the wickedness which I now begin to expose is immeasurably aggravated by the motive which prompted it. Not in any common lust for power did this uncommon tragedy have its origin. It is the rape of a virgin Territory, compelling it to the hateful embrace of Slavery; and it may be clearly traced to a depraved longing for a new slave State, the hideous offspring of such a crime, in the hope of adding to the power of Slavery in the National Government. Yes, sir, when the whole world, alike Christian and Turk, is rising up to condemn this wrong, and to make it a hissing to the nations, here in our Republic, *force*—ay, sir, FORCE—has been openly employed in compelling Kansas to this pollution, and all for the sake of political power. There is the simple fact, which you will vainly attempt to deny, but which in itself presents an essential wickedness that makes other public crimes seem like public virtues.

But this enormity, vast beyond comparison, swells to dimensions of wickedness which the imagination toils in vain to grasp, when it is understood, that for this purpose are hazarded the horrors of intestine feud, not only in this distant Territory, but everywhere throughout the country. Already the

[34]*The Congressional Globe*, 34th Congress, 1st sess., Appendix, /May 19, 1856/ pp. 529–531.

muster has begun. The strife is no longer local, but national. Even now, while I speak, portents hang on all the arches of the horizon, threatening to darken the broad land, which already yawns with the mutterings of civil war. The fury of the propagandists of Slavery, and the calm determination of their opponents, are now diffused from the distant Territory over wide-spread communities, and the whole country, in all its extent—marshaling hostile divisions, and foreshadowing a strife, which, unless happily averted by the triumph of Freedom, will become war—fratricidal, parricidal war—with an accumulated wickedness beyond the wickedness of any war in human annals; justly provoking the avenging judgment of Providence and the avenging pen of history, . . .

In now opening this great matter, I am not insensible to the austere demands of the occasion; but the dependence of the crime against Kansas upon the Slave Power is so peculiar and important, that I trust to be pardoned while I impress it by an illustration, which to some may seem trivial. It is related in Northern mythology, that the god of Force, visiting an enchanted region, was challenged by his royal entertainer to what seemed a humble feat of strength—merely, sir, to lift a cat from the ground. The god smiled at the challenge, and, calmly placing his hand under the belly of the animal, with superhuman strength, strove, while the back of the feline monster arched far upwards, even beyond reach, and one paw actually forsook the earth, until at last the discomfited divinity desisted; but he was little surprised at his defeat, when he learned that this creature, which seemed to be a cat, and nothing more, was not merely a cat, but that it belonged to and was a part of the great Terrestrial Serpent, which, in its innumerable folds, encircled the whole globe. Even so the creature, whose paws are now fastened upon Kansas, whatever it may seem to be, constitutes in reality a part of the Slave Power, which, with loathsome folds, is now coiled about the whole land. Thus do I expose the extent of the present contest, where we encounter not merely local resistance, but also the unconquered sustaining arm behind. But out of the vastness of the Crime attempted, with all its woe and shame, I derive a well-founded assurance of a commensurate vastness of effort against it, by the aroused masses of the country, determined not only to vindicate Right against Wrong, but to redeem the Republic from the thraldom of that Oligarchy, which prompts, directs, and concentrates, the distant wrong.

Such is the Crime, and such the criminal, which it is my duty in this debate to expose, and, by the blessing of God, this duty shall be done completely to the end. But this will not be enough. The Apologies, which, with strange hardihood, have been offered for the Crime, must be torn away, so that it shall stand forth, without a single rag, or fig-leaf, to cover its vileness. And, finally, the True Remedy must be shown. The subject is complex in its relations, as it is transcendent in importance; and yet, if I am honored by your attention, I hope to exhibit it clearly in all its parts, while I conduct you to the inevitable conclusion that Kansas must be admitted at once, with her present Constitution, as a State of this Union, and give a new star to the blue field of our National Flag. And here I derive satisfaction from the thought, that the cause is so strong in itself as to bear even the infirmities of its advocates; nor can it require anything beyond that simplicity of treatment and moderation of manner which I desire to cultivate. . . .

But, before entering upon the argument, I must say something of a general character, particularly in response to what has fallen from Senators who have raised themselves to eminence on this floor in championship of human wrongs; I mean the Senator from South Carolina, [Mr. BUTLER,] and the Senator from Illinois, [Mr. DOUGLAS,] who, though unlike as Don Quixote and Sancho Panza, yet, like this couple, sally forth together in the same adventure. I regret much to miss the elder Senator from his seat; but the cause, against which he has run a tilt, with such activity of animosity, demands that the opportunity of exposing him should not be lost; and it is for the cause that I speak. The Senator from South Carolina has read many books of chivalry, and believes himself a chivalrous knight, with sentiments of honor and courage. Of course he has chosen a mistress to whom he has made his vows, and who, though ugly to others, is always lovely to him; though polluted in the sight of the world, is chaste in his sight—I mean the harlot, Slavery. For her, his tongue is always profuse in words. Let her be impeached in character, or any proposition made to shut her out from the extension of her wantonness, and no extravagance of manner or hardihood of assertion is then too great for this Senator. The frenzy of Don Quixote, in behalf of his wench, Dulcinea del Toboso, is all surpassed. The asserted rights of slavery, which shock equality of all kinds, are cloaked by a fantastic claim of equality. If the slave States cannot enjoy what, in mockery of the great fathers of the Republic, he misnames equality under the Constitution—in other words, the full power in the National Territories to compel fellow-men to unpaid toil, to separate husband and wife, and to sell little children at the auction block—then, sir, the chivalric Senator will conduct the State of South Carolina out of the Union! Heroic knight! Exalted Senator! A second Moses come for a second exodus!

But not content with this poor menace, which we have been twice told was "measured," the Senator, in the unrestrained chivalry of his nature, has undertaken to apply opprobrious words to those who differ from him on this floor. He calls them "sectional and fanatical;" and opposition to the usurpation in Kansas he denounces as "an uncalculating fanaticism." To be sure, these charges lack all grace of originality, and all sentiment of truth; but the adventurous Senator does not hesitate. He is the uncompromising, unblushing representative on this floor of a flagrant *sectionalism,* which now domineers over the Republic, and yet with a ludicrous ignorance of his own position—unable to see himself as others see him—or with an effrontery which even his white head ought not to protect from rebuke, he applies to those here who resist his *sectionalism* the very epithet which designates himself. The men who strive to bring back the Government to its original policy, when Freedom and not Slavery was national, while Slavery and not Freedom was sectional, he arraigns as *sectional.* This will not do. It involves too great a perversion of terms. I tell that Senator, that it is to himself, and to the "organization" of which he is the "committed advocate," that this epithet belongs. I now fasten it upon them. For myself, I care little for names; but since the question has been raised here, I affirm that the Republican party of the Union is in no just sense *sectional,* but, more than any other party, *national;* and that it now goes forth to dislodge from the high places of the Government the tyrannical sectionalism of which the Senator from South Carolina is one of the maddest zealots. . . .

And in this same dreary catalogue faithful history must record all who now, in an enlightened age and in a land of boasted Freedom, stand up, in perversion of the Constitution and in denial of immortal truth, to fasten a new shackle upon their fellow-man. If the Senator wishes to see fanatics, let him look round among his own associates; let him look at himself.

READING NO. 35

THE NEW SENATE CHAMBER, 1859[35]

A correspondent for the New York Herald *enthusiastically describes the chamber to which the Senate moved on January 4, 1859.*

γ　　　　　　γ　　　　　　γ

. . . the Senate proceeded in a body to the new hall.

The general aspect of the new hall is light and graceful. In shape and dimensions, it is similar to the new Hall of Representatives, but to the eye appears more finely apportioned. The style and character of decoration are nearly the same in both houses, except that in the Senate the tone of color is much more subdued. The area of the floor is 80 feet by 48 feet, and of the roof 112 by 80 feet, the difference being occupied by a continuous gallery around the four sides of the apartment and capable of seating 1,200 /620/ persons. The inner roof or ceiling, of iron, is flat, with deep panels, twenty-one of which are fitted with ground glass, having in the centre of each pane a colored medallion representing the printing press, steam engine, cornucopia, and other symbols of progress and plenty. The light is supplied wholly through this window in the roof, and the effect is good—a flood of light falling on the reverend signers on the floor, while the galleries remain in half shadow. The gas apparatus is placed above the ceiling, so that the light streaming through the panes may seem like a softened effect of sunlight. The ceiling is thirty-five feet from the floor, but presents an appearance of greater altitude.

[35]*New York Herald,* January 5, 1859.

It is encrusted with floral and other embellishments in high relief, and all of iron. The floor of the chamber is covered with 1,700 yards of tapestry carpeting, having a large pattern of flowers on a purple ground. Its effect is not unpleasing. Had time permitted a carpet would have been manufactured of color and design to harmonize—as, for instance, of red stars on a buff ground. The Vice President's desk is a modest table, of mahogany, as unlike as possible to the marble bar on which the honorable Speaker /of the House/ pounds. The places of Senators are arranged in three rows.

The spectators' galleries are upholstered in drab damask, rather too blue in tone for good effect. Ample accommodation is supplied, even to the extent of a ladies' robing room. Access to the galleries is obtained through doors of maple, inlaid with bronze. The gallery set apart for the press is fitted with desks for about twenty persons, and it is understood that no one will be permitted within it unless specially accredited by the Vice President.

When the dust of a few sessions shall have taken the gloss off it, and the *genus loci* had time to settle himself, there can be little doubt that this new chamber will be found in every way more fitting than the old.

The wings of the Capitol being of the Roman Cornthian order of architecture, the interior fittings and decorations are, of course, in harmony therewith. The hall itself is approached by two grand stairways—the east, of Tennessee marble; the west, entirely of white marble, of extreme purity. Neither is yet completed, but enough is shown by the broad marble steps, the massive ballustrades of the same material, and the superb columns, with their capitals heightened with bronze, to indicate the magnificence of the design. Both stairways are lighted from the roof, with special adaptation to the walls being covered with historical paintings. This situation is considered the most favorable in the building for the execution of some work of art recording the deeds of history. . . .

The heating and ventilating arrangements are said to be the largest in the world—those of the English House of Parliament not excepted. Every portion of the Capitol—that mountainous mass of marble—is at once ventilated and warmed by one apparatus. Eight boilers convey steam to coils set in different places in the cellarage, supplying any required degree of heat, and at the same time motive power to two fans in either wing. One of these fans sends continual breezes of medicated air through the smaller apartments, while the other performs the same service for the Senate chamber. The air is graduated according to the atmospheric temperature without, and the political excitement within—during a sectional debate never to exceed 90, and on ordinary occasions to range between 70° and 73°. Thirty thousand cubic feet of air are circulated through the chamber per minute, which quantity may be increased to 80,000. The apparatus is completely under control. Any proportion of moisture may be imparted, from the delicious freshness of morning to the feeling that preludes a thunder shower, or even till the atmosphere "thaw and resolve itself into a dew."

It may be prudent to add that as each room is furnished with flues and registers, Senators, on the first symptoms of asphyxia, can protect themselves from the indiscretion of operators.

READING NO. 36

JEFFERSON DAVIS'S FAREWELL ADDRESS, JANUARY 21, 1861[36]

In a scene of unexceeded drama, Sen. Jefferson Davis takes his leave of the Senate following Mississippi's decision to secede from the Union.

γ   γ   γ

Mr. DAVIS. I rise, Mr. President, for the purpose of announcing to the Senate that I have satisfactory evidence that the State of Mississippi, by a solemn ordinance of her people in convention assembled, has declared her separation from the United States. Under these circumstances, of course my functions are terminated here. It has seemed to me proper, however, that I should appear in the Senate to announce that fact to my associates, and I will say but very little more. The occasion does not invite me to go into argument; and my physical condition would not permit me to do so if it were otherwise; and yet it seems to become me to say something on the part of the State I here represent, on an occasion so solemn as this.

It is known to Senators who have served with me here, that I have for many years advocated, as an essential attribute of State sovereignty, the right of a State to secede from the Union. Therefore, if I had not believed there was justifiable cause; if I had thought that Mississippi was acting without sufficient provocation, or without an existing necessity, I should still, under my theory of the Government, because of my allegiance to the State of which I am a citizen, have been bound by her action. I, however, may be permitted to say that I do think she has justifiable cause, and I approve of her act. I conferred with her people before that act was taken, counseled them then that if the state of things which they appre-

---

[36]*The Congressional Globe,* 36th Congress, 2d sess., /January 21, 1861/ p. 487.

hended should exist when the convention met, they should take the action which they have now adopted. . . .

I find in myself, perhaps, a type of the general feeling of my constituents towards yours. I am sure I feel no hostility to you, Senators from the North. I am sure there is not one of you, whatever sharp discussion there may have been between us, to whom I cannot now say, in the presence of my God, I wish you well; and such, I am sure, is the feeling of the people whom I represent towards those whom you represent. I therefore feel that I but express their desire when I say I hope, and they hope, for peaceful relations with you, though we must part. They may be mutually beneficial to us in the future, as they have been in the past, if you so will it. The reverse may bring disaster on every portion of the country; and if you will have it thus, we will invoke the God of our fathers, who delivered them from the power of the lion, to protect us from the ravages of the bear; and thus, putting our trust in God, and in our own firm hearts and strong arms, we will vindicate the right as best we may.

In the course of my service here, associated at different times with a great variety of Senators, I see now around me some with whom I have served long; there have been points of collision; but whatever of offense I have given which has not been redressed, or for which satisfaction has not been demanded, I have, Senators, in this hour of our parting, to offer you my apology for any pain which, in heat of discussion, I have inflicted. I go hence unencumbered of the remembrance of any injury received, and having discharged the duty of making the only reparation in my power for any injury offered.

Mr. President, and Senators, having made the announcement which the occasion seemed to me to require, it only remains for me to bid you a final adieu.

READING NO. 37

WADE-DAVIS MANIFESTO, AUGUST 5, 1864[37]

A classic defense of congressional prerogative following President Lincoln's veto of the Wade-Davis Reconstruction bill.

γ   γ   γ

A more studied outrage on the legislative authority of the people has never been perpetrated.

Congress passed a bill; the President refused to approve it, and then by proclamation puts as much of it in force as he sees fit, and proposes to execute those parts by officers unknown to the laws of the United States and not subject to the confirmation of the Senate!

The President, after defeating the law, proposes to appoint without law, and without the advice and consent of the Senate, *Military* Governors for the rebel States!

He has already exercised this dictatorial usurpation in Louisiana, and he defeated the bill to prevent its limitation . . .

The President has greatly presumed on the forbearance which the supporters of this Administration have so long practiced, in view of the arduous conflict in which we are engaged, and the reckless ferocity of our political opponents.

But he must understand that our support is of a cause and not of a man; that the authority of Congress is paramount and must be respected; that the whole body of the Union men in Congress will not submit to be impeached by him of rash and unconstitutional legislation; and if he wishes our support, he must confine himself to his executive duties—to obey and execute, not make the laws—to suppress by arms armed rebellion, and leave political reorganization to Congress.

[37]*New York Tribune,* August 5, 1864.

READING NO. 38

CHARLES SUMNER ON THE SENATE'S RULES, APRIL 12, 1866[38]

As part of a funeral oration in the Senate Chamber, Charles Sumner delivered a stirring tribute to the Senate's rules.

γ γ γ

Accustomed as we have become to the rules which govern legislative proceedings, we are hardly aware of their importance in the development of liberal institutions. They were unknown in antiquity, and they were unknown also on the European continent until latterly introduced from England, which was their original home. They are among the precious contributions which England has made to modern civilization. And yet they did not assume at once their present perfect form. Mr. Hallam tells us that even as late as Queen Elizabeth members called confusedly for the business they wished brought forward. But now, at last, these rules have become a beautiful machine by which business is conducted, legislation is molded, and debate is secured in all possible freedom. From the presentation of a petition or the introduction of a bill all proceeds by fixed processes until without disorder the final result is reached and a new law takes its place in the statute-book. Hoe's printing-press, or Alden's type-setter is not more perfect in its operations. But the rules are more even than a beautiful machine; they are the very temple of constitutional liberty.

[38]*The Congressional Globe*, 39th Congress, 1st sess., /April 12, 1866/ pp. 1911–1912.

READING NO. 39

IMPEACHMENT ARTICLE, 1868[39]

This was the principal article of impeachment against President Andrew Johnson. The Senate on May 16, 1868, by a one-vote margin, failed to agree to it.

γ   γ   γ

ARTICLE XI

That said Andrew Johnson, President of the United States, unmindful of the high duties of his office, and of his oath of office, and in disregard of the Constitution and laws of the United States, did heretofore, to wit, on the 18th day of August, A.D. 1866, at the city of Washington and the District of Columbia, by public speech, declare and affirm, in substance, that the 39th Congress of the United States was not a Congress of the United States authorized by the Constitution to exercise legislative power under the same, but, on the contrary, was a Congress of only a part of the States, thereby denying, and intending to deny, that the legislation of said Congress was valid or obligatory upon him, the said Andrew Johnson, except in so far as he saw fit to approve the same, and also thereby denying, and intending to deny, the power of the said 39th Congress to propose amendments to the Constitution of the United States; and, in pursuance of said declaration, the said Andrew Johnson, President of the United States, afterwards, to wit, on the 21st day of February, A.D. 1868, at the city of Washington, in the District of Columbia, did, unlawfully, and in disregard of the requirements of the Constitution that he should take care that the laws be faithfully executed, attempt to prevent the execution of an act entitled ''An act regulating the tenure of certain civil offices,'' passed March 2,

---

[39]*Trial of Andrew Johnson, President of the United States, Before the Senate of the United States on Impeachment by the House of Representatives* (Washington 1868), vol. 2, p. 486.

1867, by unlawfully devising and contriving, and attempting to devise and contrive, means by which he should prevent Edwin M. Stanton from forthwith resuming the functions of the office of Secretary for the Department of War, notwithstanding the refusal of the Senate to concur in the suspension theretofore made by said Andrew Johnson of said Edwin M. Stanton from said office of Secretary for the Department of War; and also by further unlawfully devising and contriving, and attempting to devise and contrive, means, then and there to prevent the execution of an act entitled "An act making appropriations for the support of the army for the fiscal year ending June 30, 1868, and for other purposes," approved March 2, 1867; and also to prevent the execution of an act entitled "An act to provide for the more efficient government of the rebel States," passed March 2, 1867, whereby the said Andrew Johnson, President of the United States, did then, to wit, on the 21st day of February, A.D. 1868, at the city of Washington, commit and was guilty of a high crime and misdemeanor in office.

READING NO. 40

WOODROW WILSON ON THE SENATE, 1885[40]

In the tradition of Alexis de Tocqueville and Thomas Hart Benton, Woodrow Wilson, as a young graduate student, tried his hand at analyzing the Senate. Unlike the others, he believed he could conduct his assessment, for an 1885 doctoral dissertation, without ever visiting the Senate. His observations are of particular interest in the light of his difficulties with the Senate while president more than three decades later.

γ   γ   γ

These, then, are the conditions of public life which make the House of Representatives what it is, a disintegrate mass of jarring elements, and the Senate what it is, a small, select, and leisurely House of Representatives. Or perhaps it would be nearer the whole truth to say that these are the circumstances and this the frame of government of which the two Houses form a part. Were the Senate not supplied principally by promotions from the House,—if it had, that is, a membership made up of men specially trained for its peculiar duties,—it would probably be much more effective than it is in fulfilling the great function of instructive and business-like debate of public questions; for its duties are enough unlike those of the House to be called peculiar. Men who have acquired all their habits in the matter of dealing with legislative measures in the House of Representatives, where committee work is every-thing and public discussion nothing but "talking to the country," find themselves still mere declaimers when they get into the Senate, where no previous question utters its interrupt-ing voice from the tongues of tyrannical committee-men, and where, consequently, talk is free to all. Only superior talents, such as very few men possess, could enable a Representative

[40]Woodrow Wilson, *Congressional Government: A Study in American Politics* (Baltimore, 1981), pp 145–147.

of long training to change his spots upon entering the Senate. Most men will not fit more than one sphere in life; and after they have been stretched or compressed to the measure of that one they will rattle about loosely or stick too tight in any other into which they may be thrust. Still, more or less adjustment takes place in every case. If a new Senator knock about too loosely amidst the free spaces of the rules of that august body, he will assuredly have some of his biggest corners knocked off and his angularities thus made smoother; if he stick fast amongst the dignified courtesies and punctilious observances of the upper chamber, he will, if he stick long enough, finally wear down to such a size, by jostling, as to attain some motion more or less satisfactory.

But it must be said, on the other hand, that even if the Senate were made up of something better than selections from the House, it would probably be able to do little more than it does in the way of giving efficiency to our system of legislation. For it has those same radical defects of organization which weaken the House. Its functions also, like those of the House, are segregated in the prerogatives of numerous Standing Committees. In this regard Congress is all of a piece. There is in the Senate no more opportunity than exists in the House for gaining such recognized party leadership as would be likely to enlarge a man by giving him a sense of power, and to steady and sober him by filling him with a grave sense of responsibility. So far as its organization controls it, the Senate, notwithstanding the one or two special excellences which make it more temperate and often more rational than the House, has no virtue which marks it as of a different nature. Its proceedings bear most of the characteristic features of committee rule. Its conclusions are suggested now by one set of its members, now by another set, and again by a third; an arrangement which is of course quite effective in its case, as in that of the House, in depriving it of that leadership which is valuable in more ways than in imparting distinct purpose to legislative action, because it concentrates party responsibility, attracts the best talents, and fixes public interest.

Some Senators are, indeed, seen to be of larger mental stature and built of stauncher moral stuff than their fellow-members, and it is not uncommon for individual members to become conspicuous figures in every great event in the Senate's deliberations. The public now and again picks out here and there a Senator who seems to act and to speak with true instinct of statesmanship and who unmistakably merits the confidence of colleagues and of people. But such a man, however eminent, is never more than *a* Senator. No one is *the* Senator. No one may speak for his party as well as for himself; no one exercises the special trust of acknowledged leadership. The Senate is merely a body of individual critics, representing most of the not very diversified types of a society substantially homogeneous; and the weight of every criticism uttered in its chamber depends upon the weight of the critic who utters it, deriving little if any addition to its specific gravity from connection with the designs of a purposeful party organization. . . .

READING NO. 41

TWO SENATES: 1875 AND 1904[41]

David Barry at the age of sixteen secured an appointment as a Senate page in 1875. Several years later he became a Washington correspondent for several midwestern newspapers. In 1904, as editor of the Providence (RI) Journal, *he looked back over a quarter century of his association with the Senate to draw some comparisons. Barry subsequently served as Senate sergeant at arms from 1919 to 1933.*

γ   γ   γ

It is largely a matter of opinion whether the Senate of 1904 measures up to the intellectual size of the Senate of 1878, or whether brains have given way to boodle, as is so popularly supposed. Those who understand the situation, however, know very well that the Senate is not a millionaires' club, but that the majority of the Senators are poor men. The millionaires are conspicuous in the yellow journals, but brains still control legislation. Not all of the brainy men in the Senate of to-day are rich, nor are all of its rich men brainy; but the rich Senator without brains has no influence on legislation as compared with the Senator with brains, either with or without the wealth. There are not a score of millionaires in the Senate, the total membership of which is ninety. But whatever the facts may be as to the influence of wealth on legislation, there is no question that in the twenty-five years that have passed since 1878 the extravagance and luxury of the Senate have kept pace with the piling-up of fortunes in the business world, and that no class of "public servants" is more petted and pampered by its own votes and at the expense of the taxpayers than the members of the United States Senate.

In 1878 a Senator of the United States provided himself out of the public treasury, in addition to his salary, with his

[41]David S. Barry, "The American House of Lords," *Pearson's Magazine,* 12 (December 1904), pp. 528–530.

mileage, his one hundred and twenty-five dollars for stationery, and one clerk, if he happened to be the chairman of a
committee. That was practically all. In 1904 a United States
Senator would sniff at one clerk, and declare it impossible to
attend to his work without two or three. Such a thing as paying
for a clerk out of his pocket, as his predecessors, up to a
comparatively few years ago, were accustomed to do, would
be regarded by the Senator of today as a crime.

Under the old rule each important committee had a clerk,
and perhaps an assistant and a messenger to wait upon the
committee when in session and attend a Senate door after the
meeting hour at 12 o'clock. The Senators who were chairmen
of committees (and, of course, these were majority Senators,
one or two small committees being allowed to the minority by
courtesy) used the committee rooms as their private offices,
and the Senators who were too young in service to be chairmen
had neither room, clerk or messenger paid for by Uncle Sam.

But does anybody think that the United States Senators of
1904, in this decade of money-making, money-spending and a
bursting treasury would manage themselves on a scale like
that? Not so. Every Senator to-day, big and little, without
regard to politics or length of service has at least one clerk who
draws his salary from the Government; each Senator of the
majority side, and almost every one of the Democrats, has a
private room in the Capitol or in the Maltby annex across the
way—a building purchased to permit the Senators to spread
themselves—and each important committee chairman has one
or two or three assistant clerks. The chairmen of the smaller
committees, many of which never meet, manage to get two
clerks by seeing to it that the ''messenger'' selected is a
stenographer and typewriter. This is a good plan for the
''messenger'' as well as the chairman, for otherwise the former
would have nothing to do. Formerly the clerks of the small and
useless committees were paid when the Senate was in session.
Now they draw annual salaries, and cases exist of clerks who
never come to Washington at all. The Senate messengers, who
formerly swung the Senate Chamber doors after 12 o'clock,
now sit about the committee rooms, and when a Senator wants
his lunch the messenger sends for a colored laborer to get it.
It is not at all the proper thing nowadays for a Senator who has

been in the body long enough to have his eye-teeth cut to eat lunch in the Senate restaurant. Only the novices and employees and the public go there. The Senator who knows a thing or two lunches in his private room. This does not mean in the general committee room, but in the little parlor connected with it, for it has been a common practice of late years to cut archways through the three-foot walls of the building to make private rooms where none were otherwise available. Formal committee room luncheons, with women as well as men as guests, and where Senate employees are waiters, are now a matter of daily occurrence.

READING NO. 42

THE CAUCUS AS AGENT OF THE SENATE'S DECLINE, 1902[42]

Moisei Ostrogorskii followed in the well-worn trail of foreign observers and political scientists seeking to explain the Senate's operations to a larger public. In 1902 he attributed the institution's apparent decline to the role of the political party caucus.

γ   γ   γ

However Congress, which usurped the powers of the executive, which gained what the latter lost, has also lapsed from the high place assigned to it by the framers of the constitution. The Caucus was one of the principal, if not the principal agent of this fall. The Senate of the United States no longer has any resemblance to that august assembly which provoked the admiration of the Tocquevilles. It would be no use looking for the foremost men of the nation there; neither statesmen nor orators are to be found in it. In wisdom, in balance, in dignity, the States' chamber is far inferior to the popular branch of Congress. The Senate no longer acts as a conservative element, as a brake for checking popular impulses, for moderating heedless ardour; on the contrary, it is this assembly which often gives the signal for extravagant conduct either in financial matters or in the sphere of foreign politics. The Senate is, for the most part, filled with men of mediocre or no political intelligence, some of whom, extremely wealthy, multimillionnaires, look on the senatorial dignity as a title for ennobling their well or ill gotten riches; others, crack wirepullers, State bosses, or representatives of large private industrial or financial concerns, find the Senate a convenient base of operations for their intrigues and their designs on the public interest; others, again, without convictions or without definite

[42]M. Ostrogorskii, *Democracy and the Organization of Political Parties* (New York, 1970), vol. 2, pp. 542–544.

or well-matured ideas but sensitive to every breath of public opinion and fond of vulgar popularity, act as the noisy mouthpieces of every movement which flatters the susceptibilities of the crowd. They represent everything save enlightened opinion, to which they do not pay the slightest heed.

And it is through the Caucus that these men, especially those of the first two categories, get into the Senate; the State Legislatures, which elect the Senators of the United States, are composed of creatures of the Machine, and they bestow the senatorial office on the favourites of the party Organization. In the States ruled by the bosses, the boss, if he wants to go into the Senate, has but to hold up his hand, and the most eminent competitor will be sacrificed to him without further ado, were he of the stamp of the Websters or the Clays. The rich men buy a seat in the Senate from the party Organization for cash, with scarcely any disguise; if they do not ''make'' the Legislature with their own money, on the method of Jay Gould, they subscribe very liberally to the funds of the Organization; and the latter, to discharge its obligation to them, procures them the dignity of Senator—it orders its liegemen in the Legislature to vote for them.

Whilst the Senate was being filled with men of an inferior type, it was assuming powers higher than those conferred on it by the constitution. It has not only encroached on the province of the executive in the matter of appointments to offices and of negotiation of treaties, but even on that of the House of Representatives; it has nullified the initiative in regard to finance, reserved by the constitution for the popular branch of Congress. By its right of amendment, of which it made an improper use, and by systematic obstruction, which consisted in keeping the bills passed by the House hung up in committee, the Senate brought the House to do its will. This usurpation was carried out, once more, with the powerful help of the Caucus. Having established the focus of the party Organization in the Senate, the Caucus gave that assembly a position of vantage over the Representatives and the executive, who are dependent on that very Organization; it placed the Senators in a sort of ambush, from which they can hit everybody without being struck themselves. They can do this with impunity because the Caucus has freed them from all responsibility; they owe nothing to public opinion, as they are indebted for their seats solely to their relations with the party Organization; and there is no fear of their being called to account on behalf of the public interest by the Machine, and still less by the State Legislature, which is supposed to have elected them and which will expire before them. This irresponsibility, ensured on the other hand by the absolute separation of powers which prevents the legislative and the executive from meeting in the light of day, has but stimulated the tendency to encroachment and to extravagant conduct which have marked the career of the Senate during the last quarter of a century.

READING NO. 43

THE MISSOURI LEGISLATURE ELECTS A SENATOR, 1905[43]

Professor George Haynes of Worcester Polytechnic Institute spent the first three decades of the twentieth century studying Senate history and procedures. At the start of the century he had become convinced that state legislative election of U.S. senators was a mistake. In support of that belief, he offered the following examples, among others, in giving a colorful account of the turmoil surrounding the deliberations of the Missouri legislature in 1905.

γ   γ   γ

Lest the hour of adjournment should come before the election was secured, an attempt was made to stop the clock upon the wall of the assembly chamber. Democrats tried to prevent its being tampered with; and when certain Republicans brought forward a ladder, it was seized and thrown out of the window. A fist-fight followed, in which many were involved. Desks were torn from the floor and a fusillade of books began. The glass of the clockfront was broken, but the pendulum still persisted in swinging until, in the midst of a yelling mob, one member began throwing ink bottles at the clock, and finally succeeded in breaking the pendulum. On a motion to adjourn arose the wildest disorder. The presiding officers of both houses mounted the speaker's desk, and, by shouting and waving their arms tried to quiet the mob. Finally, they succeeded in securing some semblance of order.

[43]George H. Haynes, *The Election of Senators* (New York, 1906), pp. 47–50.

READING NO. 44

"NEW YORK'S MISREPRESENTATIVES," 1906[44]

The following is taken from the first chapter of David Graham Phillips's Treason of the Senate.

γ   γ   γ

ONE morning, during this session of the Congress, the Senate blundered into a discussion of two of its minor disreputables, Burton and Mitchell, who had been caught with their fingers sliding about in the change pocket of the people. The discussion on these change-pocket thieves was a fine exhibition of "senatorial dignity and courtesy," which means, nowadays, regard for the honor and dignity of the American people smugly sacrificed to the Senate's craftily convenient worship of the Mumbo-Jumbo mask and mantle of its own high respectability. In closing the brief debate over his fellow-senators who had been so unluckily caught, Senator Lodge said,

"There is too much tendency to remember the senators, and to forget the Senate."

A profound criticism—profounder far than was intended, or realized, by the senator from the "interests" that center in Massachusetts.

Let us take Mr. Lodge's hint. Let us disregard the senators as individuals; let us for the moment "remember the Senate."

The treason of the Senate!

Politics does not determine prosperity. But in this day of concentrations, politics does determine *the distribution of prosperity.* Because the people have neglected politics, have not educated themselves out of credulity to flimsily plausible political lies and liars, because they will not realize that *it is not enough to work, it is also necessary to think,* they remain poor,

---

[44]David Graham Phillips, *The Treason of the Senate* (Chicago, 1964), pp. 58–60.

or deprived of their fair share of the products, though they have produced an incredible prosperity. The people have been careless and unwise enough in electing every kind of public administrator. When it comes to the election of the Senate, how describe their stupidity, how measure its melancholy consequences? The Senate is the most powerful part of our public administration. It has vast power in the making of laws. It has still vaster power through its ability to forbid the making of laws and in its control over the appointment of the judges who say what the laws mean. It is, in fact, *the final arbiter of the sharing of prosperity.* The laws it permits or compels, the laws it refuses to permit, the interpreters of laws it permits to be appointed—these factors determine whether the great forces which modern concentration has produced shall operate to distribute prosperity equally or with shameful inequality and cruel and destructive injustice. The United States Senate is a larger factor than your labor or your intelligence, you average American, in determining your income. And the Senate is a traitor to you!

The treason of the Senate! Treason is a strong word, but not too strong, rather too weak, to characterize the situation in which the Senate is the eager, resourceful, indefatigable agent of interests as hostile to the American people as any invading army could be, and vastly more dangerous; interests that manipulate the prosperity produced by all, so that it heaps up riches for the few; interests whose growth and power can only mean the degradation of the people, of the educated into sycophants, of the masses toward serfdom.

A man cannot serve two masters. The senators are not elected by the people; they are elected by the "interests." A servant obeys him who can punish and dismiss. Except in extreme and rare and negligible instances, can the people either elect or dismiss a senator? The senator, in the dilemma which the careless ignorance of the people thrusts upon him, chooses to be comfortable, placed and honored, and a traitor to oath and people rather than to be true to his oath and poor and ejected into private life.

READING NO. 45

SEVENTEENTH AMENDMENT, 1913[45]

The Seventeenth Amendment to the U.S. Constitution passed the Senate in June 1911 and was proposed to the states on May 13, 1912. Ratification was completed on April 8, 1913, when Connecticut became the thirty-sixth state to approve it. The amendment took effect on May 31, 1913.

γ   γ   γ

The Senate of the United States shall be composed of two Senators from each State, elected by the people thereof, for six years; and each Senator shall have one vote. The electors in each State shall have the qualifications requisite for electors of the most numerous branch of the State legislatures.

When vacancies happen in the representation of any State in the Senate, the executive authority of such State shall issue writs of election to fill such vacancies: *Provided,* That the legislature of any State may empower the executive thereof to make temporary appointments until the people fill the vacancies by election as the legislature may direct.

This amendment shall not be so construed as to affect the election or term of any Senator chosen before it becomes valid as part of the Constitution.

[45]*U. S. Constitution,* Amendment XVII.

READING NO. 46

IMPACT OF DIRECT ELECTION[46]

George Haynes had crusaded vigorously for adoption of the Seventeenth Amendment. Here is his assessment in 1914 of its immediate impact.

γ   γ   γ

Are there indications that popular election may impair the Senate's high tradition and prestige? It seems evident that, with the growing directness of responsibility to the people, the type of Senator is undergoing change. While it may prove to be a passing phase, due to blurred party lines, nevertheless Senatorial service is now obviously growing shorter. This involves a loss in experienced statecraft, which in the past has given to the country some of its ablest leaders. The Senators of the present day are younger than their predecessors; they have come to their membership in the foremost legislative body of the world with less of lawmaking experience than their predecessors had had. Moreover, there seems to be a distinct and psychologically explicable tendency to turn from men wise in council—who have made the reputation of the Senate in the past—to men of the more dramatic executive qualities. An aptitude for getting things done makes a stronger appeal to the voter than a capacity for deliberate—perhaps too deliberate—study of what it is wise to do. Many a Senator, whose work has been most serviceable, has had few gifts that would make him a successful votecatcher. For the future it is going to be harder for a Senator of manly independence to hold to a course which does not square with the opinion of the day; for his chance of re-election will be largely determined not by whether his acts have been wise, but by whether they have been popular. In our exultation over the prophesied banishment from the Senate of the reactionaries, the 'representatives of predatory wealth,' and

[46]George H. Haynes, ''The Changing Senate,'' *North American Review,* 200 (August 1914), pp. 232–233.

other belated survivals, we have reason for some concern lest our upper chamber is losing something of the distinction of manner, the type of mind, the poise of judgment, which have characterized our foremost Senator-statemen. In our haste to be rid of the conservative, is there no danger that we shall at the same time turn out the conservator?

READING NO. 47

RULE XXII[47]

Senate Rule XXII, providing for a limitation of debate, was first adopted in 1917. Here is the most recent version.

γ   γ   γ

Notwithstanding the provisions of rule II or rule IV or any other rule of the Senate, at any time a motion signed by sixteen Senators, to bring to a close the debate upon any measure, motion, other matter pending before the Senate, or the unfinished business, is presented to the Senate, the Presiding Officer, or clerk at the direction of the Presiding Officer, shall at once state the motion to the Senate, and one hour after the Senate meets on the following calendar day but one, he shall lay the motion before the Senate and direct that the clerk call the roll, and upon the ascertainment that a quorum is present, the Presiding Officer shall, without debate, submit to the Senate by a yea-and-nay vote the question:

"Is it the sense of the Senate that the debate shall be brought to a close?" And if that question shall be decided in the affirmative by three-fifths of the Senators duly chosen and sworn—except on a measure or motion to amend the Senate rules, in which case the necessary affirmative vote shall be two-thirds of the Senators present and voting—then said measure, motion, or other matter pending before the Senate, or the unfinished business, shall be the unfinished business to the exclusion of all other business until disposed of.

Thereafter no Senator shall be entitled to speak in all more than one hour on the measure, motion, or other matter pending before the Senate, or the unfinished business, the amendments thereto, and motions affecting the same, and it shall be the duty of the Presiding Officer to keep the time of each Senator who speaks. Except by unanimous consent, no amendment shall be proposed after the vote to bring the debate to a close, unless it

[47] U. S. Senate, *Standing Rules*, 1979 general revision, amended 1986.

216

had been submitted in writing to the Journal Clerk by 1 o'clock p.m. on the day following the filing of the cloture motion if an amendment in the first degree, and unless it had been so submitted at least one hour prior to the beginning of the cloture vote if an amendment in the second degree. No dilatory motion, or dilatory amendment, or amendment not germane shall be in order. Points of order, including questions of relevancy, and appeals from the decision of the Presiding Officer, shall be decided without debate.

After no more than thirty hours of consideration of the measure, motion, or other matter on which cloture has been invoked, the Senate shall proceed, without any further debate on any question, to vote on the final disposition thereof to the exclusion of all amendments not then actually pending before the Senate at that time and to the exclusion of all motions, except a motion to table, or to reconsider and one quorum call on demand to establish the presence of a quorum (and motions required to establish a quorum) immediately before the final vote begins. The thirty hours may be increased by the adoption of a motion, decided without debate, by a three-fifths affirmative vote of the Senators duly chosen and sworn, and any such time thus agreed upon shall be equally divided between and controlled by the Majority and Minority Leaders or their designees. However, only one motion to extend time, specified above, may be made in any one calendar day.

If, for any reason, a measure or matter is reprinted after cloture has been invoked, amendments which were in order prior to the reprinting of the measure or matter will continue to be in order and may be conformed and reprinted at the request of the amendment's sponsor. The conforming changes must be limited to lineation and pagination.

No Senator shall call up more than two amendments until every other Senator shall have had the opportunity to do likewise.

Notwithstanding other provisions of this rule, a Senator may yield all or part of his one hour to the majority or minority floor managers of the measure, motion, or matter or to the Majority or Minority Leader, but each Senator specified shall not have more than two hours so yielded to him and may in turn yield such time to other Senators.

Notwithstanding any other provision of this rule, any Senator who has not used or yielded at least ten minutes, is, if he seeks recognition, guaranteed up to ten minutes, inclusive, to speak only.

After cloture is invoked, the reading of any amendment, including House amendments, shall be dispensed with when the proposed amendment has been identified and has been available in printed form at the desk of the Members for not less than twenty-four hours.

READING NO. 48

MCGRAIN V. DAUGHERTY[48]

In an effort to take testimony in connection with the "Teapot Dome" scandal, the Senate ordered its deputy sergeant at arms, John McGrain, to arrest an uncooperative key witness. The witness, brother of former Attorney General Harry Daugherty, obtained a court-ordered release from custody on the grounds that the attempt to compel his testimony was unconstitutional as it served no legislative purpose. The U.S. Supreme Court overturned that decision in a landmark 1927 ruling.

γ   γ   γ

We are of opinion that the power of inquiry—with process to enforce it—is an essential and appropriate auxiliary to the legislative function. It was so regarded and employed in American Legislatures before the Constitution was framed and ratified. Both houses of Congress took this view of it early in their history—the House of Representatives with the approving votes of Mr. Madison and other members whose service in the convention which framed the Constitution gives special significance to their action—and both houses have employed the power accordingly up to the present time. The acts of 1798 and 1857, judged by their comprehensive terms, were intended to recognize the existence of this power in both houses and to enable them to employ it ''more effectually'' than before. So, when their practice in the matter is appraised according to the circumstances in which it was begun and to those in which it has been continued, if falls nothing short of a practical construction, long continued, of the constitutional provisions respecting their powers, and therefore should be taken as fixing the meaning of those provisions, if otherwise doubtful.

We are further of opinion that the provisions are not of doubtful meaning, but, as was held by this court in the cases

[48]47 *Supreme Court Reporter*, 328–329.

we have reviewed, are intended to be effectively exercised, and therefore to carry with them such auxiliary powers as are necessary and appropriate to that end. While the power to exact information in aid of the legislative function was not involved in those cases, the rule of interpretation applied there is applicable here. A legislative body cannot legislate wisely or effectively in the absence of information respecting the conditions which the legislation is intended to affect or change; and where the legislative body does not itself possess the requisite information—which not infrequently is true—recourse must be had to others who do possess it. Experience has taught that mere requests for such information often are unavailing, and also that information which is volunteered is not always accurate or complete; so some means of compulsion are essential to obtain what is needed. All this was true before and when the Constitution was framed and adopted. In that period the power of inquiry, with enforcing process, was regarded and employed as a necessary and appropriate attribute of the power to legislate—indeed, was treated as inhering in it. Thus there is ample warrant for thinking, as we do, that the constitutional provisions which commit the legislative function to the two houses are intended to include this attribute to the end that the function may be effectively exercised.

READING NO. 49

SENATE RESOLUTION 206, APRIL 12, 1934[49]

This resolution, typical of its kind, authorized creation of a special Senate committee to investigate the munitions industry.

γ   γ   γ

Whereas the influence of the commercial motive is an inevitable factor in considerations involving the maintenance of the national defense; and

Whereas the influence of the commercial motive is one of the inevitable factors often believed to stimulate and sustain wars; and

Whereas the Seventy-first Congress, by Public Resolution No. 98, approved June 27, 1930, responding to the long-standing demands of American war veterans speaking through the American Legion for legislation "to take the profit out of war", created a War Policies Commission which reported recommendations on December 7, 1931, and on March 7, 1932, to decommercialize war and to equalize the burdens thereof; and

Whereas these recommendations never have been translated into the statutes:

Therefore be it

Resolved, That a special committee of the Senate shall be appointed by the Vice President to consist of seven Senators, and that said committee be, and is hereby, authorized and directed—

(a) To investigate the activities of individuals, firms, associations, and of corporations and all other agencies in the United States engaged in the manufacture, sale, distribution, import, or export of arms, munitions, or other implements of war; the nature of the industrial and commercial organizations engaged in the manufacture of or traffic in arms, munitions, or

---

[49]Senate Resolution 206, 73rd Congress, 2nd sess.

other implements of war; the methods used in promoting or effecting the sale of arms, munitions, or other implements of war; the quantities of arms, munitions, or other implements of war imported into the United States and the countries of origin thereof, and the quantities exported from the United States and the countries of destination thereof; and

(b) To investigate and report upon the adequacy or inadequacy of existing legislation, and of the treaties to which the United States is a party, for the regulation and control of the manufacture of and traffic in arms, munitions, or other implements of war within the United States, and of the traffic therein between the United States and other countries; and

(c) To review the findings of the War Policies Commission and to recommend such specific legislation as may be deemed desirable to accomplish the purposes set forth in such findings and in the preamble to this resolution; and

(d) To inquire into the desirability of creating a Government monopoly in respect to the manufacture of armaments and munitions and other implements of war, and to submit recommendations thereon.

For the purposes of this resolution the committee or any subcommittee thereof is authorized to hold hearings, to sit and act at such times and places during the sessions and recesses of the Congress until the final report is submitted, to require by subpena or otherwise the attendance of such witnesses and the production of such books, papers, and documents, to administer such oaths, to take such testimony, and to make such expenditures, as it deems advisable. The cost of stenographic services to report such hearings shall not be in excess of 25 cents per hundred words. The expenses of the committee, which shall not exceed $15,000, shall be paid from the contingent fund of the Senate upon vouchers approved by the chairman.

READING NO. 50

A MAJORITY LEADER RESIGNS, FEBRUARY 23, 1944[50]

In a dramatic break with President Franklin Roosevelt, Senate Majority Leader Alben Barkley resigned his leadership position to protest the chief executive's disregard of his advice.

γ   γ   γ

Mr. BARKLEY. Mr. President, on yesterday the President of the United States sent to the House of Representatives, and indirectly to the Senate, a message vetoing the tax bill recently passed by both Houses of the Congress after 6 or 8 months of deliberation upon it. I should have preferred to discuss this veto message on a proposal to pass the bill over the President's objections, but not knowing what action the House will take, and therefore not knowing whether the Senate will be given an opportunity to vote upon the veto, I have decided to discuss it now. . . .

The President said that he had been advised by some not to veto this bill "on the ground"—to quote his own language—"that having asked the Congress for a loaf of bread to take care of this war for the sake of this and succeeding generations, I should be content with a small piece of crust."

I am one of those, Mr President, who advised the President not to veto this bill. I not only advised him, but I implored him not to veto it, because I did not then believe, and I do not now believe, that the veto which he has sent to Congress was justified. I make no apology for that. . . .

In his effort to belittle and discredit Congress throughout his veto message the President says:

"It is not a tax bill but a tax-relief bill providing relief not for the needy but for the greedy."

That statement, Mr. President, is a calculated and deliberate

[50]*Congressional Record,* February 23, 1944, 78th Congress, 2d sess., pp. 1964–1966.

assault upon the legislative integrity of every Member of Congress. Other Members of Congress may do as they please; but, as for me, I do not propose to take this unjustifiable assault lying down.

For 31 years I have continuously represented the great Commonwealth of Kentucky in the Congress of the United States—14 years in the House of Representatives—almost without opposition in my own party or in the Republican Party throughout that entire period. When my present term as a Senator shall have expired I will have served that great Commonwealth continuously for a period of 32 years. Unless I am misinformed, that constitutes a longer period of service than can be claimed by any other previous Kentuckian who has served in either branch of the Congress. When my present term in the Senate shall have expired, I will have served in this body for 18 years continuously, which is a longer period than any previous Kentuckian can claim for continuous service in the Senate.

Mr. President, out of the fullness of my heart, I entertain a profound gratitude to the people of my State for giving me the opportunity to serve them and the Nation during this tragic period of our history. On the 27th day of next July I shall have served as majority leader of this body for 7 years. You may be surprised to know, Mr. President, that, so far as I have been able to trace the record back in senatorial history, this is nearly twice as long as any other man of any political party has served as majority leader of this body.

Mr. President, this is the first time during that long service, which I had thought was honorable, when I have been accused deliberately of voting for a bill that constituted a relief measure impoverishing the needy and enriching the greedy.

Mr. President, for 12 years I have carried to the best of my ability the flag of Franklin D. Roosevelt. For the past 7 years I have carried the flag of this administration as majority leader of the Senate, and during these years I have borne that flag with pride because I felt that President Roosevelt in himself in the great crisis in the history of our country and the world constituted a dynamic leader for whom the people yearned. I dare say that during the past 7 years of my tenure as majority leader I have carried that flag over rougher territory than was ever traversed by any previous majority leader. Some times I have carried it with little help here on the Senate floor, and more frequently with little help from the other end of Pennsylvania Avenue.

Whether I have made a good majority leader, an indifferent majority leader, or a bad majority leader, the record itself will speak. There is nothing in that record that I would now change; there is nothing in that record that I would not repeat under the same circumstances that existed during this course of my legislative history. But, Mr. President, there is something more precious to me than any honor that can be conferred upon me by the Senate of the United States or by the people of Kentucky or by the President of this Republic, and that is the approval of my own conscience and my own self-respect. That self-respect and the rectitude of that conscience I propose on this occasion to maintain.

I thank Heaven that my future happiness does not depend upon whether I shall retain the post of majority leader of the Senate for another hour. As proof of that, Mr. President, and in confirmation of this statement, I have called a conference of the Democratic majority for 10:30 o'clock tomorrow morning in the conference room of the Senate Office Building, at which time my resignation will be tendered and my services terminated in the post which I now hold at this desk.

Before leaving it, Mr. President, I wish to say that I have disagreed many times with my colleagues here on both sides of the political aisle; but I have sought to earn their respect and their esteem. Before I depart from this station I wish to express my deep appreciation for the courtesies which I have uniformly received. I shall carry with me to my dying day the most sacred memories of long and honorable service in the two branches of the Congress of the United States.

Mr. President, let me say, in conclusion, that if the Congress of the United States has any self-respect yet left it will override the veto of the President and enact this tax bill into law, his objections to the contrary notwithstanding. [Prolonged applause on the Senate floor, Senators rising.]

READING NO. 51

"COMMUNISTS IN GOVERNMENT SERVICE," FEBRUARY 20, 1950[51]

With this address, Sen. Joseph R. McCarthy launched his campaign in the Senate to expose alleged Communists employed within the federal government.

γ   γ   γ

Mr. McCARTHY. Mr. President, I wish to discuss a subject tonight which concerns me more than does any other subject I have ever discussed before this body, and perhaps more than any other subject I shall ever have the good fortune to discuss in the future. It not only concerns me, but it disturbs and frightens me.

About 10 days ago, at Wheeling, W. Va., in making a Lincoln Day speech, I made the statement that there are presently in the State Department a very sizable group of active Communists. I made the further statement, Mr. President, that of one small group which had been screened by the President's own security agency, the State Department refused to discharge approximately 200 of those individuals. . . .

Mr. President, I have before me information from the State Department files, information which the President says the Senate did not have. Having this information, it is a serious question as to what should be done with it. I originally thought possibly we could hope for some cooperation from the State Department and the President. However, in going over the material and finding that all of it, of course, has been available to the State Department, for it is all from their files, it seemed that nothing would be gained by calling it to their attention again. The President, I felt, had demonstrated his lack of interest quite thoroughly during all the Hiss investigation. Then, when I sent him a telegram and said, "Mr. President, I

---

[51]*Congressional Record,* February 20, 1950, 81st Congress, 2nd sess., pp. 1952–1959.

have the 57 names; they are yours if you want them"; and when he answered by calling me a liar, I felt I could get no cooperation from the President.

Then, when the majority leader, without even discussing the matter with me, though he knew I had stated that I had the information, he made a speech in Illinois and prejudged the case, without hearing the evidence, and said, "The Senator from Wisconsin is a liar," I felt I could get no cooperation from the majority leader. It was then suggested that I ask the Committee on Expenditures in the Executive Departments to go into the matter and that I submit the names to that committee. I talked to some of the members of the committee. They thought perhaps the Committee on the Judiciary or the Committee on Foreign Relations, or both committees jointly might have jurisdiction, and they thought it should be discussed with them.

I discussed it with a number of the individuals who have been interested in the subject, digging up this information. They felt that under the present circumstances the committee could do very little, because, if we gave the committee the names and the information, and the President said, "You cannot get any information from the State Department files," they would be hamstrung. It was suggested that I draft a resolution providing that the Committee on Expenditures in the Executive Departments, or some other committee, should have the right to subpena the secret State Department files. That sounds all right on the face of it, Mr. President, but it is dangerous to go that far. . . .

I finally arrived at the conclusion that the only way to clean out the State Department, or any other Department which is infested with Communists, is not by the passage of any additional law. The only way it can be done is to secure the cooperation of the President. If we could get that, and he says that the information will be made available so that trusted staff members could go over the files, and we can be sure that the sources of information shall not be disclosed, we can clean house. I frankly think that is the only way. In line with that, I decided to submit to the Senate the detailed cases. Originally I was disturbed that I might give out information which would embarrass the investigative agencies by indirectly disclosing some of their sources of information, but I was told, "With so many commies over here having top positions, you need not fear giving the information to the Senate."

I have gone over it. Let me say, before starting, that I shall submit quite a large number of names. I think they are of importance. They all worked for the State Department at one time or another. Some are not there at the present time. Many of them have gone into work which is connected closely with the Department, for example, foreign trade, and some branches of the Maritime Commission.

I shall not attempt to present a detailed case on each one, a case which would convince a jury. All I am doing is to develop sufficient evidence so that anyone who reads the RECORD will have a good idea of the number of Communists in the State Department.

While I consider them all important, there are three big Communists involved, and I cannot possibly conceive of any Secretary of State allowing those three big Communists, who are tremendously important and of great value to Russia, to remain in the State Department. I do not believe President Truman knows about them. I cannot help but feel that he is merely the prisoner of a bunch of twisted intellectuals who tell him what they want him to know. To those who say, "Why do you not tell the State Department; why do you not give the names to the State Department?" I say that everything I have here is from the State Department's own files. I felt, when the State Department asked for the names, without being willing to cooperate or to work with us, it was saying, "Tip us off; let us know on whom you have the goods."

Case No. 1. The names are available. The Senators may have them if they care for them. I think, however, it would be improper to make the names public until the appropriate Senate committee can meet in executive session and get them. I have approximately 81 cases. I do not claim to have any tremendous investigative agency to get the facts, but if I were to give all the names involved; it might leave a wrong impression. If we should label one man a Communist when he is not a Communist, I think it would be too bad. However, the names are here. I shall be glad to abide by the decision of the Senate after it hears the cases, but I think the sensible thing to do would be to have an executive session and have a proper committee go over the whole situation. . . .

The man involved in case No. 1 is employed in the office of an Assistant Secretary of State. The intelligence unit shadowed him and found him contacting members of an espionage group. A memorandum of December 13, 1946, indicates that he succeeded in having a well-known general intervene with an Assistant Secretary in behalf of one man who is an active Communist with a long record of Communist Party connections. There is another individual who is very closely tied up with a Soviet espionage agency. There is nothing in the file to indicate that the general referred to knew those two individuals were Communists.

That is a part of the usual modus operandi. If there is one Communist in the Department, he will get some other individual to recommend another Communist so that the breed can be increased.

This individual was successful in obtaining important positions for other Communists. They were finally ordered removed from the Department not later than November 15 of the following year. Subsequent to that time, however, both of them still had access to secret material.

A memorandum of November 2, 1946, pointed out that this individual and the previously mentioned Communists whom he succeeded in having placed were connected with an alleged Russian espionage agency. Nevertheless, this individual still occupies an important position in the State Department. I should like to point out at this time, however, that the security group, which was then operating in the State Department, was apparently doing a good job. It presented the entire picture to the Secretary of State. This individual who, the investigative agency of the State Department says, is a Communist, got a general innocently to bring two other Communists into the State Department, and he is today in the State Department and has access to the secret material. As I say, his name is certainly available to any Senate committee that wants it. . . .

This is a case to which I particularly invite the Senate's attention. The files show two very interesting facts. A major portion of the file was removed. Papers refer to information in the file which is nonexistent. Upon contact with the keeper of the records, he stated that, to the best of his knowledge, the major portion of the file had been removed. He did not mention any name, but he said, "He was put in some highbrass job about 2 years ago."

I am inclined to think that this individual's name may be known from the information which I shall give here.

The file shows two things. It shows, first, that this individual had some of his clothing picked up, with unusual material in it, and, second—and this is important—it shows that the State Department and the President had prepared material which was to be sent to a foreign government. The file shows that before the material left the State Department it was in the hands of the Kremlin in Moscow. Do Senators follow me? The State Department's own investigative file shows that some secret material, which was being transmitted to another nation, before it even left this country for the other country, showed up in Moscow. So far, that is not too significant. However, the file shows that this particular individual, who has held one of the most important positions at one of the listening posts in Europe, was shadowed, that he was found to have contacted a Soviet agent, and that the Soviet agent was then followed to the Soviet Embassy, where the agent turned the material over to the Soviet Embassy. Do Senators follow me? This is what the secret State Department file shows: First, the papers get to Moscow in some mysterious manner, and, second, this individual, who is now one of our foreign ministers, contacts a Russian espionage agent, and that agent is followed to the Russian Embassy, where the material is handed over. This is no secret to the State Department.

Incidentally, I might say that I promised the press I would have copies of this material for their use. However, in view of the fact that I have nothing completely ready at this time, and must refer to the documents before me, which I cannot turn over to the press, I do not have anything to give them. I am sorry. I shall try, however, to give them now the material I have, and shall try to make the dates and places as clear as I can.

READING NO. 52

"DECLARATION OF CONSCIENCE," JUNE 1, 1950[52]

In this eloquent address, Sen. Margaret Chase Smith leads the Senate assault on Joseph McCarthy's anti-Communist crusade.

γ   γ   γ

Mr. President, I would like to speak briefly and simply about a serious national condition. It is a national feeling of fear and frustration that could result in national suicide and the end of everything that we Americans hold dear. It is a condition that comes from the lack of effective leadership in either the Legislative Branch or the Executive Branch of our Government.

That leadership is so lacking that serious and responsible proposals are being made that national advisory commissions be appointed to provide such critically needed leadership.

I speak as briefly as possible because too much harm has already been done with irresponsible words of bitterness and selfish political opportunism. I speak as simply as possible because the issue is too great to be obscured by eloquence. I speak simply and briefly in the hope that my words will be taken to heart.

I speak as a Republican. I speak as a woman. I speak as a United States Senator. I speak as an American.

The United States Senate has long enjoyed worldwide respect as the greatest deliberative body in the world. But recently that deliberative character has too often been debased to the level of a forum of hate and character assassination sheltered by the shield of congressional immunity.

It is ironical that we Senators can in debate in the Senate directly or indirectly, by any form of words, impute to any

---

[52]*Congressional Record,* June 1, 1950, 81st Congress, 2d sess., pp. 7894–7895.

American who is not a Senator any conduct or motive unworthy or unbecoming an American—and without that non-Senator American having any legal redress against us— yet if we say the same thing in the Senate about our colleagues we can be stopped on the grounds of being out of order.

It is strange that we can verbally attack anyone else without restraint and with full protection and yet we hold ourselves above the same type of criticism here on the Senate Floor. Surely the United States Senate is big enough to take self-criticism and self-appraisal. Surely we should be able to take the same kind of character attacks that we ''dish out'' to outsiders.

I think that it is high time for the United States Senate and its members to do some soul-searching—for us to weigh our consciences—on the manner in which we are performing our duty to the people of America—on the manner in which we are using or abusing our individual powers and privileges.

I think that it is high time that we remembered that we have sworn to uphold and defend the Constitution. I think that it is high time that we remembered that the Constitution, as amended, speaks not only of the freedom of speech but also of trial by jury instead of trial by accusation.

Whether it be a criminal prosecution in court or a character prosecution in the Senate, there is little practical distinction when the life of a person has been ruined.

Those of us who shout the loudest about Americanism in making character assassinations are all too frequently those who, by our own words and acts, ignore some of the basic principles of Americanism:

The right to criticize;

The right to hold unpopular beliefs;

The right to protest;

The right of independent thought.

The exercise of these rights should not cost one single American citizen his reputation or his right to a livelihood nor should he be in danger of losing his reputation or livelihood merely because he happens to know someone who holds unpopular beliefs. Who of us doesn't? Otherwise none of us could call our souls our own. Otherwise thought control would have set in.

The American people are sick and tired of being afraid to speak their minds lest they be politically smeared as "Communists" or "Fascists" by their opponents. Freedom of speech is not what it used to be in America. It has been so abused by some that it is not exercised by others.

The American people are sick and tired of seeing innocent people smeared and guilty people whitewashed. But there have been enough proved cases, such as the Amerasia case, the Hiss case, the Coplon case, the Gold case, to cause nationwide distrust and strong suspicion that there may be something to the unproved, sensational accusations.

As a Republican, I say to my colleagues on this side of the aisle that the Republican Party faces a challenge today that is not unlike the challenge that it faced back in Lincoln's day. The Republican Party so successfully met that challenge that it emerged from the Civil War as the champion of a united nation—in addition to being a Party that unrelentingly fought loose spending and loose programs.

Today our country is being psychologically divided by the confusion and the suspicions that are bred in the United States Senate to spread like cancerous tentacles of "know nothing, suspect everything" attitudes. Today we have a Democratic Administration that has developed a mania for loose spending and loose programs. History is repeating itself—and the Republican Party again has the opportunity to emerge as the champion of unity and prudence. . . .

The Democratic Administration has greatly lost the confidence of the American people by its complacency to the threat of communism here at home and the leak of vital secrets to Russia through key officials of the Democratic Administration. There are enough proved cases to make this point without diluting our criticism with unproved charges.

Surely these are sufficient reasons to make it clear to the American people that it is time for a change and that a Republican victory is necessary to the security of this country. Surely it is clear that this nation will continue to suffer as long as it is governed by the present ineffective Democratic Administration.

Yet to displace it with a Republican regime embracing a philosophy that lacks political integrity or intellectual honesty would prove equally disastrous to this nation. The nation sorely needs a Republican victory. But I don't want to see the Republican Party ride to political victory on the Four Horsemen of Calumny—Fear, Ignorance, Bigotry, and Smear.

I doubt if the Republican Party could—simply because I don't believe the American people will uphold any political party that puts political exploitation above national interest. Surely we Republicans aren't that desperate for victory.

I don't want to see the Republican Party win that way. While it might be a fleeting victory for the Republican Party, it would be a more lasting defeat for the American people. Surely it would ultimately be suicide for the Republican Party and the two-party system that has protected our American liberties from the dictatorship of a one party system.

As members of the Minority Party, we do not have the primary authority to formulate the policy of our Government. But we do have the responsibility of rendering constructive criticism, of clarifying issues, of allaying fears by acting as responsible citizens.

As a woman, I wonder how the mothers, wives, sisters, and daughters feel about the way in which members of their families have been politically mangled in Senate debate—and I use the word "debate" advisedly.

As a United States Senator, I am not proud of the way in which the Senate has been made a publicity platform for irresponsible sensationalism. I am not proud of the reckless abandon in which unproved charges have been hurled from this side of the aisle. I am not proud of the obviously staged, undignified countercharges that have been attempted in retaliation from the other side of the aisle.

I don't like the way the Senate has been made a rendezvous for vilification, for selfish political gain at the sacrifice of individual reputations and national unity. I am not proud of the way we smear outsiders from the Floor of the Senate and hide behind the cloak of congressional immunity and still place ourselves beyond criticism on the Floor of the Senate.

As an American, I am shocked at the way Republicans and Democrats alike are playing directly into the Communist design of "confuse, divide, and conquer." As an American, I don't want a Democratic Administration "whitewash" or "cover-up" any more than I want a Republican smear or witch hunt.

As an American, I condemn a Republican "Fascist" just as much as I condemn a Democrat "Communist." I condemn a Democrat "Fascist" just as much as I condemn a Republican "Communist." They are equally dangerous to you and me and to our country. As an American, I want to see our nation recapture the strength and unity it once had when we fought the enemy instead of ourselves.

It is with these thoughts that I have drafted what I call a "Declaration of Conscience."

READING NO. 53

RESOLUTION OF CENSURE, DECEMBER 2, 1954[53]

In a special post-election session, the Senate met to deal with charges against Sen. Joseph R. McCarthy. Those charges resulted in adoption of the following resolution of "condemnation."

γ   γ   γ

Resolved, That the Senator from Wisconsin [Mr. MC-CARTHY] failed to cooperate with the Subcommittee on Privileges and Elections of the Senate Committee on Rules and Administration in clearing up matters referred to that subcommittee which concerned his conduct as a Senator and affected the honor of the Senate and, instead, repeatedly abused the subcommittee and its members who were trying to carry out assigned duties, thereby obstructing the constitutional processes of the Senate, and that this conduct of the Senator from Wisconsin, [Mr. MCCARTHY] is contrary to senatorial traditions and is hereby condemned.

SEC. 2. The Senator from Wisconsin [Mr. MCCARTHY] in writing to the chairman of the Select Committee To Study Censure Charges, Mr. WATKINS, after the Select Committee had issued its report and before the report was presented to the Senate charging three members of the Select Committee with "deliberate deception" and "fraud" for failure to disqualify themselves; in stating to the press on November 4, 1954, that the special Senate session that was to begin November 8, 1954, was a "lynch party"; in repeatedly describing this special Senate session as a "lynch bee" in a Nationwide television and radio show on November 7, 1954; in stating to the public press on November 13, 1954, that the chairman of the Select Committee, Mr. WATKINS, was guilty of "the most unusual,

[53]*Congressional Record*, December 2, 1954, 83rd Congress, 2d sess., pp. 16394–16395.

most cowardly thing I've heard of'' and stating further: ''I
expected he would be afraid to answer the questions, but didn't
think he'd be stupid enough to make a public statement''; and
in characterizing the said committee as the ''unwitting hand-
maiden,'' ''involuntary agent'' and ''attorneys-in-fact'' of the
Communist Party and in charging that the said committee in
writing its report ''imitated Communist methods—that it
distorted, misrepresented, and omitted in its effort to manufacture a plausible rationalization'' in support of its recommendations to the Senate, which characterizations and charges
were contained in a statement released to the press and inserted
in the CONGRESSIONAL RECORD of November 10, 1954, acted
contrary to senatorial ethics and tended to bring the Senate into
dishonor and disrepute, to obstruct the constitutional processes
of the Senate, and to impair its dignity; and such conduct is
hereby condemned.

READING NO. 54

"RESPONSIBILITY OF THE INDIVIDUAL SENATOR: ITS DISINTEGRATION"[54]

On February 23, 1959, Sen. William Proxmire launched an attack on what he considered the heavy-handed leadership style of Senate Majority Leader Lyndon Johnson.

γ   γ   γ

Today I shall talk about how the total disappearance of the Democratic Party caucus as an instrument of decision or even information has contributed to this situation. In later talks I shall discuss the effect of this surrender of right and duty on the role of our Democratic Policy Committee. I shall also discuss the consequences to the interests of the States themselves. Later I shall talk about how this evaporation of individual senatorial responsibility offends the obligations of this body to the party on whose platform we have run for election. I will also talk about the effect of this situation on the vital function of the Senate as a great deliberative body. Finally, I shall discuss how this has concentrated a unique degree of power in the hands of the majority leader, and I shall examine in detail the full implications of this concentration of power.

Mr. President, I know it will be said that party matters of this kind should be discussed only in party circles—privately, behind closed doors. There are two reasons why I have decided to make this a public discussion. First, I think this is very much the public's business. With my party the overwhelmingly dominant force in this powerful body, the public has a right to sit in on a full critical discussion of who exercises this power, how, and why.

Frankly, I have not discussed these proposals with the leadership, although I have been told by colleagues that they have tried this in the past with uniformly discouraging results.

---

[54]*Congressional Record*, February 23, 1959, 86th Congress, 1st sess., pp. 2814–2820.

Also I am reminded of a Herblock cartoon showing a happy, smiling and hungry lion, labeled "Congressional leaders," leading into the lion's cave a Congressman carrying a banner labeled "reform." The caption on the cartoon is "Step into my office, lad, and tell me all about it." The floor of the cave is littered with the bareboned skeletons of previous Congressmen who have followed the suggestion of this happy lion.

Secondly, there is a very practical reason why I have taken this issue to the floor of the Senate. There is no other place where I can take it. The Democratic conference or caucus of the Senate is in fact dead—as I shall show shortly.

It will be said also that this kind of public talks on the floor of the Senate itself will accomplish no good, and may do serious harm; that it is foolish and useless.

Mr. President, I disagree, and there is precedent to support my position. I think I can show in the course of the speeches I shall make that there has never been a time when power has been as sharply concentrated as it is today in the Senate. But a similar problem of power concentration has confronted Senators in the past. The first step to its solution has been to talk about it: To pull it out in the cleansing scrutiny of public debate and national consideration. Before I am through I hope to point the way toward at least some modest reforms. And I honestly hope to achieve at least a beginning.

THE DEMOCRATIC CAUCUS

Here lies the Democratic caucus

Conceived by senatorial responsibility

And born with the Democratic Party—1800

Assassinated at the hand of senatorial indifferences—1953

"She labored faithfully and well to make Senatorial leadership responsible to all the people."

VITAL ROLE OF CAUCUS

Mr. President, there is one body and only one body to which all Democratic Senators and only Democratic Senators belong. That is the Democratic conference—in past years called the Democratic caucus. This is the fountainhead of Democratic power in the Senate. The policy committee, the steering committee, the chairmen of all committees, the party whip, and, yes, the majority leader himself, all owe their offices to this convocation of all Democratic Senators, which also directs the assignment of Democratic members to all committees. During much of the history of the Senate the party conference or caucus has given all Democratic Senators their opportunity to exercise their right and fulfill their duty in determining our party's program and policies.

Mr. President, what has happened to that opportunity?

I took office in this body on August 29, 1957. Since that time the Democratic Party has had exactly two senatorial conferences or caucuses. The first was the first week in January 1958. This was the first Democratic Party caucus in this body for 1 full year. The second took place just last month. So this party in the Senate has been moving along at the rate of one conference or caucus a year. What caucuses! The caucus is not only immensely important, it offers the one and only opportunity for most of us as Democratic Senators to have a word to say about our Democratic program, the legislation this majority Democratic Party of ours will take up during the session.

What I am calling for is a greater degree of democracy in our party in the Senate. And the first step toward this democracy is regular meetings of our party membership to permit all Senators to know where the leadership intends to take us, and to permit the membership, if it cares to do so, to indicate whether or not it wants to go there.

In a later speech I shall discuss in detail the effect of this surrender of responsibility by Democratic Senators on our obligation to the Democratic Party we represent and its platform. Suffice it to say here that without genuine caucuses there is no way we can exercise the responsibility every Democratic Senator shares to hold our leadership accountable to that platform. And, of course, without a caucus the whole process by which our party's program is rationalized and compromised to fit as well as possible the interests of every section of the country—this process is short circuited. This, too, I shall discuss in detail at a later date. And, Mr. President, without any significant caucuses of our party the policy committee assumes a degree of responsibility that is large and serious. I shall talk about that later also.

PROXMIRE PURPOSE

Mr. President, in conclusion, the junior Senator from

Wisconsin was not sent to this body to delegate his authority as a Senator to any other Senator, no matter how able, wise, or good that Senator may be. This Senator is going to continue to call on the leadership to tell him what programs are to be proposed, when they are to be considered, and why. And when the leadership does inform me, I am going to do all I can to recover the traditional power U.S. Senators have had in the past to take part in determining how our leadership should act for our party and country.

I am not as sanguine about this, perhaps, as some may think I am, so I close with a quotation from William the Silent, which indicates my attitude on this entire great question. This is the only quotation that hangs in my office:

"It is not necessary to hope in order to undertake, or to succeed in order to persevere."

Mr. President, before I came on the floor I was puzzled and rather curious to know what kind of reaction there would be to my speech on the part of my colleagues, inasmuch as this is a very difficult speech to give. It is probably even more difficult to listen to. I wish to thank my colleagues for their willingness to give of their time to listen to the speech, and the fact that there are a number of my colleagues on the floor who came to listen to it without being solicited. It was a very hard and difficult speech for me to make.

READING NO. 55

"THE SENATE AND ITS LEADERSHIP," NOVEMBER 27, 1963[55]

Senate Majority Leader Mike Mansfield had planned to deliver this defense of his leadership style on November 22, 1963. The assassination of President Kennedy caused him simply to insert these remarks in the Congressional Record *several days later.*

γ   γ   γ

Mr. MANSFIELD. Mr. President, some days ago blunt words were said on the floor of the Senate. They dealt in critical fashion with the state of this institution. They dealt in critical fashion with the quality of the majority leadership and the minority opposition. A far more important matter than criticism or praise of the leadership was involved. It is a matter which goes to the fundamental nature of the Senate.

In this light, we have reason to be grateful because if what was stated was being said in the cloakrooms, then it should have been said on the floor. If, as was indicated, the functioning of the Senate itself is in question, the place to air that matter is on the floor of the Senate. We need no cloakroom commandos, operating behind the swinging doors of the two rooms at the rear, to spread the tidings. We need no whispered word passed from one to another and on to the press.

We are here to do the public's business. On the floor of the Senate, the public's business is conducted in full sight and hearing of the public. And it is here, not in the cloakrooms, that the Senator from Montana, the majority leader, if you wish, will address himself to the question of the present state of the Senate and its leadership. The Senator from Montana has nothing to conceal. He has nothing which is best whispered in the cloakrooms. What he has to say on this score will be said

[55]*Congressional Record,* November 27, 1963, 88th Congress, 1st sess., p. 22858.

here. It will be said to all Senators and to all the members of the press who sit above us in more ways than one.

How, Mr. President, do you measure the performance of this Congress—any Congress? How do you measure the performance of a Senate of 100 independent men and women—any Senate? The question rarely arises at least until an election approaches. And, then, our concern may well be with our own individual performance and not necessarily with that of the Senate as a whole.

Yet that performance—the performance of the Senate as a whole—has been judged on the floor. Several Senators, at least, judged it and found it seriously wanting. And with the hue and cry thus raised, they found echoes outside the Senate. I do not criticize Senators for making the judgment, for raising the alarm. Even less do I criticize the press for spreading it. Senators were within their rights. And the press was not only within its rights but was performing a segment of its public duty which is to report what transpires here.

I, too, am within my rights, Mr. President, and I believe I am performing a duty of the leadership when I ask again: How do you judge the performance of this Congress—any Congress? Of this Senate—any Senate? Do you mix a concoction and drink it? And if you feel a sense of well-being thereafter decide it is not so bad a Congress after all? But if you feel somewhat ill or depressed then that, indeed, is proof unequivocal that the Congress is a bad Congress and the Senate is a bad Senate. Or do you shake your head back and forth negatively before a favored columnist when discussing the performance of this Senate? And if he, in turn, nods up and down, then that is proof that the performance is bad?

With all due respect, Mr. President, I searched the remarks of the Senators who have raised the questions. I searched them carefully for I do not make light of the criticism of any Member of this body. I searched them carefully for any insight as to how we might judge accurately the performance of this Senate, in order that we might try to improve it.

There is reference, to be sure, to time-wasting, to laziness, to absenteeism, to standing still, and so forth. But who are the timewasters in the Senate, Mr. President? Who is lazy? Who is an absentee? Each Member can make his own judgment of his individual performance. I make no apologies for mine. Nor will I sit in judgment on any other Member. On that score, each of us will answer to his own conscience, if not to his constituents.

But, Mr. President, insofar as the performance of the Senate as a whole is concerned, with all due respect, these comments in timewasting have little relevance. Indeed, the Congress can, as it has—as it did in declaring World War II in less than a day—pass legislation which has the profoundest meaning for the entire Nation. And by contrast, the Senate floor can look very busy day in and day out, month in and month out, while the Senate is, indeed, dawdling. At one time in the recollection of many of us, we debated a civil rights measure 24 hours a day for many days on end. We debated it shaven and unshaven. We debated it without ties, with hair awry and even in bedroom slippers. In the end, we wound up with compromise legislation. And it was not the fresh and well-rested opponents of the civil rights measure who were compelled to the compromise. It was, rather, the exhausted, sleep-starved quorum-confounded proponents who were only too happy to take it.

No, Mr. President, if we would estimate the performance of this Congress or any other, this Senate or any other, we will have to find a more reliable yardstick than whether, on the floor, we act as timewasters or moonlighters. As every Member of the Senate and press knows, even if the public generally does not, the Senate is neither more nor less effective because the Senate is in session from 9 a.m. to 9 p.m. or to 9 a.m. the next day. In fact, such hours would most certainly make it less effective in present circumstances.

Nor does the length of the session indicate a greater or lesser effectiveness. We live in a 12-month nation. It may well be that the times are pushing us in the direction of a 12-months Congress. In short, we cannot measure a Congress or a Senate by the standards of the stretchout or of the speedup. It will be of no avail to install a timeclock at the entrance to the Chamber for Senators to punch when they enter or leave the floor.

There has been a great deal said on this floor about featherbedding in certain industries. But if we want to see a featherbedding to end all featherbedding, we will have the Senate sit here day in and day out from dawn until dawn, whether or not the calendar calls for it, in order to impress the boss—the American people—with our industriousness. We may not shuffle papers as bureaucrats are assumed to do when engaged in this art. What we are likely to shuffle is words— words to the President on how to execute the foreign policy or administer the domestic affairs of the Nation. And when these words pall, we undoubtedly will turn to the court to give that institution the benefit of our advice on its responsibilities. And if we run out of judicial wisdom we can always turn to advising the Governors of the States or the mayors of the cities or the heads of other nations on how to manage their concerns.

Let me make it clear that Senators individually have every right to comment on whatever they wish and to do so on the floor of the Senate. Highly significant initiatives on all manner of public affairs have had their genesis in the remarks of individual Senators on the floor. But there is one clearcut, day-in-and-day-out responsibility of the Senate as a whole. Beyond all others, it is the constitutional responsibility to be here and to consider and to act in concert with the House on the legislative needs of the Nation. And the effectiveness with which that responsibility is discharged cannot be measured by any reference to the clocks on the walls of the Chamber.

READING NO. 56

COMMENT ON IMPEACHMENT, OCTOBER 15, 1986[56]

The conclusion of the Harry Claiborne Impeachment trial in the Senate at the end of the 1986 session prompted Sen. Charles McC. Mathias, chairman of the Senate Impeachment Committee, to make these observations on the nature of the impeachment process and its application to that trial.

γ   γ   γ

MR. MATHIAS. Mr. President, Prof. Raoul Berger has observed that while impeachment in this country has been "largely a means for the ouster of corrupt judges," it was in England " 'the chief institution for preservation of the government.' " In the 198 years since it first assembled in New York, the Senate has removed only five civil officers of the United States, all judges. While this supports the observation that impeachment in this country has been used narrowly, we must be mindful of the larger purpose, "the preservation of the government," that is served by the framers' decision to import this English institution into our national charter.

The framers did not specify the procedures which the Senate should use when trying impeachments, other than that the Senate shall have "the sole Power to try all Impeachments," that "/w/hen sitting for that Purpose, /Senators/ shall be on Oath or Affirmation," that "/w/hen the President of the United States is tried, the Chief Justice shall preside," and that "no Person shall be convicted without the concurrence of two-thirds of the Members present." Beyond these requirements, the Constitution grants to the Senate discretion, through its authority to "determine the Rules of its Proceedings," to choose the means of implementing its impeachment trial responsibilities.

---

[56]*Congressional Record,* October 15, 1986, 99th Congress, 2d sess., pp. S16350–S16353 (daily edition).

The Senate's impeachment procedures must serve three objectives. They must enable the Senate to determine if there is sufficient evidence to convict an officer of the United States of a high crime or misdemeanor. They must enable the officer to defend himself against the accusation of the House of Representatives. Finally, in adopting procedures to aid in "the preservation of the government," the Senate must be careful not to diminish its ability to perform the other functions of the government which it is seeking to preserve. . . .

The Constitution provides that the Senate shall have the power to "try" impeachments. If the word "try" imported into the Constitution the exact specifications of a judicial trial, then the Senate might have little latitude to define its rules of proceedings. However, the Framers did not intend to obligate the Senate to replicate all features of a judicial trial. Hamilton recognized that the Senate "can never be tied down by such strict rules, either in the delineation of the offence by the prosecutors, or in the construction of it by the judges, as in common cases serve to limit the discretion of courts in favor of personal security." Justice Story expressed the similar opinion that "it is obvious that the strictness of the forms of proceeding in cases of offences at common law is ill adapted to impeachments."

Instead, the requirement that conviction on impeachment be by "trial," I believe, was intended to fulfill the Framers' intent that the Senate act in "judicial character as a court." The Framers intended that the Senate perform this judicial function impartially, "to preserve, unawed and uninfluenced, the necessary impartiality between an individual accused, and the representatives of the people, his accusers."

In my opinion, the Senate performed its judicial task /in the 1986 Claiborne trial/ with complete impartiality. There were many outside of the Senate who thought that this impeachment should have taken the Senate only several hours to resolve after the House exhibited its articles in early August. The Senate determined, instead, that Judge Claiborne should have available to him the subpoena power of the Senate to bring here witnesses who could testify to the tax transactions in 1979 and 1980. These witnesses were examined and cross-examined by counsel and also questioned by members of the committee over

7 days of hearings. The full Senate received briefs from the parties and then heard closing arguments from the managers, from Judge Claiborne's counsel, and from Judge Claiborne. The Senate deferred its decision whether to hear witnesses in open Senate until it heard and considered these arguments. Senators then deliberated with great care prior to voting. In every sense the Members of the Senate fulfilled their special impeachment oath to "do impartial justice according to the Constitution and laws."

READING No. 57

TELEVISION COVERAGE IN THE SENATE[57]

On February 6, 1986, Senate Democratic Leader Robert C. Byrd, a major proponent of televising the Senate's proceedings, offered these arguments in support of his case.

γ　　　　　　γ　　　　　　γ

TELEVISION COVERAGE IN THE SENATE

Mr. BYRD. Mr. President, in 1944 the first resolution calling for the broadcasting of Senate floor proceedings was introduced. Forty-two years have intervened. We have spent almost half a century debating whether or not to permit our floor proceedings to be televised. Senator Hubert Humphrey told us: "A 20th Century Congress cannot be content with employing 18th or 19th Century technology." It is 1986. We are leaving the 20th century and approaching the 21st century. Yet we still have not found a way to go beyond the technology of the 19th century in communicating with the American public. If we do not act quickly to embrace the communications technology of the 20th century, we may find that in the 21st century, the Senate will have lost its relevance.

There are at least three compelling arguments for supporting the televising of Senate floor proceedings. There is a democratic argument, there is an institutional argument, and there is an educational argument. . . .

Let us give the American people a more informed basis on which to judge what the Senate is and what the Senate does.

We are doing the people's business here. We do not need to fear their scrutiny. The Senate is a body of able and intelligent people. When we have given the public a chance to observe us closely, they have responded favorably. Let us look at some historic episodes to verify this.

---

[57]*Congressional Record*, February 6, 1986, 99th Congress, 2d sess., pp. S1107–S1111 (daily edition).

The highest public opinion rating for the Congress in recent memory was registered in 1974. In that year, the Nation had a chance to observe the House Judiciary Committee conducting impeachment hearings. The American people saw a group of serious, throughtful, and reasonable men and women doing their job, and they were impressed with what they saw. The opinion polls reflected that fact.

The year before, 1973, the Nation gathered daily around its television sets to watch the Senate Watergate Committee conduct its hearings under the leadership of Senator Sam Ervin. A survey conducted by Broadcasting Magazine showed that 85 percent of all U.S. households had tuned in to some portion of the Watergate hearings. Senator Ervin was not a product of the television age. He did not style his hair. He did not surround himself with media advisers. Yet, he became a folk hero. He may not have had the polish of a news anchor. But he had wisdom and character. And the American people saw that and responded favorably to it. . . .

To give this debate some historical perspective, I remind Senators—and it has been said on this floor several times that in 1789, and indeed for the first 5 years of its existence, the U.S. Senate met behind closed doors. That policy was the target of as much criticism then as our failure to open our Chamber to television is today. In fact, the 18th century opponents to opening the doors of the Senate Chamber to the public have much in common with those in the 20th century who oppose opening the Senate Chamber to television. They feared that, with the public in attendance, Senators would pander to the galleries with rhetorical speeches long on style but short in substance. There would be so many speeches, they warned, that the Senate would no longer be able to carry out its responsibilities in an efficient manner. Sometimes we feel that is the case around here, but it is not because we allowed the public to sit in the visitors' galleries. And, in response to the 20th century opponents, I do not believe that televising our proceedings to a national audience will have that effect either. . . .

Mr. President, the coming of television to the U.S. Senate is not an occurrence to be feared—it is an opportunity to be seized. Let us not run from the public. Let us meet them where they already are—out yonder on the airwaves. The age of electronic communication is no longer the wave of the future. It is the reality of the present. Let us embrace this moment and become part of it.

The Senate has done this in the past. When we opened our doors to the public and the press in the 18th century, no more than three reporters were in attendance. However, in the early years of the 19th century their numbers grew steadily, and in 1857 the Congress responded by establishing Press Galleries in the Capitol. In the last quarter of the 19th century, the spread of telegraph communication began. Newspapers across the country were suddenly able to receive instantaneous wire-service reports of events in Congress. This heightened the American people's interest in congressional news. Again, the American people responded favorably to this new and timely access and so did the Congress. By 1919, both Chambers had adopted the policy of holding open committee hearings on important legislative proposals.

In the 1920's, advances in radio technology again transformed mass communications. In the following two decades, news magazines and political periodicals began to appear on the scene. Now there were even more journalists on Capitol Hill, and the appetite for congressioanl news on the part of the American public continued to grow. By 1944, in response to the growing demand, the Congress had established the galleries for radio correspondents and for the periodical press. Between the years of 1945 and 1979, television brought the proceedings of various Senate committees into the homes of millions of American viewers. Interest in the legislative branch grew as a result of this exposure and now, in the 1980's, we are again being asked to respond to that interest.

The historic pattern has repeated itself. New technology enhances the communication process. It brings greater access to the Congress. The American people respond with greater interest. Now let us do what our predecessors have done throughout the history of the Congress. Let us respond favorably. Let us embrace contemporary technology and the opportunities it provides to enhance our democracy and prepare our future generations for their participation in that democracy.

FOR FURTHER READING

1. Aiken, Goerge D., *Aiken: Senate Diary* (Brattleboro, VT, 1976).
2. Anderson, Clinton P., *Outsider in the Senate* (New York, 1970).
3. Asbell, Bernard, *The Senate Nobody Knows* (New York, 1978).
4. Auerbach, Jerold S., *Labor and Liberty: The La Follette Committee and the New Deal* (Indianapolis, IN, 1966).
5. Bailey, Thomas A., *Woodrow Wilson and the Great Betrayal* (New York, 1945).
6. Baker, Bobby, *Wheeling and Dealing* (New York, 1978).
7. Baker, Richard Allan, *Conservation Politics: The Senate Career of Clinton P. Anderson* (Albuquerque, NM, 1985).
8. _____, *The United States Senate, A Historical Bibliography* (Washington, 1977).
9. Baker, Ross, *Friend and Foe in the United States Senate* (New York, 1980).
10. Baxter, Maurice G., *One and Inseparable: Daniel Webster and the Union* (Cambridge, MA, 1984).
11. Benedict, Michael Les, *A Compromise of Principle: Congressional Republicans and Reconstruction, 1863–1869* (New York, 1974).
12. Benton, Thomas Hart, *Thirty Years' View* (New York, 1854–1856).
13. Bogue, Allan G., *Earnest Men, Republicans of the Civil War Senate* (Ithaca, NY, 1981).
14. Bowen, Catherine D., *Miracle at Philadelphia* (Boston, 1966).
15. Brown, Everett, *William Plumer's Memorandum of Proceedings in the United States Senate, 1803–1807* (New York, 1923).
16. Burdette, Franklin L., *Filibustering in the Senate* (Princeton, NJ, 1940).
17. Byrd, Robert C., ''Addresses on the History of the U.S. Senate,'' *Congressional Record,* 1980–1987.
18. Coit, Margaret, *John C. Calhoun* (Boston, 1950).

19. Congressional Quarterly, *Guide to Congress* (Washington, 1982).

20. Cotton, Norris, *In the Senate: Amidst the Conflict and Turmoil* (New York, 1978).

21. Cunningham, Noble, E. *The Process of Government Under Jefferson* (Princeton, NJ, 1978).

22. Donald, David, *Charles Sumner and the Coming of the Civil War* (New York, 1960).

23. _____, *Charles Sumner and the Rights of Man* (New York, 1970).

24. Drury, Allen, *A Senate Journal, 1943–1945* (New York, 1963).

25. Griffith, Robert, *The Politics of Fear: Joseph R. McCarthy and the Senate* (Lexington, KY, 1970).

26. Hamilton, Holman, *Prologue to Conflict: the Crisis and Compromise of 1850* (New York, 1964).

27. Haynes, George H., *The Senate of the United States*, 2v. (Boston, 1938).

28. Jacob, Kathryn Allamong, ed., *Guide to Research Collections of Former United States Senators, 1789–1982*, Sen. Doc. 97-41 (Washington, 1983).

29. Javits, Jacob K., *Javits: The Autobiography of a Public Man* (Boston, 1981).

30. Johannsen, Robert W., *Stephen A. Douglas* (New York, 1973).

31. Josephy, Alvin M., *On the Hill, A History of the American Congress* (New York, 1979).

32. Kennedy, John F., *Profiles in Courage* (New York, 1955).

33. Kerr, Clara H., *The Origin and Development of the United States Senate* (Ithaca, NY, 1895).

34. Lodge, Henry Cabot, *The Senate of the United States* (New York, 1921).

35. Lowitt, Richard, *George Norris, The Triumph of a Progressive* (Urbana, IL, 1978).

36. Maclay, William, *The Journal of William Maclay* (New York, 1965).

37. Main, Jackson T., *The Upper House in Revolutionary America, 1763–1788* (Madison, WI, 1967).

38. Matthews, Donald R., *U.S. Senators and Their World* (Chapel Hill, NC, 1960).
39. Merrill, Horace S. and Marion G., *The Republican Command, 1897–1913* (Lexington, KY, 1971).
40. Miller, James A., *Running In Place, Inside the Senate* (New York, 1986).
41. Ornstein, Norman, et al., *Vital Statistics on Congress* (Washington, 1984).
42. Oshinsky, David M., *A Conspiracy So Immense: The World of Joe McCarthy* (New York, 1983).
43. Patterson, James, *Mr. Republican: A Biography of Robert A. Taft* (Boston, 1972).
44. Phillips, David Graham, *Treason of the Senate* (Chicago, 1964).
45. Redman, Eric, *The Dance of Legislation* (New York, 1973).
46. Reedy, George, *The U.S. Senate, Paralysis or a Search for Consensus* (New York, 1986).
47. Riddick, Floyd, *Senate Procedure, Precedents and Practices,* Sen. Doc. 97-2 (Washington, 1981).
48. Riedel, Richard L. *Halls of the Mighty: My 47 Years at the Senate* (Washington, 1969).
49. Ripley, Randall, *Power in the Senate* (New York, 1969).
50. Rogers, Lindsay, *The American Senate* (New York, 1926).
51. Rothman, David J., *Politics and Power: the United States Senate, 1869–1901* (Cambridge, MA, 1966).
52. Schulz, George J., *Creation of the Senate,* Sen. Doc. 75-45 (Washington, 1937).
53. Shaffer, Samuel, *On and Off the Floor: Thirty Years as a Correspondent on Capitol Hill* (New York, 1980).
54. Smith, Elbert B., *Magnificent Missourian: The Life of Thomas Hart Benton* (Philadelphia, 1958).
55. Solberg, Carl, *Hubert Humphrey, A Biography* (New York, 1984).
56. Swanstrom, Roy, *The United States Senate, 1787–1801,* Sen. Doc. 99-19 (Washington, 1985).
57. U.S. Senate, *Senate Election, Expulsion and Censure Cases From 1793 to 1972,* Sen. Doc. 92-7 (Washington, 1972).

58. _____, *Senate Manual,* Sen. Doc. 98-1 (Washington, 1984).
59. Van Deusen, Glyndon G., *The Life of Henry Clay* (Boston, 1937).
60. _____, *William Henry Seward* (New York, 1967).
61. White, William S., *Citadel, the Story of the U.S. Senate* (New York, 1957).
62. Widenor, William C., *Henry Cabot Lodge and the Search for an American Foreign Policy* (Berkeley, CA, 1980).
63. Young, James S., *The Washington Community, 1800–1828* (New York, 1966).

INDEX

257